THE STORY OF THE
SPITFIRE

THE STORY OF THE
SPITFIRE

AN OPERATIONAL AND COMBAT HISTORY

KEN DELVE

The History Press

Cover illustrations: Front: The classic and unmistakable shape of the Spitfire, SN code of 243 Squadron. (Ken Delve Collection); *Back:* Jerry Jarrold and Spitfire in the Western Desert. (Jerry Jarrold)

First published 2007 by Greenhill Books/Lionel Leventhal Ltd.
This paperback edition first published by the History Press 2016
Published by arrangement with Greenhill Books/Lionel Leventhal Ltd.

The History Press
The Mill, Brimscombe Port
Stroud, Gloucestershire, GL5 2QG
www.thehistorypress.co.uk

British Library Cataloguing in Publication Data.
A catalogue record for this book is available from the British Library.

ISBN 978 0 7509 6528 6

Printed and bound in Great Britain by TJ International Ltd.

Contents

List of Illustrations   7

Foreword by Alfred Price   9

Introduction: Fighter Tactics – Principles   11

1   Development   15

2   Into Battle   30

3   Battle of Britain   36

4   'There I Was' – Tactical Training   53

5   Offensive Operations – Europe   65

6   D-Day and Beyond   89

7   Over the Desert and Italy   103

8   Jungle Operations   112

9   Carrier Operations   124

10   Reconnaissance Operations   156

11   Post-1945 Operations   163

12   Spitfire Warbird   168

Annexes

A   Variant Data and Squadrons   170

B   RAF Orders of Battle – Spitfire Squadrons   210

C   Spitfire Prototype Trial   219

D   AFDU Tactical Trials: Spitfire VB versus Fw 190   222

E   AFDU Trial: Spitfire VB Clipped-wing versus Standard Version   224

F   AFDU Tactical Trials: Spitfire Mark VI   226

G   AFDU Short Tactical Trials: Spitfire VIII   229

H   AFDU Trial: Spitfire VIII JF299 with Tear-drop Canopy   231

I	AFDU Tactical Trials: Spitfire Mark IX	234
J	AFDU Tactical Trials: Spitfire Mark IX versus Fw 190	238
K	AFDU Comparative Trials: Spitfire IX versus Mustang X	240
L	AFDU Tactical Trials: Spitfire XII	244
M	AFDU Tactical Trials: Spitfire Mark XIV	248
N	AFDU Tactical Trials: Spitfire Mark F.21 LA201	254
O	Tactics Used by Spitfire Day Fighter/Bomber Squadrons of 2nd TAF	258

Bibliography   266

Index   269

List of Illustrations

Plates appearing between pages 128 and 145

1	Spitfires of 611 Squadron at Duxford in 1939	129
2	The Spitfire IA was the first operational variant	129
3	Sqn Ldr R. H. Leigh, Officer Commanding 66 Squadron	130
4	Teddy St Aubyn of 616 Squadron	131
5	Mark IIB of 91 Squadron being serviced	131
6	Flt Sgt Sherk in Spitfire VB of 129 Squadron	132
7	The Spitfire Mark V was an interim solution but was produced in large numbers	132
8	Spitfires of 64 Squadron run up at Hornchurch, May 1942	133
9	Engine change at Audley End in April 1943	133
10	Captain Don Willis of the US 8th Air Force, April 1943	134
11	The Spitfire VIII saw most of its service in the Middle East and Far East	134
12	Spitfires being serviced at a central location in the build-up to D-Day	135
13	The Spitfire IX was considered by many combat pilots to be the best variant	136
14	Spitfire IXC MK264 of the Polish 308 Squadron	136
15	Pilots of 80 Squadron pose at West Malling in July 1944	137
16	Spitfire VIII MT714 of 43 Squadron being serviced	137
17	Rear-quarter view of Spitfire XIV	138
18	Aircraft belonging to No 61 Operational Training Unit	138
19	The Spitfire LF.XVI spent much of its time as a fighter-bomber	138
20	Pristine Spitfire V (Trop) in the snow in January 1942	139
21	Jerry Jarrold with a modified Spitfire IX of 80 Squadron	140
22	The groundcrew service aircraft in Italy, 1944	141
23	Another rough-and-ready airstrip for 111 Squadron	141
24	Sqn Ldr Neil Wheeler of OC 'B' Flight of 140 Squadron	142
25	Fitting oblique camera to Spitfire; reconnaissance was a key role	142

26   Major work underway on an aircraft of 136 Squadron   143
27   Spitfire FR.18 of 208 Squadron firing-up   144
28   Fleet Air Arm Seafires during the Korean War   144
29   The Mark 24, the end of the line for the Spitfire   144

Line illustrations

A   Luftwaffe recognition three-view of Spitfire I   176
B   Luftwaffe recognition three-view of Spitfire V   182
C   2nd Tactical Air Force diagram of ideal strafing attack profile   265
D   2nd Tactical Air Force diagram of dive-bombing profile   265

Foreword

There have been numerous books on the Spitfire, but in fact there still remains a great deal to be explored and explained about this iconic aircraft. In *The Story of the Spitfire* the author has certainly taken a new line by concentrating on the aircraft as an evolving fighting machine, and outlining the tactics and methods it employed in action. To strengthen his text he makes extensive use of official reports and summaries, plus first-person published and unpublished accounts by pilots who flew the Spitfire.

An important section in this book concerns the development of effective training courses to prepare RAF fighter pilots for combat. These were aimed at pilots flying all fighter types, not just the Spitfire, but as the war progressed the latter predominated. Making incremental improvements to the performance of the aircraft was all very well, but that counted for little if the pilots lacked the skills necessary to handle the aircraft in action. To the layman the business of training is less 'sexy' than flying in combat, but the former is essential if the latter is to be performed effectively.

During the Battle of Britain in the summer of 1940, RAF Fighter Command suffered heavy losses in pilots. Some of the hastily trained replacements arrived at their operational squadrons with as little as ten hours' flying in the type they were to take into action. These unfortunates found themselves at the bottom of an enormous learning curve. The lucky ones who survived their initial baptisms of fire would become effective in action, but that would take time.

Fortunately for Fighter Command, the large-scale daylight attacks on Great Britain tapered off in the autumn of 1940. That reduced the scale of its losses, removing the extreme pressure on squadrons to send inexperienced pilots into action. It also allowed time to pick through the hard-won lessons of combat, and put these to good use.

First and foremost, the increased time given to training was aimed at teaching pilots to survive in combat, to give them a sense of situational awareness that reduced their chance of being surprised by an attacking enemy. The majority of pilots shot down in fighter-versus-fighter combat never saw their assailant before their aircraft suffered hits. When they were likely to meet the enemy in the air, pilots were taught to scan the sky around their aircraft systematically, take a quick glance at the instrument panel to check all was well, then repeat the process.

Secondly, it was important to train pilots in air-to-air gunnery, to enable them to engage the enemy effectively. At the beginning of the Second World War, the gunnery training given to RAF fighter pilots varied between poor and non-existent. In a series of incremental steps, it took until the middle of the war to make good this deficiency. Then the combat effectiveness of RAF fighter pilots increased markedly.

As Annexes the author includes a range of service trials reports produced by the RAF's Air Fighting Development Unit. These interesting 'warts and all' documents reveal how well the different versions of the Spitfire compared with contemporary Allied and German fighter types.

The author describes the Spitfire's employment in its various roles, as air superiority fighter, fighter-bomber, reconnaissance aircraft and as a navalised fighter to operate from aircraft carriers. Above all else, his account shows the amazing versatility of Reginald Mitchell's original design to meet a specific RAF requirement for a short-range interceptor fighter.

Alfred Price
2007

Introduction:
Fighter Tactics – Principles

The world of fighter tactics is awash with accrued wisdom that provides a general basis for all fighter operations regardless of the aircraft type. This book concentrates on the tactical employment of the Spitfire in its air-to-air and air-to-ground roles and, whilst reference is made when appropriate to the 'accrued wisdom', this aspect is not the focus of attention. One of the great fighter pilots of the Second World War, A. G. 'Sailor' Malan, learnt his trade flying Spitfires with 74 Squadron and in 1941 his 'Ten Rules of Air Fighting' were circulated as guidance for fighter pilots. The ten rules were ones that would have been recognised by contemporary German aces such as Adolf Galland, and understood by First World War aces such as Albert Ball, although not all the rules were applicable in the same way in that earlier conflict; similarly, they could be found on the wall of an Israeli fighter squadron in the 1973 war with Egypt, and many would not be out of place in a modern air combat scenario, where all that has changed is the application of the same core principles.

Malan's Rules of Air Fighting were:

1 Wait until you see the whites of his eyes. Fire short bursts of one or two seconds, and only when your sights are definitely 'ON'.
2 Whilst shooting, think of nothing else, brace the whole of your body, have both hands on the stick, concentrate on your ring sight.
3 Always keep a sharp lookout, 'Keep your finger out!'
4 Height gives you the initiative.
5 Always turn and face attack.
6 Make your decisions promptly. It is better to act quickly even though your tactics are not the best.
7 Never fly straight-and-level for more than thirty seconds in the combat area.
8 When diving to attack, always leave a proportion of your formation above to act as top guard.
9 INITIATIVE, AGGRESSION, AIR DISCIPLINE, and TEAMWORK are words that MEAN something in air fighting.
10 Go in quickly – punch hard – get out!

This is all good stuff but it does not provide a framework on which to assess the tactical capability of an aircraft. There are a number of factors that play a part in the success of any fighter aircraft; these can be summarised as:

1 Performance, primarily manoeuvrability.
2 Armament, which includes guns and gun sights.
3 Resilience to damage of the airframe, engine and systems.
4 Tactics, which includes leadership and training.
5 Pilot skill, meaning training rather than innate skill.
6 Luck.

Whilst the 'Ten Rules of Air Fighting' provide a generic set of principles, it is hard to define any one of them in respect to a particular aircraft type, but by looking at the six factors mentioned above it is possible to provide both objective and subjective appraisals of an aircraft. However, this still does not provide a single appraisal of an aircraft since it is the combination of factors that gives the overall picture of capability – invariably measured as success or failure. This can be summed up as 'the pilot with the best aircraft will not always win' and the other factors, especially tactics and training, will mitigate the 'armchair' result that statistics would otherwise predict.

The air fighting principles laid down by 'Sailor' Malan were 100 per cent appropriate to the Spitfire pilot and his training should have been aimed at providing him with the skills, including what is now referred to as 'situational awareness' to fight his aircraft in an effective and successful manner.

For example, as far as this book is concerned it is assumed that all fighter pilots of the period knew that they had to search the sky for the enemy and that to fly straight-and-level for more than a few seconds was a recipe for disaster. These are not specific Spitfire points; where they will be alluded to is in regard to aspects such as visibility from the cockpit, a major factor in successful lookout and one that was related to the airframe – for the Spitfire this meant changes from the early canopy style with too much 'ironwork' and limited visibility to a tear-drop canopy with a cut-down rear fuselage. Height was always seen as a major factor in air combat as it gave an initiative to an attacker, and again aircraft performance was a factor in this, both in terms of Service ceiling and climb time to height. This too is mentioned in the book where appropriate, and data on such performance can be found in the Annexes.

Before leaving this brief consideration of generic fighter tactics it is worth mentioning a pamphlet that was published in late 1940 or early 1941 by No 13 Group. The 'Forget-Me-Nots for Fighters' contained 'pearls of wisdom' from the experiences of the Battle of Britain and used cartoons to illustrate the points made. The booklet was issued during AVM Saul's tenure as Air-Officer-Commanding, and in his foreword he states:

This book is the outcome of discussion amongst the Training Staff on the best and simplest way to bring to the notice of new Fighter Pilots certain salient points in air fighting, which it is essential that they should master before taking their places as operational pilots in Fighter Squadrons. The various points illustrated are by no means comprehensive, and it must be clearly understood that only the main points which a new Fighter Pilot should know before going into action are included. These have been compiled on the advice and guidance of many well-known and proved Fighter Pilots, who have willingly co-operated in placing their knowledge and experience at the disposal of their younger brother pilots.

In selecting the motto of the Three Musketeers – 'all for one and one for all' – to put at the head of this Foreword, I have done so because it expresses what should be the creed to every Fighter Pilot. Never forget that you are an essential cog in the wheel, and if you break or fail it will let down your brother pilots, and the grimness of war allows for no such weakness.

Air fighting is a combination of skill and courage, which, allied with confidence and experience, makes the Fighter Pilot master of his trade.

The salient 'Forget-Me-Nots' applied to all single-seat fighters and should be borne in mind when reading pilot accounts or aircraft details in this book.

Air Fighting Development Unit

Finally, this book makes significant use of the reports issued by the Air Fighting Development Unit (AFDU); indeed, the majority of the Annexes are the reports relating to tactical trials of the various Spitfire Marks. The AFDU was formed in July 1940 from the Air Fighting Development Establishment, which had been formed in 1934 at Northolt to evaluate Service types. The importance of this unit cannot be overstated and it was staffed by experienced pilots whose task was to evaluate new aircraft, both in terms of handling and performance and, in most cases, in tactical trials against other aircraft, allied and enemy. The AFDU borrowed aircraft, and sometimes pilots, from operational squadrons, if it was deemed appropriate, and their reports carried a great deal of credibility. What is less certain is what effect the reports actually had in terms of changes being made or useful information being relayed to the operational units or appropriate training units.

Performance trials were also conducted by the Aircraft and Armament Experimental Establishment (AAEE) and it was they who promulgated performance data and handling notes for pilots, but they did not get involved in tactical evaluations. This book does not, therefore, include detailed reports from the AAEE.

Ken Delve
2007

~ 1 ~

Development

The Second World War was into its third day, 5 September 1939, when Spitfire Is of 65 Squadron scrambled from their base at Hornchurch in search of an unidentified 'raider'. They returned having found nothing, but in effect this sortie opened the operational career of a fighter that, more than any aircraft, has come to symbolise the RAF's fighter war from 1939 to 1945. If you ask any aircraft enthusiast to name the aircraft they would most like to fly in – and to own – the Spitfire is invariably top of the list. During the war the propaganda machine, which played a vital role in maintaining the morale of the British public, made great play of the importance of the Spitfire, with campaigns such as the Spitfire Fund, through which everyone was asked to contribute metal to the war effort; turning pots and pans into Spitfires was never much more than a slogan but it was highly effective as a morale booster. The Germans too held the aircraft in high regard, with the famous, but misquoted, phrase from a German fighter ace (sometimes held to be Adolf Galland) asking Hermann Goering for a 'squadron of Spitfires' (as immortalised in the film *The Battle of Britain*).

The Spitfire design developed from prototype K5054 with an all-up weight (AUW) of 5,439lb and using a 990hp Rolls-Royce Merlin 'C' engine giving a top speed of 342mph, to the Seafire Mark 47 with a final AUW of 10,700lb using a Rolls-Royce Griffon 87 engine of 2,035hp giving a maximum speed of 440mph. Other performance figures had also seen marked increases, although not all changes were for the better. The Spitfire was one of the few fighters of the period to undergo such a development, from the genesis of high-performance piston monoplane fighters to the limits of the development potential for this airframe/engine combination.

So just how justified was the 'Spit's' reputation as a combat aircraft? A veritable library of books has been published about this aircraft, ranging from detailed technical histories to racy biographies from pilots; this present book takes a look at the operational aspects of the Spitfire by looking at its combat record through official documents, especially the trials and evaluation reports, and the personal accounts of those who flew the aircraft. It is not a blow-by-blow account of the aircraft and it only covers the aircraft's technology and equipment where they are relevant to the combat element.

Origins

The concept of the fighter aircraft had been born in the First World War where manoeuvrability was one of the key performance criteria; for the Royal Flying Corps/Royal Air Force, the experience with monoplanes had been an unhappy one and the war ended with small highly agile bi-planes, armed with two 0.303-in guns as the standard day fighter. The situation did not change over the next twenty years and the RAF's fighter squadrons continued to fly a range of delightful little fighters that by the late 1920s had all but lost touch with the realities of a future air war – but as the RAF's doctrine, tactics and training also had not changed, everything in the fighter garden appeared rosy. It was not until the early 1930s that a more realistic specification was issued for a future fighter, and even then, as we shall see, it was short-sighted in many key aspects. Specification F10/35 was in many respects a disaster as far as a fighter that would eventually see action in the Second World War was concerned. It encapsulated the fighter doctrine of the mid-1930s and as such is worth examining; the following extracts illustrate the major points.

Specification F10/35.
Requirements for Single-Engine Single-Seater Day and Night Fighter

General
The Air Staff require a single-engine single-seater day and night fighter which can fulfil the following conditions:

   a Have a speed in excess of the contemporary bomber of at least 40mph at 15,000ft.
   b Have a number of forward firing machine guns that can produce the maximum hitting power possible in the short space of time available for one attack.

Performance
   a Speed. The maximum possible and not less than 310mph at 15,000ft at maximum power with the highest possible between 5,000 and 15,000ft.
   b Climb. The best possible to 20,000ft but secondary to speed and hitting power.
   c Service ceiling. Not less than 30,000ft is desirable.
   d Endurance. ¼ hour at maximum power at sea level, plus one hour at maximum power at which engine can be run continuously at 15,000ft. This should provide ½ hour at maximum power at which engine can be

run continuously (for climb, etc.), plus one hour at the most economical speed at 15,000ft (for patrol), plus ¼ hour at maximum power at 15,000ft (for attack).

Armament
Not less than 6 guns, but 8 guns are desirable. These should be located outside the airscrew disc. Re-loading in the air is not required and the guns should be fired by electrical or means other than Bowden wire. It is contemplated that some or all of these guns should be mounted to permit a degree of elevation and traverse with some form of control from the pilot's seat.

Ammunition
300 rounds per gun if 8 guns are provided and 400 rounds per gun if only 6 guns are installed.

View
   a The upper hemisphere must be so far as possible unobstructed to the view of the pilot to facilitate search and attack. A good view for formation flying is required.
   b A field of view of about 10 degrees downwards from the horizontal line of sight over the nose is required for locating the target.

Handling
   a A high degree of manoeuvrability at high speeds is not required but good control at low speeds is essential.
   b The aircraft must be a steady firing platform.

It is interesting to look at how the fighter requirement had changed during the 1930s to explain the development of both the aircraft's capabilities and the tactical doctrine. During the 1930s the basic concepts were still those that had been developed in the latter years of the First World War; with no significant combat experience in the 1920s and in the absence of conflict (and funding) no appreciable development of technology or tactics, this was not really surprising. The main fighter specification that eventually led to the new generation of fighters was F7/30 for a 'Single-Seater Day and Night Fighter'. This Specification was dated October 1931 and the General Requirements paragraph included statements such as 'a satisfactory fighting view is essential and designers should consider the advantages offered in this respect by the low wing monoplane or pusher'. The main requirements for the aircraft are:

   a Highest possible rate of climb.
   b Highest possible speed at 15,000ft.
   c Fighting view.
   d Capability of easy and rapid production in quantity.
   e Ease of maintenance.

This was a lengthy document and amongst the key provisions was that the 'aircraft must have a high degree of manoeuvrability'. By the time of F10/35 this requirement had been toned down as being 'not required'. The aircraft was to have provision for four 0.303-in Vickers guns and a total of 2,000 rounds of ammunition, with a minimum supply of 400 rounds per gun, as well as being able to carry four 20-lb bombs. It stated that two of the guns were to be in the cockpit, with interrupter gear if required, and the other two in cockpit or wing. There was no requirement for an enclosed cockpit and the pilot's view was a prime concern: 'the pilot's view is to conform as closely as possible to that obtainable in "pusher" aircraft'. Virtually all of these requirements could be said to apply to an aircraft that suited the latter part of the First World War, a Sopwith Camel or Bristol Fighter, but with (slightly improved) performance. If the manufacturers had followed these requirements to the letter then the Spitfire and Hurricane might never have been born.

In terms of overall air doctrine the emphasis was increasingly on the bomber – the 'war-winning' weapon that will always get through no matter what the defenders try and do. Whilst the basic provisions of F7/30 could be said to describe an agile, manoeuvrable fighter, those of F5/34 (dated 16 November 1934) tipped the balance to what is best described as a bomber destroyer. The introduction to this Specification stated that:

> the speed excess of a modern fighter over that of a contemporary bomber has so reduced the chance of repeated attacks by the same fighter(s) that it becomes essential to obtain decisive results in the short space of time offered for one attack only. This specification is issued to govern the production of a day fighter in which speed in overtaking the enemy at 15,000ft, combined with rapid climb to this height, is of primary importance. In conjunction with this performance the maximum hitting power must be aimed at, and 8 machine guns are considered advisable.

No mention here of manoeuvrability; what is needed is to catch the enemy (meaning enemy bomber) and hit him hard in a single attack. All of this was encapsulated in F10/35 but with the added provisions under 'Handling' that emphasised the requirement for the fighter to be 'a steady gun platform' in which a 'high degree of manoeuvrability at high speeds is not required'. Of course, the British were not alone in this fighter theory and in Germany the Bf 110 came from a similar bomber-destroyer requirement. The latter proved a disaster in day fighting and if the RAF's new day fighter had been of a similar ilk then the Battle of Britain would have been short-lived – and lost. Rather than entering the annals as one of the great fighters, a Spitfire to this requirement would have followed the Defiant into the records as a glorious failure (as a day fighter).

Yet the Spitfire, and its Hurricane stablemate, was built broadly in line with the Air Ministry Specification, so how come it avoided the potential pitfalls?

The Spitfire is Born

On 28 December 1934 the Air Ministry issued Specification F37/34 to reflect the design proposed by Supermarine for F7/30, although at this stage only four guns were incorporated and the prototype would use the PV12 engine from Roll-Royce. This latter was a significant development as the PV12 became the Merlin and it was the airframe/engine combination that made the Spitfire a success. The contract for a prototype was signed on 3 January 1935 and detailed design work, including close cooperation with Rolls-Royce, commenced. This book does not focus on the development of the aircraft (the best study of that subject is *Spitfire: The History* by Eric Morgan and Edward Shacklady), but there are various elements of that tale of development that had a significant impact on the Spitfire's combat capability and are thus central to our story.

Under the prototype contract a four-gun installation had been agreed but by early April 1935 Mitchell had received the detail of Specification F10/35, which called for six or eight guns. It was inevitable that the successful fighter would need to incorporate this number of guns and in a 26 April 1935 meeting with Squadron Leader Sorley from the Air Ministry, Mitchell stated that he could adapt the prototype to take eight guns but that the bomb provision of the Specification would have to be deleted and the fuel capacity would be reduced to sixty-six gallons, both measures to save weight. Sorley supported the changes, as did the Deputy Chief of the Air Staff (DCAS), but others expressed concern at the reduction in fuel capacity. Air Commodore Verney (Director of Technical Developments) stated 'I am not in favour of reducing the tankage, as this could be done in production models if required; it is always much easier to decrease than increase, and experience shows that as engine power goes up we often wish to add extra tankage. Nor need the aeroplane be flown with full tanks.' These were prophetic words for, as we will see, 'short legs' (lack of fuel) was a problem that later plagued the Spitfire. In May Verney wrote to the Air Ministry to clarify a number of points concerning the new fighter, one of which concerned the armament:

As I understand it the view of the Air Staff is that the fighter's opportunities will be so fleeting that nothing but the maximum rate of fire in a minimum time is worth having. While agreeing with this, I feel sure that the trend of weapon development must be to increase the range of attack. My suggestion is for a single-seater fighter with 8 guns in the no allowance position either in the wings or fuselage, plus the COW [Coventry Ordnance Works] gun in the fuselage. Such a fighter could attack from the rear at a range of 100 to 500 yards using its COW gun. When the range had closed sufficiently the machine guns will be used.

The question of cannon versus machine guns was to continue to be hotly debated throughout the war. Verney's point of view appears to have been glossed over and at this stage the requirement was fixed at eight machine guns with 300 rounds per gun.

The name Spitfire first appeared in Supermarine records in late June but it was not yet sanctioned by the Air Ministry, and officially it was still the Supermarine Type 300. The prototype (K5054), fitted with a Rolls-Royce Merlin 'C', took to the air at Eastleigh, Southampton on 5 March 1936 in the hands of 'Mutt' Summers. It was a highly successful first flight with no major problems and for those observing from the ground the aeroplane 'looked right'; and history has proven that aeroplanes that look right usually are right. It was, however, only an aerodynamic and initial performance check and there was a great deal of development work still to be done, not only on the basic aircraft but more particularly to turn it into what it was meant to be – a weapon of war. For those interested in the development of the Spitfire the best 'hands-on' accounts are those by the aircraft's two main test pilots, Jeffrey Quill (*Spitfire, a Test Pilot's Story*) and Alex Henshaw (*Sigh for a Merlin*).

Before looking at the Spitfire's introduction to service and combat, there are a few aspects of the aircraft that need to be covered when considering its combat capability. These can be grouped under the headings of armament, self-protection, cockpit, visibility and performance, to which can be added tactics and training. The last three are covered in detail in each of the subsequent chapters but it is convenient to overview the first three in this introductory chapter.

Arming the Spitfire

One of the provisions of the Specification was that of armament and it is worth looking at this in a bit more detail. The standard armament for British fighters in the First World War was rifle-calibre (0.303-in) machine guns, primarily the Vickers. Forward-firing, through, over or around the propeller, or in rear cockpits (front cockpits in pusher types) operated by another crew member, the reasonably high rate of fire of the guns was very effective against the wood-and-fabric types of the First World War and the 1920s. Indeed, in view of the weight of the guns and bullets it was generally desirable to restrict the number of guns. The advent of larger aircraft with more engines, and the introduction of metal structures, led to lively debate on the number and calibre of guns required by fighters.

In the 1930s the Air Fighting Committee undertook a number of trials into fighter armament and a July 1935 paper concluded that the provision of eight guns (of 0.303-in calibre) would: 'provide a means of obtaining a decisive result in the minimum of time while at the same time increasing the chances of obtaining this result at longer ranges'. A paper the previous year had investigated the use of larger calibre guns, primarily 20-mm Hispano cannon and concluded that the heavier weight of the cannon – whereby one 20-mm cannon plus sixty rounds of ammunition weighed the same as four Brownings and 300 rounds of ammunition – was a disadvantage and when this was added to the cannon's aiming problems and slower rate of fire the machine-gun calibre Browning was best. In June 1935 a trial took place at Shoeburyness with eight 0.303-in guns being aimed at a metal aircraft target positioned tail-on to the guns. Assuming a two-second sight-on burst (256 rounds) 109 hits were recorded, including fourteen through the seats. The same set-up with a 20-mm cannon allowed for only seventeen rounds fired in the same period, although the resultant holes were much larger. The engine-mount system for cannon was considered a problem and it was concluded that if four such guns could be wing mounted they would prove an effective weapon. Although cannon armament was used by both RAF fighter types in the Battle of Britain, albeit in limited numbers, it was to prove problematical, especially with the Spitfire. However, the effectiveness of the machine-gun calibre Browning was also called into question, especially against increasingly well-armoured bombers. However, the RAF's weapon of choice was the 0.303-in Colt-Browning and whilst cannon-armed (20-mm) aircraft entered service in 1940 it was some time before the teething troubles were overcome and the cannon became a main armament, and a later exclusive armament, for the Spitfire.

A number of enhancements to the Spitfire weaponry were made in late 1939; for example, reflector sights were fitted in September and October and by December most of the Brownings had been modified to the Mk II with a modified muzzle attachment. Such changes were often the result of analysis by the Fighter Command Armament Section, who also looked at the question of gun harmonisation.

> At the start of the war all guns on Hurricanes and Spitfires were harmonised to give both a lateral and a vertical dispersion. Later the guns of some aircraft were harmonised to give a circular dispersion. On 19 December 1939 one squadron (No 111) harmonised its guns to give a rectangular dispersion of 12ft by 8ft at 250 yards. Later, after experimentation with nine squadrons, it was decided that all Hurricanes and Spitfires in the Command should harmonise their guns in accordance with the pattern of the British Air Force in France,

whereby all guns converged on a point at 250 yards. (Fighter Command Diary)

Harmonisation, and the range at which a pilot should open fire, caused much debate, and whilst the instructions for the former were laid down – although not always followed – the latter was more a matter of personal choice, as we shall see later. Fighter Command Battle Orders stated that the eight-gun fighters were to be loaded in the following way:

Starboard:	No 4 Gun	Ball	*Port:*	No 1 Gun	Ball
	No 3 Gun	AP		No 2 Gun	Ball
	No 2 Gun	Ball		No 3 Gun	AP
	No 1 Gun	AP		No 4 Gun	Ball

The guns were numbered from inboard to outboard; for night operations the only variation was for the No 4 Gun on each side to have one round in ten of B.Mk IV incendiary ammunition. Generally, there appears to have been few problems with either the AP or Ball ammunition.

It was also important to have an effective gun-sight and whilst early production aircraft had a simple ring-and-bead sight, provision had been made for a reflector sight; the RAF evaluated a number of such sights and in May 1938 chose the GM2 for its new fighters. Gun-sights continued to be developed throughout the war and various Spitfire Marks had different sights, although most were variations on the basic reflector design.

Self-Protection

It is now taken for granted that critical systems in an aircraft, such as fuel tanks – and the pilot – are protected from the effects of enemy fire, but this concept was not an automatic one in fighters such as the Spitfire. It was, for example, only in early 1940 that consideration was given to fitting rear armour in the cockpit of the Spitfire. The argument against such protection was weight, with the armour versus performance trade-off. Major considerations included bullet-proof (armoured) glass for windscreens, armour for the cockpit and protection for the fuel tanks, which later involved self-sealing tanks to prevent fumes igniting (a problem that made Japanese fighters such as the Zero highly vulnerable as they chose to ignore self-protection). In addition to the purely practical benefit of protecting the aircraft and pilot was the morale effect of knowing that there was at least some protection against enemy fire.

In general terms the Spitfire was no better and no worse than its contemporaries in respect of self-protection, although it is usually stated that the Hurricane was able to take more punishment. Cannon strikes could punch major holes in the metal structure of the Spitfire and, depending on the location of the strike, it could be either catastrophic or barely noticeable; the fuel tanks were always an area for concern but more devastating was damage to the control surfaces that made the aircraft unflyable. It is usually considered that to cause critical damage to an aircraft you need to keep the sight on for a minimum of two seconds (a figure we still used in the Tornado!), but if you went for the cockpit you could 'neutralise' the aircraft in half a second by hitting the most critical system of all, the pilot. To hold a manoeuvring aircraft in your sights for two seconds is not easy but it is true that most pilots were reluctant to shoot at the cockpit; if the pilot was hit as part of the general spraying of his aircraft with gunfire, so be it – but generally he was not directly targeted.

The use of armour-plate behind the pilot was a way of countering part of this random fire as it was still considered that most attacks would be from the stern and there was little that could be done to defend against a lateral attack, whilst the engine provided good protection from a frontal shot. However, the engine was also one of the most vulnerable systems in any aircraft and whilst the Merlin was rugged and reliable it was still prone to damage: a single bullet with a lucky hit was all that was necessary to take it down. The tell-tale stream of glycol from the punctured cooling system, or a plume of grey-to-black smoke from a critically damaged engine invariably spelt the end of the aircraft. Again, the Spitfire was no worse than its contemporaries in the early part of the war, although when the type took on the ground-attack role later in the war it did have a poorer record than types such as the Typhoon, of which more later.

Cockpit

A general comment made by many Spitfire pilots was that the aircraft 'fitted like a glove' and that the pilot therefore felt very much part of the aircraft; in comparison the Bf 109 was considered by pilots to be 'like a straight-jacket' and the Mustang 'like an armchair'. Jeffrey Quill remarked on the 'snug' cockpit when he strapped in for his first Spitfire flight:

> The cockpit was narrow but not cramped. I sat in a natural and comfortable attitude; the rudder pedals were adjustable, the throttle and mixture controls were placed naturally for the left hand and the seat was easily adjustable up or down. The retractable undercarriage selector lever and hydraulic hand-pump were situated to the right of the seat. The instrument panel was tidy, symmetrical and logically laid out. The windscreen was of curved perspex, which gave a good deal of optical distortion, but it had a clear-view glass panel for vision dead ahead in the line of the gunsight. The sliding canopy

was straight-sided and operated directly by hand, with a latch which engaged the top of the windscreen. With the seat in the fully raised position there was very little headroom – but at once I felt good in the cockpit. (Quill, *Spitfire, a Test Pilot's Story*)

As fighter pilots came in all shapes and sizes, the snug nature of the Spitfire was to cause some difficulty, although a great deal of flight time could be with the cockpit open, making life for the taller pilots a little more comfortable. The later Marks with blown bubble canopies were somewhat better.

There were few adverse comments about the internal layout, other than the switching of hands on take-off for undercarriage operations. In combat the basic idea was left hand on throttle and right hand on control column (as it is in modern combat aircraft); the control column was well-placed and comfortable to use, with a circular upper portion that included the all-important gun button. As with all fighter cockpits there was never enough room but it was not restrictive in combat, and it was relatively easy to escape from if everything went wrong.

Visibility and Lookout

In terms of visibility the Spitfire was far better than its first main opponent, the Bf 109, which had far too much 'ironwork' in the canopy and was probably the worst of all the early fighters in this respect. Jeffrey Quill took time away from his test-pilot duties to fly operational sorties in the Battle of Britain and in his autobiography he stated that this experience showed up

> one or two glaring defects which needed urgent action . . . The Spitfire was fitted with a thick, armoured-glass panel at the centre of its windscreen but the side panels were of curved Perspex and the optical distortion from these made long-distance visual scanning extremely difficult. I was determined to have the design altered, and indeed I succeeded in getting optically true glass into the side panels by 1941. (Quill, *Spitfire, a Test Pilot's Story*)

Many people assume that lookout is simply a matter of looking out of the cockpit, but it actually requires specific techniques of scanning and eye manipulation:

> I always knew, or at least was given the advice and followed it, to look at each sector – not just a glance around looking everywhere, you know, up and behind, not giving myself time to recognise anything. But look at a sector and decide whether there was or there wasn't anything there. Then I'd look at another sector and do the same thing. I found that the best policy if you really wanted to look at something. ('Rosie' Mackie, quoted in his biography: Avery with Shores, *Spitfire Leader*)

Combat experience had quickly shown the need to improve the rear view and whilst the 'rear-view mirror' was of great benefit it was not the whole answer. Fighter pilots had to learn to swivel their heads, and usually wore scarves to help 'lubricate' the neck, and were taught the principle of actually looking for aircraft. Once again, knowledge of the problem and its solution, coupled with training was an absolute must – sadly it was in short supply in the early part of the war.

Problems with the rear view was another lesson that Jeffrey Quill took away from his Battle of Britain ops with 65 Squadron:

> Also necessary was an improvement in direct rearwards vision. I did not quite see how this could be achieved in the short term, although probably something could be done in the way of further bulging of the canopy [this was done]. In the longer term I believed that a big change must be made to the lines of the rear fuselage and the shape of the canopy. This would take time but in the immediate future I could try to draw attention to the urgency of the need. (Quill, *Spitfire, a Test Pilot's Story*)

The Spitfire canopy underwent a number of modifications during the early and middle years of the war, culminating in clear-vision tear-drop canopies with exceptional visibility. The rear fuselage was also modified in some variants with a cut-down section to further improve the rearward visibility, although it had a detrimental effect on stability.

Whilst blister hoods were intended to improve visibility, jettisonable hoods were intended to improve pilot survivability by making it easier to escape from the aircraft when the time came. By December 1940 development work was underway on jettisonable hoods and schemes that had been put forward by 72 Squadron, Supermarine, Martin-Baker and ATS Hamble were duly inspected by Fighter Command's technical branch. Sadly, the records of the technical branch include no details, other than a reference to the blister-hood debate: 609 Squadron state that blister hoods for the Spitfire are unsatisfactory whereas 421 Flt state that they are a 'great improvement'. No 609 Squadron had been evaluating tear-drop perspex blister hoods since June 1940 following earlier trials by 65 Squadron. However, Mark VIII JF299 was the first to appear with a tear-drop canopy and cut-back fuselage (mid-1943), a combination whose rearward view attracted the comment that: 'this is an enormous improvement over the standard Spitfire rear view. The pilot can see quite easily round to his fin and past it, almost to the further edge of the tailplane. The whole field of search is increased appreciably.'

Performance

In the fight the only important performance considerations were whether the pilot could 'defend and survive' or 'attack and kill', with the need to defend or to attack switching in moments. Ignoring for now the training, experience, confidence and luck elements, the core of this is the aircraft's ability to turn better than the opposition or to out-climb, out-dive or simply have a better speed range in order to close or escape. Throughout its career, the Spitfire was generally considered to be amongst the best in terms of its ability to turn, although as we will see in a later chapter the tactical advice was never to try a turning fight with Japanese fighters such as the Zeke. In the European war the Spitfire usually had the edge in this department, although the appearance of the Fw 190 shaved off most of the Spitfire Vs advantages.

In respect to climb and dive the Spitfire was average, and in the early years of the war the engine limitations in negative-G (no fuel injection and therefore no fuel feed) meant that it was often poorly placed against the Bf 109. In most of the tactical scenarios of the Battle of Britain the Spitfires were at a disadvantage, often still climbing to height when they came upon the enemy. The 'Hun in the Sun' was definitely at an advantage.

Performance is a combination of engine performance and airframe aerodynamics, including control authority, and the Spitfire had two superb core engines in the Merlin and Griffon, although both had their fair share of problems, as will be mentioned in subsequent chapters. Overall performance varied greatly between the Marks of Spitfire and this is one of the subjects addressed in more detail in the following chapters.

Tactics

The pre-war prescribed Fighter Command attacks comprised six basic attack formations designed with slow and poorly armed bombers as the target, with the prime concern being that whenever possible 'fighters should attack enemy bomber formations in equal numbers by astern and quarter attacks from the same level'. It looked neat and worked well on peace-time exercises in the 1920s and 1930s but it was totally inappropriate to air combat by 1940.

> Fighter Command adhered to the orthodox methods of attack, i.e. in vic formation if possible, or in line astern, from the rear, either above or below. The Command did not approve of beam attacks, which called for accurate sharp-shooting in the fractional time when the beam of the enemy was exposed. Nor for similar reasons did it approve of the deflection shot. (Fighter Command Diary)

This rigid adherence to out-of-date tactics was not a Spitfire-specific problem, although it had a direct bearing on the aircraft's combat record in the early part of the war.

Into Service

The prototype was delivered to the AAEE at Martlesham Heath on 26 May 1936 for an initial series of performance and handling tests, the prime concerns being to confirm the top speed and to assess the aircraft's suitability for the 'average squadron pilot'. The report on the latter was positive and the top speed was recorded as 349mph. An initial production order for 310 Spitfires was awarded on 3 June 1936 and the RAF had its second monoplane fighter (the Hurricane being the first). Vickers-Armstrongs (owners of Supermarine) gave the Air Ministry a costing of £3,500 per aircraft for the first 100, and £2,500 for the next 210 aircraft. Somewhat later it became the norm to quote £5,000 as the cost of a fully equipped Spitfire and this was the figure used in the Spitfire Fund campaign.

The Martlesham pilots flew K5054 on further trials during summer 1936, a major report being issued after the September handling trials. The 'Summary of Flying Qualities' stated that:

> The aeroplane is simple and easy to fly and has no vices. All controls are entirely satisfactory for this type and no modification to them is required, except that the elevator control might be improved by reducing the gear ratio between the control column and elevator. The controls are well harmonised and appear to give an excellent compromise between manoeuvrability and steadiness for shooting. Take-off and landing are straightforward and easy.
>
> The aeroplane has rather a flat glide, even when the under-carriage and flaps are down and has a considerable float if the approach is made a little too fast. This defect could be remedied by fitting higher drag flaps.
>
> In general the handling of this aeroplane is such that it can be flown without risk by the average fully trained service fighter pilot, but there can be no doubt that it would be improved by having flaps giving a higher drag.

The full report is included at Annexe C. The comment that: 'the controls are well harmonised and appear to give an excellent compromise between manoeuvrability and steadiness for shooting' is an interesting one and had its roots in the RAF's accepted fighter requirement that an aircraft should be able to intercept and destroy bombers — fighter-versus-fighter air combat was not high on the list – air doctrine held that the destructive potential of modern bombers was the major threat and thus had to be countered.

By the end of the year the eight Brownings had been fitted and in February 1937 the aircraft returned to Martlesham once more for the gun-firing evaluation – with an eight-gun fighter still a thing of wonder for the

RAF. All went well with gun-butt tests on the ground and with air-firing at lower altitudes, but when the aircraft climbed to height the guns proved far more problematic. Being located in the wings meant that the guns had to be cocked prior to take-off and that the pilot could do nothing in the event of a stoppage. At height the oil in the breeches, which were unheated, was unable to cope with the combination of low temperature and low pressure with the result that five of the guns would not fire at all and the best result was one gun that managed 171 rounds before it too froze. This was totally unacceptable for a fighter, but should not have been a great surprise. The solution lay in heating the gun bays and in ensuring that the oil was the right type, although it was to take some time for the gun heating problem to be sorted out. The Martlesham report also criticised the GD5 reflector sight and recommended adoption of the GM5 sight, which was duly done. The gun problem did not, though, go away:

> Another thing which browned us off were the faults which had shown up in our machines [autumn 1940, Spitfire I, 74 Squadron]. The peacetime pilots must have really goofed off – we had to ask if they ever fired their guns way up in the icy cold. Did they ever test the bloody things to see if they'd work. On one of our first high-altitude battles we, 74, had only nine machine-guns fire out of 96. The oil had frozen, locking breech mechanisms solid. Now all guns were lubed with refrigerator oil, then wiped almost dry. (Spurdle, *Blue Arena*)

Despite the problems, the Spitfire had shown its potential and it was hoped that first deliveries of production aircraft would take place by mid-1937; however, there were a number of production problems and the delivery date slid backwards. The first production Spitfire flew in May 1938 and the RAF's first production Spitfire, K9788, went to Martlesham Heath in July 1938 for trials and the following month (4 August), whilst K9789 was delivered to 19 Squadron, commanded by Sqn Ldr Henry Cozens, at Duxford to begin that unit's re-equipment from Gauntlets. More aircraft arrived and the two Duxford squadrons – 19 and 66 – began intensive 'service trials' in order to iron out any problems. Initial snags that gave rise to adverse comment included poor starting, oil leaks and lack of headroom for tall pilots!

With the death of R. J. Mitchell in June 1937 the mantle of taking the Spitfire into production and further development was taken on by Joe Smith as chief designer. His desire to develop the aircraft further was not necessarily well received in certain circles at the Air Ministry and whilst it is not the role of this book to go into the politics of this period it is worth stating that the Spitfire was in danger of being almost still-born. There were some in the Ministry, in part angered by the early problems of production and delivery that saw no future for the Spitfire and were already considering alternative production options for the Supermarine works at Southampton. The legend was almost killed before it had been tested in battle. However, by December 1938, No 19 Squadron had its full complement of sixteen aircraft – less than a year before war broke out. The standard establishment for a fighter squadron was set at sixteen aircraft to give four flights each with four aircraft.

War

At the outbreak of the Second World War on 3 September 1939, the RAF had over 300 Spitfires in service — a major achievement considering that the first unit had only re-equipped in August 1938 and that by March the following year only four squadrons had received the new fighter. In that first month of the war the company produced thirty-three Spitfires, bringing the total production to 341 (by summer 1940 production was running at around 130 aircraft a month). The initial production problems evident following the first flight of the prototype had been largely overcome but they had resulted in a significant delay in the type's entry to service. The stage was set, the players were moving into position, all that remained was for the aircraft to prove itself in combat.

~ 2 ~

Into Battle

First Shots

The Spitfire's first combat engagement during the Second World War proved to be something of a farce. In the so-called Battle of Barking Creek on 6 September 1939 the Spitfires of 74 Squadron were alerted to the presence of 'an aircraft' by anti-aircraft fire and so went to investigate. In the subsequent air combat they shot down two Hurricanes of 56 Squadron; not an auspicious start to a combat career. Aircraft recognition was a much-practised art but what seemed obvious in a crew-room when staring at silhouettes or models on the ceiling was far less so in the high-speed action that was modern air combat. 'Friendly fire' remained a major problem throughout the war and Spitfires were fired on by all manner of friendly forces, air, ground and sea – as well as by other Spitfires.

The first definite combat for Fighter Command's Spitfires came on 16 October when Red Section of 603 Squadron scrambled from Turnhouse to engage Ju 88s of KG30 that were attacking shipping in the Firth of Forth. One of the bombers was shot down, whilst a second German aircraft was claimed by 602 Squadron. The Spitfire's tally-sheet had started.

Deliveries increased in the early part of 1940 and more Spitfire squadrons became operational. It is fortunate that at this stage of the war the calls upon Fighter Command were still light; this not only allowed time for more aircraft to be delivered but also gave squadrons the opportunity to work up to operational readiness with their aircraft. As Commander-in-Chief of Fighter Command, Hugh Dowding had decreed that none of the Spitfire units should be sent to France as part of the air component of the British Expeditionary Force, this duty falling instead to the Hurricane units. Whilst the fighter squadrons remained in the UK, one Spitfire moved to France to begin a whole new career in the photographic reconnaissance role; thus, N3071 became a PR.1A and was detached to Seclin, France from where, in the hands of Flt Lt 'Shorty' Longbottom, it flew its first operational mission on 18 November (see Chapter 10, 'Reconnaissance Operations').

However, the German offensive launched on 10 May 1940 smashed the Anglo-French defences and the RAF's air elements were soon overworked and under pressure; the Hurricane units fought well but there were many who considered that now was the time to send the Spitfires in to join the battle. Pressure was applied by the French but Dowding held firm, believing that the main battle was yet to come and that he would need every fighter, especially the Spitfires, when the Germans attacked England. Nevertheless, Spitfire units were placed on alert to fly offensive patrols over the Continent, which soon led to a number of air combats.

June 1940, while these first significant air battles involving Spitfires were taking place, also saw a new production facility commence deliveries. P7260 was the first Spitfire delivered from the Castle Bromwich plant, which provided a great increase in the production capability at a time when Spitfires were in huge demand. The Castle Bromwich factory eventually produced some 12,000 Spitfires, well over half of the total numbers built.

The experiences of the early combats were put to good use as RAF fighter squadrons refined their tactics and trained hard for the inevitable air assault on Britain. The delay in the assault was a result of the Luftwaffe's need to reorganise after recent losses and to establish itself at new bases ready for the attack on Britain. It was a supremely confident Luftwaffe that opened the battle on 10 July 1940. On 16 July Hitler issued Directive No 16, Operation Sea Lion, for the invasion of Britain, with the proviso that before invasion could take place 'the British Air Force must be eliminated to such an extent that it will be incapable of putting up any sustained opposition to the invading troops'. Over the next few months the Spitfire became a legend and the Hurricane became 'the other aircraft'.

A Fighter Command report considered the question of Spitfire versus Hurricane, in respect to 'manoeuvrability in air fighting':

the attached notes concerning the relative manoeuvrability of Spitfire versus Hurricane are forwarded for the information of pilots. They are the result of combat tests by experienced pilots and the principles will apply against hostile aircraft of similar performance.

It was found that the Hurricane will easily out-turn the Spitfire in a simple tailchase, and bring guns to bear in two or three turns. A tailchase is therefore of advantage to the Hurricane, but fatal to the Spitfire. The correct tactics for the Spitfire against the Hurricane (or any hostile aircraft with better turning circle but lower speed) are as follows:

Approach in such a way that the guns are brought to bear as soon as it is within range, if possible by a surprise attack from above. Maintain the attack only as long as the sights are on. If the attack is not decisive, and sights cannot be kept on owing to the turn of the other aircraft, break off instantly. If the aircraft turns away and tries to escape, the Spitfire has the immediate and decisive advantage, provided the pilot does not lose sight of the enemy. If the slower aeroplane with better turning circle is flown by a very skilful pilot, it is difficult for the pilot of the Spitfire to get the sights on for more than a moment, and make an effective attack, unless he can use the element of surprise by making the enemy pilot lose sight of him. The Spitfire pilot can, however, retain the initiative and sooner or later bring off a decisive attack by exercising patience in attaining the most favourable position well above the enemy. It is considered that higher speed is much more valuable than smaller turning circle, provided the sacrifice of quick turn is not out or proportion to the gain in speed. Other factors being equal, the aircraft with the greater speed has the advantage both strategically and tactically, over that with the better turning circle. It is considered that a combat between two fighter pilots of great experience and equal skill, one in the Spitfire and the other in a slower but more 'manoeuvrable' type would result in a victory for the pilot of the Spitfire.

First Combats – The Channel and France

It was during the Dunkirk evacuation that Fighter Command's Spitfires were at last released to go and tangle with the enemy, and even then their operations were confined to coastal districts. Spitfires of 66 Squadron were the first to operate over Europe: six aircraft flying with Defiants of 264 Squadron; the formation bounced and damaged a lone Ju 88. The following day the first real air battle was fought, with the Spitfires and Defiants engaging a formation of Ju 87 Stukas escorted by Bf 109s – the first time that the German fighters met Spitfires. The RAF pilots shot down five of the enemy (only one Bf 109), for the loss of six of their own (one Spitfire). However, the Allied ground forces rapidly succumbed to the blitzkrieg tactics of the enemy and the evacuation of British and French troops took place in late May and early June from the French port of Dunkirk. The area was subjected to heavy air attacks and in view of the critical nature of the situation Fighter Command flew intensive operations over and around the Dunkirk area. One such mission flown by Spitfires of 19 Squadron on 26 May resulted in a claim of six Ju 87s and six Bf 109s for no loss.

In the same month, the British had the opportunity of carrying out comparative tests with a captured Bf 109E, courtesy of the French. Plt Off Adolf 'Sailor' Malan, plus Spitfire, was detached from 74 Squadron for this task. The general conclusion following the trials was that the Spitfire was superior to the Bf 109 in most areas of performance; tactical advice included such comments as 'another effective form of evasion with the Spitfire was found to be a steep, climbing spiral at 120mph; in this manoeuvre the Spitfire gained rapidly on the Me 109, eventually allowing the pilot to execute a half roll on to the tail of his opponent.' One important result, although this was also due to lessons learned by the Hurricane squadrons in France, was to harmonise the fighter's guns at 250 yards instead of the standard 400 yards. Interestingly, but not surprisingly, German trials of a Bf 109 against a captured Spitfire suggested that the latter was generally inferior; the great fighter pilot Werner Molders commented that

> it handles well, is light on the controls, faultless in the turn and has a performance approximately that of the Me 109. As a fighting aircraft, however, it is miserable. A sudden push forward on the stick will cause the motor to cut . . . in a rapidly-changing air combat situation the motor is either overspeeding or else is not being used to the full.

However, after the two types had been involved in a number of real combats over England, it was generally accepted that the Bf 109 had the edge in all areas except that of turning performance; the standard evasion tactic for the German pilots was a steep dive, taking advantage of the fuel-injected engine – the Spitfire pilot wishing to follow his adversary would have to roll his aircraft onto its back and pull into the dive in order to keep positive-G forces on the Rolls-Royce Merlin. Successful fighter pilots such as Johnnie Johnson preached the inadvisability of going after diving targets that were leaving the battle.

Operational Spitfires had two-pitch propellers, which turned out to be one of those good ideas that was proved detrimental; early combats had shown that the Spitfire needed more height and more speed, with a suggestion that the inherent power of the Merlin was being restricted by the propeller. After some debate and with 65 Squadron leading the field with a 'semi-official' inquiry to de Havilland concerning conversion of their aircraft to a constant-speed unit, by August 1940 every Spitfire (and Hurricane) in the Command had been given the modification. It was an amazing accomplishment, with the production of the mod kits by de Havilland and the field modification by de Havilland engineers and RAF ground crew. At around the same time the RAF began to use 100 octane as standard fuel, rather than the old 87 octane, with an appreciable increase in engine performance.

Cannon-armed Spitfire IBs entered service with 19 Squadron in spring 1940 (initial trials with a pair of cannon had been made with a Spitfire at Drem in late 1939 and cannon as a weapon had been evaluated in the mid-1930s – see Chapter 1, 'Development'). Typical of the combat reports relating to the new guns was that for 16 August:

> A Flight of 19 Squadron was sent to intercept a raid near Clacton and joined combat with Bf 110s. Although three were claimed for no loss the cannons performed badly and only two pilots had no stoppages and all were handicapped by no tracer. Pilot commented that 'when the 20mm guns were

fired accurately the effects on the Me 110s was most gratifying'. (Air Historical Branch Narrative)

However, at this juncture the view of the CO (Sqn Ldr R. Pinkham) was that his boys would have scored far more kills if they had been flying standard eight-gun aircraft. Regarding the effectiveness of 0.303-in guns against some German bomber types, with their increasing amounts of armour protection, there were numerous instances of fighters using up all their ammunition with no apparent result; it was soon apparent that the heavier punch of the cannon was the way forward but it would be some time before an effective armament combination was universally in use.

Spitfire II

The Spitfire II entered service with 611 Squadron in August 1940, as the Mark IIA equipped with the standard eight 0.303-in Brownings; the Spitfire IIB, with its cannon armament, did not enter service until the following March (with 222 Squadron). Externally the new variant was almost identical to the Mark I but it was more powerful with its Merlin XII engine, and it also had a number of other refinements, including a pressurised water-glycol cooling system and a Coffman cartridge starter. Production of the new variant was centred at Castle Bromwich. This plant eventually produced 921 Spitfire IIs, of which 750 were the IIA version. In September 1940 one of the first production aircraft was sent to Boscombe Down for evaluation and comparative trials with a Spitfire I. The overall conclusion was there was little to choose in terms of performance between the two variants. However, as with all combat aircraft the Spitfire was increasingly burdened with extra weight and drag, the two items of significance being armour-plate – heavy but essential – and IFF aerials, which caused airflow drag. When Miroslav Liskutin joined 145 Squadron at Catterick, the Squadron was equipped with a mix of Spitfire IIA and IIB. His view was that the IIA was an

> excellent aircraft for all aspects of flying and particularly for aerobatics. This variant seemed to be the best in its class, although there was a limit of 20 seconds for inverted flying. The danger of inadvertently exceeding the limit was minimal as the engine always picked up promptly and there was no detectable signs of damage. For air firing purposes the Spitfire was undoubtedly an excellent gun platform. The only disadvantage came from the distribution of weapons along the wing, which called for a harmonizing pattern at a given distance. As a rule, these harmonizing patterns were planned for an impact grouping at 250 yards or 300 yards, creating a circle of 3 feet in diameter. Different harmonization patterns were used for special purposes. Minor variations were allowed to individual pilots who requested it. (Liskutin, *Challenge in the Air*)

The Brownings had 300 rounds per gun, enough for seventeen seconds of fire, and the cannon had sixty rounds per gun, enough for eight seconds; Liskutin's comment on the latter weapon was 'the destructive potential of these weapons with their standard ammunition gave us the confidence of being equal or superior to the Luftwaffe fighters.' Many pilots liked to keep a few rounds back for the run to home in case they were intercepted or given a golden opportunity of a quick shot, this was particularly true later when the Spitfires were roving over enemy territory on the offensive. However, as there was no round counter in the cockpit it was always an estimate of how much ammunition was left, based on a mental calculation of how many seconds of firing there had been so far – and in combat that was a hard calculation to keep going.

A number of Spitfire IICs were produced, but this did not, as it did in later Marks, indicate use of the 'C' Wing but denoted that these aircraft were modified for air-sea rescue work. The Spitfire IIA combat debut came in the later part of the Battle of Britain and it is to that conflict – and the establishment of the Spitfire legend that we now turn.

~ 3 ~

Battle of Britain

Oberleutnant Friedrich-Wilhelm Koch was an observer with the Heinkel-equipped 3 Staffel/Kampfgeschwader 4 (3/KG4). Koch and his crew, Oberfeldwebel Hermann Draisbach, Oberfeldwebel Rudolf Ernst and Feldwebel Alfred Weber had already flown in Poland, Norway, France and on 1 July 1940 were making their first attack on Britain. Three Heinkel 111s took off from Wittmundhafen in northern Germany late in the afternoon on what was the unit's first daylight attack against Britain. Their target was a chemical works at Middlesbrough. Like most Luftwaffe aircrew they were confident in themselves, their aircraft, and in the prospects of another easy victory.

> ... Already after the first machine-gun bursts of my radio operator in the upper rear position, the gun had suffered a malfunction. From this moment on, the Spitfires could perform their attacks unhindered and from close range. One after the other made his run. Each time a Spitfire launched his attack, a noisy stream of bullets rushed through our aircraft. At first the instrument panel was shot to pieces, then one engine was put out of action. Next, the landing gear came down and the flaps flew off. After the second engine was also put out of action and the starboard ailerons had been shot away, the Spitfires left their crippled victim and returned to their base. The pilot, without instruments, flaps, ailerons, a damaged rudder and propellers that could not be feathered, struggled with the controls, miraculously keeping the aircraft flying. Now after the continuous rattling noise of the bullets had stopped, it became dead and quiet in the aircraft. My pilot asked me to guess the speed and altitude since he had no instruments and was fully occupied in struggling with the controls. (Goss, *The Luftwaffe Bombers' Battle of Britain*)

Some crew made it into dinghies when aircraft ditched and they were picked up by HMS *Black Swan*.

The Spitfire legend was born with the Battle of Britain, which, some would have us believe 'it' won; as is often the case with such 'historical facts' this one is far from an accurate reflection of either the event or the aircraft, and yet no matter how many words are written to expound on the subject the basic 'truth' will no doubt remained enshrined!

Table 1: Battle of Britain: Fighter Command Strength

	10 July 1940				31 October 1940			
	Sqns	IE	Serv	Ac/Cr	Sqns	IE	Serv	Ac/Cr
Hurricane	27	432	582	344	34	544	561	399
Spitfire	19	304	320	226	19	304	294	227
Defiant	2	32	39	24	2	32	39	10
Blenheim	6	96	92	62	6	96	61	46
Totals	54	864	1033	656	61	976	955	682

Notes: October 1940 does not include half-squadron of Gladiators
IE = Initial Establishment (the authorised issued strength)
Serv = serviceable
Ac/Cr = serviceable with crew

Statistics are always more complex than they first appear; for example, for 10 July Table 1 shows 582 serviceable Hurricanes and only 320 serviceable Spitfires – so there were 262 more serviceable Hurricanes available. However, the column for serviceable aircraft *with* a (serviceable!) pilot shows a different picture in terms of combat effectiveness, with only 118 fewer Spitfires than Hurricanes. Table 2 gives a more detailed look at Fighter Command's Order of Battle for August 1940, showing the composition of each operational Group in respect of aircraft types.

Table 2: Fighter Command Order of Battle, August 1940

Aircraft	Squadrons	Total Sqns
No 10 Group		
Blenheim	604	1
Hurricane	87, 213, 238	3
Spitfire	92, 152, 234, 609	4
No 11 Group		
Blenheim	25, 600, FIU	3
Hurricane	1, 17, 32, 56, 85, 111, 145, 151, 501, 601	10
Spitfire	41, 64, 65, 74, 266, 610	6
No 12 Group		
Blenheim	23, 29	2
Hurricane	46, 229, 242	3

Aircraft	Squadrons	Total Sqns
Spitfire	19, 66, 222, 611	4
Defiant	264	1
No 13 Group		
Blenheim	219	1
Hurricane	3, 73, 79, 232, 245,249, 253, 263, 504, 605, 607	11
Spitfire	54, 72, 602,603, 616	5
Defiant	141	1
Other	804, 808	2
Note: The complete Orders of Battle for August 1940 and September 1940 are at Annexe B		

The Order of Battle for August 1940 shows twenty-seven Hurricane squadrons and nineteen Spitfire squadrons, with No 11 Group – the real front-line in this stage of the battle – having ten Hurricane and only six Spitfire squadrons. The situation had changed little in the Order of Battle for September, with twenty-nine Hurricane squadrons and seventeen Spitfire squadrons – so why is it that the Spitfire is seen as the type that won the Battle?

The Battle of Britain consisted of a number of reasonably distinct phases:

I   10 July to 12 August: attacks on coastal shipping, plus limited attacks on radar installations and airfields.

II   13 August to 6 September: attacks on airfields and associated installations in an attempt to gain air superiority.

III   7 September onwards: attacks on London.

IV   Late September to end of October: daylight fighter raids.

At first the British accepted the challenge and sent up Hurricanes and Spitfires to engage the German units. The Hurricanes were out of date and their performance was far inferior to that of the Messerschmitt fighter as regards both maximum speed in level flight and rate of climb. Though the Spitfire was more manoeuvrable in turning, its maximum speed was 20–30 km per hour less. German ammunition and armament were manifestly better than those of the British. The RAF lost the greater number of fighters. But even more important than these technical drawbacks were the out-moded tactics used by the British fighters. Generally speaking, they flew in close formation of squadron strength in order to peel off immediately before making an attack. German fighters, on the other hand, flew in wide, open formations, a tactic evolved and perfected in the Spanish Civil War. About 15 days after the beginning of this phase of the Battle the British adopted the German style of flying.

The question of comparative fighter performance is one that has occupied many thousands of words and is frequently clouded by partisan viewpoints – did the rugged nature of the Hurricane make it better able to survive being hit? was the armament of the German fighters far superior? did the Spitfire really win the Battle? and so on. The qualitative nature of the pilots and – as Galland points out – the tactics being employed have also to be taken into consideration. 'The Luftwaffe entered the Battle with a confident, almost cocky, attitude and hence their morale was superb. The RAF fighter pilots were still largely untried and they faced what appeared to be an invincible war machine that had swept previous opponents away' (Adolf Galland).

Aircraft performance was all important: 'Above 5,000ft I could not out-dive or out-climb the Me 109, so if my Spitfire's superior manoeuvrability could not be used, pretending to be shot-down was a good strategy. At low altitudes, with emergency engine boost, the Spitfire allowed for three minutes of extra power, and was definitely better all-round in performance than the Me 109' (Jan Zurakowski, 234 Squadron).

Tactics, however, continued to cause the RAF problems and whilst some COs soon realised that the old tactics were not suitable for the high-speed air combat of fighter-on-fighter, others were slow to change. In his autobiography, *Wing Leader*, Johnnie Johnson commented that 'the presence of the aggressive hard-hitting 109s would not permit our fighters the time necessary to carry out elaborate manoeuvres. Tactics must be simple … always keep your head turning. It takes about 4 seconds to shoot-down a fighter – so look around every three!' Over the summer months of 1940 the RAF fighter pilots had much to learn.

On 31 July, the day that the RAF recognises as the start of the Battle, a flight of Spitfires of 66 Squadron from Coltishall was scrambled to intercept one of the regular early-morning German reconnaissance flights, they succeeded in finding the oft-elusive aircraft and 'opened' the score by shooting it down. Later in the day a major German attack developed on shipping in the Dover area; amongst the fighter squadrons that pitched into the air battle was 74 Squadron,

Plt Off Cobden, leading Yellow Section, followed Blue Section down. He picked out a straggling Do 17 and disabled its starboard engine. He then delivered a second attack on the bomber, but as he was breaking away, was set upon by a group of Me 109s and his Spitfire was riddled with their fire … engaged emergency boost and broke away from his attackers in a steep climbing turn.

It had been a typical encounter: into the fray; identify a target; close, give it a burst or two; keep looking around and don't stay on a straight course for more than a few seconds; where once the sky was full of aircraft it is now empty! This was the first 'dogfight' involving more than 100 aircraft and the RAF had come out well. Total German losses for the day were recorded as twelve aircraft, whereas the RAF's only loss had been Hurricane P3671 of 111 Squadron.

Daily combats became the norm, ranging from only a few aircraft to major air battles fought over and around convoys. Without the vital information provided by the RAF's radar network and fighter direction system, Fighter Command would have suffered far greater losses and achieved much less. The single greatest advantage, however, was that of fighting over one's own territory – damaged aircraft could be recovered and repaired and pilots, having been shot down, would often find themselves back in the air again the following day. This latter point is a vital one as Fighter Command's greatest problem during the battle was one of insufficient aircrew *not* insufficient numbers of aircraft.

The Spitfire 'mystique' was already being established on all sides. Most German combat reports speak of being attacked by Spitfires, even when there were none anywhere near the actual combat; the British public were soon being encouraged to 'sponsor a Spitfire'. For the sum of £5,000 an organisation or individual could 'buy' a Spitfire for the defence of the country; indeed, a high proportion of Spitfires leaving the factories were sponsored in such a fashion and presentation aircraft became a common sight – to the extent that whole squadrons acquired the name of the sponsor. All those thousands of citizens who donated pots, pans, railings and other metal items to the Spitfire Fund had visions of their contribution eventually forming part of a Spitfire! At a time when most of the war news was bad such morale-boosting exercises were essential.

Although the RAF fighters were taking to the air to meet the Luftwaffe attacks on convoys, the air battles were not going as the German planners had predicted and a change of strategy was required. Thus on 1 August Hitler ordered the Luftwaffe to 'overpower the British Air Force with all the forces at its command in the shortest possible time'. The strategy outlined a policy of attacks on flying units, their ground installations and the aircraft industry. Luftwaffe planners translated this into *Adlerangriffe* (Eagle Attack) – a progressive campaign to destroy the RAF on the ground and in the air. There were accurate attacks on 12 August against radar stations and airfields, Lympne, Hawkinge and Manston airfields being hit hard. This last attack caught the Spitfires of 65 Squadron as they were getting airborne but, despite this, all but one of the fighters made it safely into the air. The airfields of No 11 Group remained the primary target and by mid-afternoon on 15 August every fighter in the Group was airborne to counter the more than 300 German raiders. At the end of the day the losses were recorded as forty-five German aircraft and thirteen RAF aircraft, although this does not include aircraft destroyed on the ground; at Detling, for example, twenty-two aircraft were destroyed by the air attack. As part of a plan to swamp the defences, raids were flown by Luftflotte 5 against targets in the Midlands and the north. Unknown to the German planners, a large and important convoy was due to depart Hull at midday and so the East Coast radar stations were at a high state of readiness and vigilance. Taking off at 1000 hours from their bases in Norway and Denmark, the German bombers had a two-hour flight to the British coast – and no fighter escort. Just after midday, controllers at the East Coast radar sites detected two raids, and fighter squadrons – including 616 Squadron – were brought to maximum readiness. The Staxton Wold radar station plotted a raid of over forty aimed at the fighter stations of Church Fenton and Leconfield. No 616 was scrambled and ordered to patrol over Flamborough Head. The call came just as the two flights were in the process of changing over the readiness duty, which enabled the whole squadron to scramble. Such was the spirit that on hearing the scramble, Fg Off Moberley, who was on a day's leave, leapt into a spare Spitfire and roared off fifteen minutes behind his colleagues. Fourteen Spitfires scrambled, and for its first major battle the squadron's sections were:

Red: Robinson (CO), Hellyer, Smith, Westmorland.
Yellow: Bell, Brewster, Walker.
Blue: Gillam, Murray, Marples.
Green: Dundas, Casson, Hopewell, Moberley.

The squadron was vectored to patrol over Flamborough, and at 1315 hours it intercepted a formation of around fifty Ju 88s of KG30. Squadron pilots reported that the enemy was flying in a very poor formation, with several stragglers. Flt Lt Denys Gillam, leading Blue Section, was the first to spot the enemy, at 19,000ft, and immediately led the section into the attack. Plt Off Marples got in the first burst and as he broke away, Gillam took over; he kept up a continuous fire as the Ju 88 dived to 6,000ft, jettisoning its bombs. Part of the tail broke away and the aircraft turned onto its back, enveloped in flames, before crashing into the sea. Meanwhile Marples, having pulled off from his first attack, immediately pursued another bomber, getting in two bursts before it entered cloud with one engine smoking. He then saw two other bombers north of Scarborough and gave chase, firing short bursts. One aircraft wheeled to port and dived to ground level, but Marples could only harass the bomber as it flew at 100ft – he had run out of ammunition. Plt Off Murray (Blue 2) saw two Ju 88s flying through broken cloud at 10,000ft; they were in close formation and one was smoking badly. He fired three long bursts and, a second or two after the last burst, both bombers caught fire. He did not see them crash but it is most unlikely that they were able to make it back to Denmark. Plt Off Hugh Dundas, leading Green Section, saw Denys Gillam lead Blue Section into the attack and after Marples broke away, having severely damaged his second aircraft, Dundas closed in and fired a three-second burst, setting both engines on fire. Plt Off Buck Casson (Green 2) had followed Dundas in, but being poorly placed he broke away to intercept a lone bomber heading out to sea at 5,000ft. After two quarter attacks, the enemy dived to 1,000ft – with the rear gunner keeping up a steady fire. Casson fired two more bursts and the aircraft dived to sea level, at which point Dundas re-appeared and, with Casson out of ammunition, took over the attack. By now, there was no return fire and the enemy bomber was last seen at very low level with smoke pouring from its port engine.

Red Section also attacked the main bomber force, with the CO, Sqn Ldr Robinson, damaging one bomber before he ran out of ammunition. Flt Lt Hellyer, accompanied by Plt Off Smith, dived astern a Ju 88, and fired all his ammunition into it; Smith then took over and fired a series of short bursts until the bomber suddenly dived steeply into the sea.

By now, the bombers were completely split up and a number of individual actions took place. Sgt Hopewell picked out a lone Ju 88 and hit it in both wings. The bomber took violent evasive action and turned inland; Hopewell continued to fire into the engines and pieces started to break off. Shortly afterwards the bomber crashed three miles northwest of Bridlington. Sgt Westmoreland also attacked a lone bomber; firing two short bursts from 400 yards he set the port engine on fire, after which one of the crew bailed out. Finally, Fg Off Moberley arrived on the scene after his late take-off. He had been listening on the radio and decided to head towards Flamborough, but before reaching the area he spotted a twin-engined aircraft low over the sea. He dived to 2,000ft and identified a Ju 88 with smoke coming from one engine (probably the aircraft that had been attacked by Westmoreland). He made two or three attacks before the bomber's starboard engine stopped and the aircraft crashed into the sea. In just a few minutes, 616 Squadron claimed eight enemy bombers destroyed and six seriously damaged – for no loss. As the Squadron was soon to discover, it was a different war to that being fought in the south.

By 18 August it had become official policy that, whenever possible, the Spitfire squadrons should engage the enemy fighters, leaving the Hurricanes to attack the bombers. This proved impossible to enforce as all too often a single squadron, of whichever type, found itself alone facing over 100 German bombers and fighters! By the third week of August the situation was becoming critical, with severe damage to a number of airfields and an increasing shortage of trained pilots; expedients such as shortening the length of the Operational Training Unit course provided more pilots, but with less experience.

A few days after its success against KG30, 616 Squadron was ordered south, to Kenley. At 1845 hours on 22 August, fourteen Spitfires scrambled to patrol over Hawkinge at 15,000ft. With no customers they turned towards Dover; no sooner had they arrived when they were bounced by twelve Bf 109s, Green Section being on the receiving end. Almost immediately, Plt Off Dundas's aircraft was hit and he was wounded in the arms and legs. With his controls shot to bits and his aircraft on fire, Dundas tried to bail out but could not open his hood. He spun down out of control from 12,000ft and finally managed to escape from his aircraft at 800ft. Another 109 was attacking Green 3 and Sgt Wareing dived onto the enemy's tail, following it in a steep dive to port. After being hit by a number of short bursts fired from 300–400 yards, the German fighter levelled out and slowed down, giving Wareing the opportunity to fire another burst, which set the 109 on fire. Honours were more or less even on this encounter but it was not long before the intensity of the battle led to heavy losses.

After a quiet start to 25 August the Squadron scrambled twelve aircraft at 1820 hours to patrol over Maidstone and intercept raids aimed at the airfields in Kent. Over Canterbury, they intercepted fifteen to twenty Dornier Do 17 bombers flying at 17,000ft escorted by up to twenty Bf 109s flying in a staggered line at 20,000ft. A number of 109s were engaged and damaged; Fg Off Moberley shot down one and Plt Off Bell attacked another that was on the tail of a Spitfire. Sgt Ridley managed to disengage from the main dogfight with the 109s and closed on one of the bombers, shooting it down into the sea. However, the squadron paid dearly. Both Sgt Westmoreland and Sgt Wareing failed to return and it was soon confirmed that the former had been killed when his Spitfire crashed near Canterbury.

The situation was even worse the following day: in a number of scrambles the Squadron's pilots found themselves at a disadvantage and were mauled by the German fighters; the day cost 616 Squadron seven aircraft, with two pilots killed and three wounded badly enough that they played no further part in the Battle of Britain. This particular unit had suffered heavily in less than a week but they were not unique; the RAF was struggling. RAF and Luftwaffe loss rates assumed similar proportions, and remained so through to early September; the Battle was very much in the balance. The overall German strategy was working. Some squadrons virtually ceased to exist in a single day. Then it all changed.

On the night of 24 August London was bombed; Churchill ordered a retaliatory raid on Berlin the following night. In a speech on 4 September Hitler decreed that he would wipe out British cities. To certain Luftwaffe leaders this seemed an ideal way of forcing the 'few remaining' RAF fighters to take to the air and be destroyed. By late afternoon on 7 September 1940, some 400 bombers and 600 fighters converged in waves on London. The defending fighters rose to meet them but it was to be a day of mixed fortunes, with some squadrons suffering heavy losses and others claiming high scores for little loss. All too often it depended on how well the ground controllers had predicted the situation and thus put the fighters in an advantageous position. The controllers were getting better and the aircraft supply situation was reasonable, which meant that the Spitfire squadrons were never truly short of aircraft, although the careers of some aircraft lasted only a few days – as did some pilots. Some squadrons were still having trouble with tactics.

> I switched on the reflector sight and tucked myself in under my leader. Yellow sparkles flickered from the front of the bomber as it seemed to float up towards us. Things banged and clanged off my plane's wings and even off the windscreen. I was frozen into following my leader. I was formatting under him far too closely and suddenly saw the streams of empty cartridge cases spewing out of the vents under his wings and flashing all around me. I couldn't fire for fear of hitting the jinking, diving machine so close in front of me and we flashed past the bomber to climb and curve back and dive again in a quarter stern attack. (14 September 1940, Spurdle, *Blue Arena*)

'Spud' Spurdle's autobiography provides an excellent insight into Spitfire ops in the Battle of Britain (and beyond) and does not try to gloss over the problems of training, morale and integration, or his own initial problem coming to terms with air combat. The use of pre-war tactics such as the stern quarter attack and the slavish adherence to combat pairs, with the No 2 sticking with his leader, lingered even in experienced units such as 74 Squadron. After a week of intensive raids, followed by days when nothing seemed to happen, the Battle was set for its climax. The Luftwaffe planned one final blow to smash the remnants of Fighter Command. However, the Command was in good shape after a quiet week and squadrons were at the most effective strength they had been for some time. As the first raids of 15 September built up, the RAF's fighters rose to meet the threat and soon all the squadrons of No 11 Group and a number of others from No 12 Group were engaged. Although the losses on both sides have been debated ever since, it was nevertheless a defining day as the culmination of the campaign to date, and caused Hitler to postpone Operation Sea Lion. By 1120 hours the Command had twelve squadrons airborne covering the southeast approaches to London; the Duxford Wing (or five squadrons) was up a few minutes later to patrol Hornchurch. The Spitfires of 72 Squadron were first into action:

> I was Tennis Leader when ordered to patrol Canterbury with 92 Squadron, 72 leading. While I was on patrol I was ordered to attack fighters. I ordered the Squadron into line astern and dived down on the fighters out of the sun,

as we dived I ordered the Squadron into echelon starboard, thus attacking as many fighters (Me 109s) as possible. The Me 109 which I attacked half-rolled as I opened fire and before he could dive away he caught fire and exploded. I was then attacked by five other Me 109s. I did a steep turn to starboard and continued to turn until I out-turned one Me 109 which was on my tail. I gave him two short bursts and he burst into flames. I then spun down to get away from more Me 109s which dived down on me.

The Luftwaffe certainly recognised the threat from the Spitfire and late September brought a concerted effort against centres of production. The Supermarine works at Woolston were attacked on 24 September by two waves of bombers. On this occasion damage was only light but one air-raid shelter was hit, causing deaths amongst the workforce. However, two days later the factory was hit again and this time damage was far more severe. Dispersal plans had already been made and this attack hastened their implementation. Nevertheless, German intelligence remained good and the Westland works at Yeovil, then in the process of tooling-up for Spitfire production was attacked and damaged at the end of the month. Overall production fell from 133 aircraft in August to just fifty-nine in October. However, the situation soon recovered and provision of aircraft never became a major factor. Table 3 shows the Spitfire squadrons and their claims and losses.

The last weeks of the Battle saw the combat debut of the Spitfire II, the first unit, 611 Squadron at Digby having re-equipped in August, with three further squadrons in September. In addition to various modifications that the RAF had been requesting, and in many case retrofitting to Mark Is, the new variant had a Merlin XII engine and a pressurised water-glycol cooling system, as well as a cartridge starter. In overall terms there was little to choose between the performances of the Spitfire I and II and externally they were almost indistinguishable. The exception to this was a batch of aircraft that were fitted with a forty-gallon fuel tank semi-blended into the port wing. Whilst this certainly aided range and endurance, it reduced most aspects of performance, including speed, climb and ceiling. Only three units – 66, 118 and 152 squadrons – operated this Mark II, with – it would appear – little enthusiasm. The search for extra range and endurance would continue to haunt the Spitfire.

Table 3: Battle of Britain Spitfire Squadrons

Sqn	Main Airfields	COs	Claim	Loss
19 Sqn	Duxford, Fowlmere	S/L P. C. Pinkham+ S/L B. J. Lane	60½	7
41 Sqn	Catterick, Hornchurch	S/L H. R. Hood+ S/L R. C. Lister S/L D. O. Finlay	89	32
54 Sqn	Rochford, Hornchurch, Catterick	S/L J. A. Leathart S/L D. O. Finlay S/L T. P. Dunworth	52	20
64 Sqn	Kenley, Leconfield, Biggin Hill, Coltishall	S/L N. C. Odbert S/L A. R. Macdonnell	39½	13
65 Sqn	Hornchurch, Turnhouse	S/L D. Cooke S/L H. C. Sawyer+ S/L A. L. Holland S/L G. A. Saunders	31	15
66 Sqn	Coltishall, Kenley, Gravesend, West Malling	S/L R. H. Leigh	53½	25
72 Sqn	Acklington, Biggin Hill, Croydon, Coltishall	S/L R. A. Lees S/L A. R. Collins+ S/L E. Graham	66	23
74 Sqn	Hornchurch, Wittering, Kirton-in-Lindsey, Coltishall	S/L F. L. White S/L A. G. Malan	45	11
92 Sqn	Pembrey, Biggin Hill	S/L P. J. Sanders S/L A. M. Maclachlan S/L J. A. Kent	78½	32
152 Sqn	Acklington, Warmwell	S/L P. K. Devitt	61	20
222 Sqn	Kirton-in-Lindsey, Hornchurch	S/L H. W. Mermagen S/L J. H. Hill	53	15
234 Sqn	St Eval, Middle Wallop	S/L R. E. Barnett S/L J. S. O'Brien+	69	17
266 Sqn	Wittering, Tangmere, Eastchurch, Hornchurch	S/L J. W. Hunnard S/L R. L. Wilkinson+ S/L D. G. Spencer S/L P. G. Jameson	14	11
602 Sqn	Drem, Westhampnett	S/L G. C. Pinkerton S/L A. V. Johnstone	84	15
603 Sqn	Turnhouse, Hornchurch	S/L E. H. Stevens S/L G. L. Denholm	67	30

Sqn	Main Airfields	COs	Claim	Loss
609 Sqn	Middle Wallop	S/L H. S. Darley S/L M. L. Robinson	97	14
610 Sqn	Biggin Hill, Acklington	S/L A. T. Smith+ S/L J. Ellis	58	20
611 Sqn	Digby	S/L J. E. McComb	18	2
616 Sqn	Leconfield, Kenley, Coltishall, Kirton-in-Lindsey	S/L M. L. Robinson S/L H. F. Burton	28	14
Total claims and losses for Spitfire squadrons			1064	336
Notes: + = Killed in Action; Only first two initials of CO's name given				

Night Operations

Digby, 6 June 1940:

Air Raid alarm at 0005, lasting until 0215. A calm, cloudless, starry night, but no moon. Three pilots in succession sent up, patrolling various points in the Sector at 20,000ft, but no contact made. It is the general opinion amongst the pilots that the Spitfire is unsuitable for night flying, owing to the pilot being blinded by his exhaust flames. If blinkers are fitted, that difficulty is diminished, but the difficulty of landing is increased. Further, fore and aft control is very light, necessitating constant reference to the instruments, so that there is a constant adjustment of eyesight between the lighted instruments and the dark skies. (611 Squadron Operations Record Book – ORB)

Less than two weeks later, on 18/19 June the first significant night attack by the Luftwaffe took place – and two Spitfire squadrons were involved in the defence. The targets for the He 111s of KG4 were the airfields of Honington and Mildenhall and the bombers, flying solo attacks, were told not to expect any night fighters. One of the 74 Squadron pilots scrambled that night was Flt Lt 'Sailor' Malan, his combat report showed that the Spitfire was not as totally ineffective at night as the 611 Squadron ORB suggested.

... I climbed towards an enemy aircraft which was making for the coast and held in a searchlight at 8,000ft. I positioned myself astern and opened fire at 200 yards, closing to 50 yards, with one burst. I observed bullets entering the enemy aircraft and had my windscreen covered in oil. Broke off left and immediately below, as enemy aircraft scrambled out of beam ...

This first successful combat took place near Foulness Island in the Thames Estuary and Malan soon picked up another raider near Southend, the He 111 being clearly visible in a searchlight beam. '. . . I gave two five-second bursts and observed bullets entering all over the enemy aircraft with slight deflection as he was turning to port. Enemy aircraft emitted heavy smoke and I observed one parachute open very close . . . I followed him down until he crashed in flames near Chelmsford.'

A number of Blenheims were also airborne and one Heinkel was on the receiving end of a simultaneous attack by a 23 Squadron Blenheim and Fg Off 'Johnnie' Petre's 19 Squadron Spitfire. The latter was hit by return fire when his aircraft was illuminated by searchlights and as it burst into flames he was forced to bale out. Another 19 Squadron pilot also made contact, Fg Off George Ball, stalking a Heinkel that he picked up in the searchlights north of Southend. Two good bursts of machine-gun fire wrecked the Heinkel, which crashed in the Thames.

Although the RAF gradually developed its night fighter force using two-seat aircraft such as the Blenheim, equipped with AI (airborne intercept – radar), single-seaters such as the Spitfire continued to be used for night defence as 'cat's eye' fighters. The main problem was that of finding the target and, whilst the ground controllers became increasingly expert at guiding aircraft to the general area of a target, and even setting up a basic interception, the system was not accurate enough, especially in height estimations, markedly to reduce the need for the fighter pilot to acquire the target visually from some distance. Spitfires scrambled to patrol or intercept relied on searchlights to pick out aircraft and then they would fly in that direction to try and close for an engagement. Estimating range at night was difficult, as was maintaining decent night vision – especially when the guns were fired. None of these problems was unique to the Spitfire. However, where the type did suffer more than its colleagues such as the Hurricane was in the general difficulty of landing the aircraft at night, a combination of its approach pattern and undercarriage.

The Battle Ends

The raid on 31 October marked, in official RAF terms, the end of the Battle of Britain. The Luftwaffe had been defeated and the Spitfire had experienced what many consider to have been its finest hour. This is, of course, a very simplified picture and does no justice to the other elements of Fighter Command, not least the Hurricane units, which played critical roles during the Battle. The top-scoring Spitfire unit in the Battle had been 602 Squadron with a claims board of 102 enemy aircraft (the overall top squadron was the Hurricane-equipped 303 Squadron).

In the late autumn, the Luftwaffe employed more fighter sweeps, at times with hundreds of aircraft involved throughout the day, in an attempt to wreak final destruction on the RAF's fighter force; on most occasions the tactic was seen for what it was and Fighter Command did not respond. The development of hit-and-run fighter-bomber tactics was, however, to cause problems for Fighter Command.

Spitfire Legend?

A Fighter Command report stated that in November 1940 the Command had brought down 190 enemy aircraft, of which 113 fell to Spitfires and seventy-five to Hurricanes and 'despite the fact that Spitfires had flown two-thirds of the operational hours flown by Hurricanes they brought down 20% more enemy aircraft and suffered 17% less casualties.' This would seem to be a clear indication that the kill ratio of the Spitfire was markedly better. How true a picture was this?

The Battle of Britain was essentially fought by Spitfire Is equipped with eight machine guns; the number of cannon-armed aircraft and Spitfire IIs was fairly irrelevant to the overall statistics. Table 4, dated November 1940, gives the performance range (speeds) for the Spitfire I but, as with most performance statistics, they mean little except as a comparison with other types – and in general most single-seat fighters in the Battle were similar in speed range, although a few mph here and there could prove significant. The differences in performance were more important in respect of combat elements such as turn (manoeuvrability), climb and dive; speed was of course a factor if you were trying to run away from, or catch, another aircraft.

One post-war RAF study of the Battle stated:

> During August Sqn Ldr A G Malan commented that his Spitfire was no better than a 109 at that altitude (27,000ft). Pilots of 74 Sqn had earlier commented that they easily outfought 109s up to 20,000ft. This was one of the earliest indications of a merit of the 109 – its excellent performance above 25,000ft compared to the Spitfire and especially the Hurricane.

On 6 October 1940 Churchill asked the Secretary of State for Air for 'figures of total losses of Hurricane and Spitfire during the months of August and September'. Table 5 shows these results.

Table 4: Performance Table – Spitfire I

Height	Gate	Buster	Line	Scramble
0ft	282/291	249/257	151/152	161/161
5,000ft	303/290	267/257	163/152	172/161
10,000ft	324/289	286/256	176/152	186/161
15,000ft	346/287	305/252	190/152	195/155
20,000ft	360/276	315/241	207/152	201/146
25,000ft	348/245	301/210	226/152	208/126

Notes: First figure is TAS (True Air Speed) and second is ASI (Air Speed Indicator), both mph
Gate – top speed
Liner – economical speed
Buster – max cruising speed
Scramble – best climb speed
Table dated 29 November 1940

Table 5: Total Losses of Hurricane and Spitfire, August and September 1940

	August 1940			September 1940		
	Hurricane	Spitfire	Total	Hurricane	Spitfire	Total
Enemy action	238	143	381	228	134	362
Accident	15	11	26	15	8	23

One of the remarkable things about these figures is just how similar they are for each of the two months that were the height of the Battle. Table 6 makes interesting reading in that loss rates in combat are similar when you take into account the fact that for most of the period there was an average of nineteen Spitfire squadrons, supplying 220 or so 'aircraft plus pilot' each day, whereas the Hurricane statistics show an average of thirty squadrons providing 370 'aircraft plus pilot'. Bearing in mind these figures, the table also demonstrates that the accident rate with the Spitfire remained higher than that of the Hurricane.

According to some recent research the Spitfire suffered a loss rate of approximately 4 per cent during major air combats (6 per cent for the Hurricane) and its average kill to loss ratio was 1.8 to 1 (1.34 to 1 for the Hurricane). This would tend to suggest that the Spitfire was only marginally more successful than its counterpart. However, these statistics are at variance with those in Table 3 above, which show 1,064 victories for 336 losses – a kill ratio of over 3 to 1. There will always be debate on questions such as this, especially with official records showing distinct differences. The bottom line is that both British fighter types shot down more German aircraft than they lost themselves, both had aircraft and pilots that were recovered to fight again, the essential equation in the Battle – but that for a variety of reasons, including the 1940s version of 'spin-doctoring', the Spitfire was turned into a legend for both home and enemy consumption. It would be true to say that the Spitfire did not deserve the epithet legend because of its Battle of Britain participation but that the epithet was fully justified by its overall contribution to Allied air power in the Second World War.

Table 6: Losses, 1 August 1940 to 31 October 1940

Month	Category	Combat Loss		Destroyed on Ground		Flying Accidents	
		Hurricane	Spitfire	Hurricane	Spitfire	Hurricane	Spitfire
Aug	Cat 2	49	55	10	10	38	35
	Cat 3	220	118	15	5	18	14
Sep	Cat 2	95	80	1	0	60	56
	Cat 3	228	130	1	2	21	13
Oct	Cat 2	29	36	10	2	48	38
	Cat 3	76	60	1	0	25	15
Total	Cat 2	173	171	21	12	146	129
	Cat 3	524	208	17	7	64	42

Notes: Cat 2 = Repairable but not at unit
Cat 3 = Total loss

Final Thoughts – And Onto the Offensive

Dowding had every right to be pleased with the performance of his fighter squadrons but he was also realistic enough to know that the Battle had been finely balanced and that there were many lessons to be learnt. One of these concerned fighter leadership and he later wrote: 'the quality of the RAF's tactical leadership was a matter of vital importance . . . some of the worst losses of the Battle had been caused by the mistakes of inexperienced Squadron Commanders . . . in future promotions to command will be of officers who have proved their abilities as Flight Commanders.'

The Spitfire I had come out of the Battle as a solid air-combat fighter; considering the lack of time that the squadrons had to equip and train with the type its kill to loss ratio was reasonable. There were problems with the aircraft, with Fighter Command tactics and with the quality of the training and there was much work to do in further developing the aircraft. Some of the aircraft-related elements have already been referred to but there was one that had been apparent since the early flight trials, had been very noticeable during the Battle, and simply had to be rectified. At high speeds the Spitfire's controls, primarily the ailerons, were very heavy; this was a very severe limitation on combat manoeuvrability. 'My mind went back to the many occasions of struggling with both hands on the stick at well over 400mph on the clock, swearing and sweating profusely as one always did and feeling totally restricted in manoeuvre.' (Quill, *Spitfire, a Test Pilot's Story*). The aileron problem was one that Jeffrey Quill and others had noticed from the first trials but at the time it was not the most important issue and it was only when high-speed combat became a reality that the problem took on a tactical significance. This was both frustrating and dangerous for pilots, who were used to an aircraft that was light and responsive, yet positive, on the controls throughout most of the flight envelope. It was not a problem that was confined to the Spitfire: trials on a captured Bf 109 revealed a similar, if not worse, state of aileron control above 400mph. By late 1940 a solution had been found. The use of metal-skinned ailerons with a thin trailing edge transformed the aileron control and an urgent modification programme was instigated.

Although minor raids still took place, the great air battles of 1940 had ceased. The Luftwaffe licked its wounds, rebuilt its strength and began taking on new tasks in other operational theatres. Meanwhile the RAF continued to expand its aircraft strength both with new bombers and with an ever-increasing number of Spitfire units. Never again would major air battles take place by day over the UK – it was time for the RAF to move from defence to offence, and for the Spitfire to truly earn its 'legend' epithet.

~ 4 ~

'There I Was' – Tactical Training

This book focuses on the Spitfire as a weapon of war by looking at its tactical employment, and whilst the facts and figures of performance, armament and the aircraft-associated aspects are of course crucial, they are only one element of what makes an aircraft 'combat effective'. An equally important aspect is how to make best use of that weapon system – and that comes down primarily to training and tactics. Reference is made to training and tactics in the relevant chapters, but many of the principles and practices that applied to similar fighter types also applied, or with little variation, in all theatres and applications of the Spitfire. The bulk of this book is a chronological or by theatre of operation examination of the Spitfire, but this chapter cuts across that formula to look in general at the question of tactical training as well as picking up a number of the 'combat effectiveness factors' mentioned in the Introduction.

Initial thoughts on the Spitfire from Wg Cdr Evan 'Rosie' Mackie DSO DFC, the top RNZAF ace:

> In the air it seemed to have enough power to do anything. It flew like a dream in turns. At the same time one realised that there was sting in the tail – it was a real weapon itself. You had to come to grips with the fact that although it was a beautiful sleek machine, it was basically just a weapon. (quoted in Avery with Shores, *Spitfire Leader*)

Training

A major conference took place in early 1942 to discuss aircrew training; in the report the section on Fighter Command opened with a series of statements as to what was required of a fighter pilot.

> Except for greater speed, higher ceiling, fire-power and armour, there is essentially little difference between aerial combat to-day and that in the latter

part of the last war. Speed has been gained at the expense of manoeuvrability, but the fleeting instants in which targets present themselves are compensated for by greatly-increased fire-power. Thus, the first requirement of a pilot who has learned to handle his aircraft is an ability to seize his limited opportunities, and, having done so, to shoot accurately when an opportunity is presented. Such work calls for an instant response from hand and eye, together with the capacity to endure a considerable strain concentrated into a short but decisive period of time. (SD349: 'Aircrew Training: Report on the Conference held in the United Kingdom January/February 1942')

The report went on to address a number of key elements, extracts of which are included below.

Aircraft performance:

A good fighter pilot must feel himself part of his aircraft. He must be well aware of its powers of manoeuvrability at all altitudes and in every condition of weather, its offensive power, and its vulnerability to attack.

Gunnery:

He should have a capacity for taking infinite pains to perfect the tactical side of flying and most important of all, gunnery. In the last war the most successful fighter pilots spent much time on the ground in perfecting their gunnery and in devising new methods of attack; and no system of training can fully succeed if it does stimulate the same interest and enthusiasm.

Fuel awareness:

While the speed of a fighter is great, its endurance is small and the constant concern of a pilot is his petrol consumption ... a pilot cannot achieve an economical standard unless he is trained to understand the capabilities and limitations of his engine and can extract the best performance from it.

Aircraft recognition and lookout:

It is vital that a fighter pilot should be trained to recognise friend from foe at the first glance and at maximum distance. This entails constant practice, and intensive study of models and photographs throughout the training period. The importance of 'rubbernecking' must be instilled into every pupil from the very beginning of his training, so that the whole time he is flying he is studying the sky and making a mental note of the type, position, course and height of every aircraft he sees. He must be made to realise that for every aircraft he does see there is probably another he does not; and that he must be watchful and alert from the moment that he enters his aircraft.

Oxygen and blacking-out:

The rate of climb, ceiling and speed of fighter aircraft are responsible for several problems, principal among them are oxygen and blacking-out. One object of training should be to kill the fallacy that oxygen is necessary for height only. It is, of course, essential at high altitudes, but it is also necessary long before the need for it becomes physically apparent to the pilot if his mental alertness is to be kept at concert pitch. Pilots must realise that oxygen has as its principal function the improvement of fighting efficiency at all altitudes, and that the correct drill is vital to safety and success. In blacking-out it is not generally realised that many successive tight turns or immoderate weaving have accumulative effect on the circulation, tending to early fatigue and possible blackout. Training should teach the pilot to realise instinctively what he can and cannot do without incurring the risk of blackout.

Remember, this was a 1942 report – with two full years of Fighter Command operations on which to base some of the points covered by the conference. Before we look in more detail at the training of Spitfire pilots, the report highlights a number of other aircraft-related issues that need comment. There were a number of things that killed Spitfire pilots, from enemy action to bad luck and carelessness. Most of these could be mitigated by training and most were, of course, not restricted to the Spitfire but could be lumped under the general heading of 'aviation', especially aviation in wartime.

It is not our purpose to look in detail at any of these but there are a few that crop up fairly regularly in squadron, group and command records. In a previous chapter we have already alluded to night operations and the high incidence of landing accidents, although most of these resulted in injury and aircraft damage rather than pilot fatalities. However, night and bad weather, combined or separate, were a major problem and the total losses to this element were high, although difficult to quantify. Disorientation has always been a killer for aircrew but it was not truly recognised and trained for until the 1950s and many a single-seat pilot in the Second World War would at best have lost control and baled out or at worst gone down with his aircraft. The Spitfire was not blessed with protection from icing; the engine with its water–glycol mix had some anti-icing protection but the carburettor was still vulnerable. The airframe was even worse; there was no anti-ice or de-ice protection and no warning system.

Pilots were warned to avoid icing conditions, but that was often easier said than done; as a day fighter the Spitfire's normal operating environment was clear of cloud where the bad guys be found and destroyed, but seeking cloud cover as protection against superior numbers or evading a better fighter was a standard tactic. Once the aircraft started to ice-up the only option was to get out of the icing layer – by climbing or descending – as soon as possible and wait for the ice to melt, preferably before it had too adverse an effect on airframe or controls.

As the 1942 report mentioned, oxygen was of critical importance to fighter pilots both for survival at height and for performance in high-workload conditions at any height. The Spitfire's oxygen system was reasonably effective but there were numerous recorded instances of losses being put down to oxygen failure or mismanagement. Squadron records often mention an aircraft falling out of formation and plunging to earth for no apparent reason, and with no response to anguished calls from colleagues. These losses were usually stated as oxygen failure or the pilot forgetting to select his oxygen. Following a particular spate of such mysterious losses of Spitfire VBs the Accident Branch report stated:

> it had been found that firing the VB's cannons damages, in some ways, or dislocates the oxygen regulating apparatus so that thereafter the rate of supply cannot be regulated . . . The greater the length of piping the more chance there was of a stoppage of supply due to a collection of condensation freezing, with the result that the pilot would black out [oxygen starvation to the brain].

In an earlier chapter we mentioned the Spitfire's lack of fuel; all fighter pilots must develop fuel awareness: it is both embarrassing and potentially lethal to run short of fuel (as fast-jet aircrew I have been there!). In this respect the Spitfire was one of the worst of the fighters as it had a thirsty engine, especially when combat settings were being used, and in the heat of battle it was all too easy to neglect the fuel gauges, which themselves were notoriously unreliable (a feature shared by most contemporary aircraft). When operating over the UK this was not so much of a problem as there were plenty of airfields to pancake into and refuel, or if it was really desperate there were fields to land in, although the weak undercarriage of the Spitfire liked reasonable grass surfaces rather than ploughed fields.

However, when the fighters started to range over Europe and further, the easy options were no longer available and pilots had to be prudent and know when the time had come to head for home. Over the desert you could land almost anywhere but fuel had to come to you; over the jungle there was usually nowhere to land other than a limited number of airfields and landing strips. It was essential that leaders were aware of the fuel states of the members of their formation, which would invariably be worse than their own. Other than adding more fuel there was little that could be done from an aircraft point of view, except improve gauging and add warning lights, so it was all a matter of training, airmanship and experience.

The final element to pick out of the report before focusing on performance and tactical issues is G, referred to in the report as 'blacking-out'. High-performance air combat involves pulling large amounts of G, whereby the body increases its apparent weight (gravity effect). A tight turn or a snap pull to climb will produce an instant G-loading, the exact degree of which depends on the degree of the action, but 4G–5G is not unusual. The main effect of this as far as the pilot is concerned is the physiological one of blood pooling, whereby under positive-G the blood attempts to 'go south' towards the feet, meaning that the head (and brain) are amongst the first areas to be affected; this leads to the phenomenon of grey-out and then black-out. Again, this is not the place to go into detail of the effect and how to counter it, but it was a distinct problem for the Spitfire and one that was not always recognised or trained for.

> I held my fire on the Hun as we screamed together and, as I saw the smaller details of his kite, I heaved back on the stick. My face dragged down and strained on my skull, my mask nearly broke my nose and everything went brown and then black. I held the stick hard back and kicked on left rudder – that'll fox the bastard. The black-out faded and for an ageless instant I couldn't see a single plane. (Spurdle, *Blue Arena*)

Until the adoption of G-suits later in the war, and even then with few Spitfire squadrons being issued such equipment, the only solution to G was knowledge and understanding of its existence and training in how to ameliorate its affects. The author could find little evidence of such training for Spitfire pilots.

Conversion to Type and Operational Conversion

There are two main elements in training for a particular aircraft – conversion to type and operational conversion, the latter including weapons. Training is one of the first elements to suffer when time is in short supply and for the RAF in 1940 there was never enough time; the urgent needs of the operational squadrons led to reductions in training time and a consequent lessening of the pilot's effectiveness when he arrived on his squadron. Johnnie Johnson noted this in his excellent biography *Wing Leader*: 'Our time at Hawarden was spent in learning how to fly the Spitfire; during my few days there I never fired the eight guns or took part in any tactical training – this would come later, if there was time.'

AVM Sholto Douglas (ACAS in late 1930s) later wrote that, based on his First World War experience, he was in favour of initial type and combat training:

> We had to devote precious time and effort in the squadrons to giving them their final training, and no matter how hard we tried they were still only half trained when they went into battle. As a result of that we suffered very heavy casualties. I was determined that should not happen again and when my chance came as a senior officer on the Air Staff, I pressed hard for the formation of those initial training units.

The average Operational Training Unit (OTU) course by late 1941 was forty hours on type – four times longer than it had been in 1940 but still not enough, especially in respect of tactics and gunnery. A great deal of time was spent honing the skills of pilots to enable them to get onto enemy aircraft, and it is strange that so little was done to ensure that they had a good standard of marksmanship once they got there. Less than three of the forty hours were spent on actual firing, and cine-gun seemed of limited use in comparison.

Miroslav Liskutin, a Czech pilot who subsequently served with a number of Spitfire squadrons, was on No 10 Course at No 58 OTU, Grangemouth in summer 1941. He was one of thirty pilots on the six-week course – and six of them were killed in flying accidents, a higher than usual rate but a fact of life at training units such as this. In his biography *Challenge in the Air*, Liskutin recalled:

> the ground school instructors gave us the principles for using our aircraft's guns for combat. This was followed by lectures on local firing practice and the air firing followed in great haste. It is difficult to describe my pleasant surprise when, on my first attempt at firing onto a flying target I achieved 16% of hits. My result had turned out to be one of the best at Grangemouth at that time.

He was right to be pleased with that percentage; for most pilots an average score was nearer to 5 per cent.

It was a similar story at 53 OTU when Ralph Sampson (later Wg Cdr) had his 'laying on of hands'. In his biography, *Spitfire Offensive*, he recounts the final flying exercise at Hawarden, an air combat against Flt Lt Geoffrey Banham (ex-Battle of Britain pilot):

> pupils who had preceded me all had the same dismal experience to recount. Each confirmed that no sooner had the dogfight commenced than Geoff and his Spitfire were on their tail, and each knew that if this had indeed been the real thing that would have been promptly shot down. A sobering thought for us embryonic air fighters.
>
> Flt Sgt Payne told me 'the moment he gets on your tail, roll the Spitfire onto its back, open the throttle wide, pull the stick hard back into your stomach and just before the vertical, slam the stick hard to one side. The aeroplane will then go into a series of barrel rolls, gathering speed all the time. This manoeuvre makes it impossible for another pilot to follow, let alone get in any telling shot.'

Sampson followed the advice and promptly lost control, eventually recovering and returning to Hawarden – the only one of his course not to have been shot down.

The peak year for Fighter Command's OTU strength was in 1942 and five of the eleven units were for Spitfire conversion:

52 OTU – Aston Down
53 OTU – Llandow
57 OTU – Eshott
58 OTU – Grangemouth
61 OTU – Rednal

The strength of the OTUs varied from time to time, as did their composition in terms of aircraft types, but in general by mid-1941 the Spitfire OTUs had a main strength of Spitfires, a mix of Marks, plus a complement of trainers, usually Masters, and a small number of target-towing types for air-to-air gunnery. As an example, the establishment of No 58 OTU at Grangemouth was increased with effect from 24 February 1941 to 51+17 Spitfires (these figures reflect 51 aircraft IE – In Establishment – and 17 aircraft IR – In-use Reserve), 17+5 Masters and 4+2 target-tow aircraft.

It has been standard practice for many years to have a dual-control trainer for operational types to make the conversion to type and initial weapon training more effective. A two-seat Spitfire for this purpose, the T.8, did eventually appear but only in the post-war period and even then it was a private venture development and not an Air Ministry request. A twin-sticker had been mooted as early as 1941 but the panic at that stage was for operational Spitfires and not trainers, and anyway the 'system' was happy that the existing concept of using an advanced trainer such as the Harvard provided enough of a lead-in for the average pilot. There is no doubt that a two-seat trainer Spitfire at the OTUs would have saved lives by reducing accident rates but it is questionable as to what improvements in actual training there would have been.

The only Spitfire user to have an operational trainer during the war was the Russian Air Force, who converted a number of Mark IXs into Mark IX UTI (Uchebno Trenirovochnii Istrebityel – fighter trainer) but these must have been a nightmare for the instructor in the rear seat as his forward vision was virtually zero. When the Supermarine Mark VIII (later T.VIII of T.8) trainer appeared in 1946 it had a raised rear cockpit to overcome some of the vision problems. A number of nations did order trainer conversions of the Mark VIII and Mark IX but this was the tail-end of the Spitfire's life and the RAF was not interested. Confirmed users included Egypt, India, Ireland and the Netherlands.

Training on the Squadron

One of the classic scenes in the film *The Battle of Britain* is when a Spitfire pilot makes a hash of his landing – given a Verey to wave him off because the undercarriage wasn't down, followed by a bouncing landing. When met by the CO with the question 'how many hours do you have on Spitfires?' his answer was '10½, sir'. 'Let's make it 11 before Jerry has you for breakfast.' As they walk to their aircraft the other pilots make the comment 'spring chicken to shite hawk in one easy lesson'. The point is, however, a very valid one for 1940: not only were pilots arriving with very little tactical training, they were arriving with very few flying hours on type.

A general comment made by many Spitfire pilots is that they were given very little tactical training, either in training or on the squadron. In 1940 Spitfires (and Hurricanes) were in short supply and were needed in the squadrons; there were very few to spare for the training units and pilots had to make do with whatever types were available. However, the policy of leaving such additional type experience and tactical training to the squadrons was massively flawed. It was workable in 1939 and even into early 1940 with the Phoney War, although it very much depended on the attitude of the CO and his senior pilots, some of whom saw 'sprog' pilots as more trouble then they were worth. Where training did exist it usually focused on formation flying and the approved Fighter Command attacks, both of which were of limited tactical value.

In August 1940 Johnnie Johnson was posted to 19 Squadron at Duxford with a total of 205 hours in his logbook, of which twenty-three were on Spitfires. The promised extra training was not forthcoming as the squadron was having problems with its new cannon armament: 'I don't know how we shall find time to train you chaps. We've simply got to get these things working first.' The concept of on-squadron training was totally flawed, especially at a time when the squadrons were hard-pressed to maintain operational status. Most flight and squadron commanders did the best they could and tried to shield new boys from ops until they had built up a few more hours and had flown a few mock combats. Sadly, for many a bright young Spitfire pilot his first combat experience was often his last.

The situation varied from unit to unit and depended to a large degree on the attitude of the squadron commander, and to a lesser extent the flight commanders or even senior (experienced) pilots.

We had a great deal of respect for 'Crash' Curry [Sqn Ldr John Harvey Curry DFC]. He set about really putting us through our paces with 'tail-chasing'. A small formation of say four aircraft went off and he would do all sorts of attacks on us, 'out of the sun', 'up and under' and really gave us a hard time. He was a magnificent pilot, nobody could touch him – he had his own 'Flying Circus' in Texas before the war. He did not approve of the RAF gun-sight and had his own built into his aircraft. He was out 'polishing' his Spitfire almost every day until it gleamed, and no airman was allowed to go near it. (Jerry Jarrold, 80 Squadron)

Crew-room Chat?

Wg Cdr 'Rosie' Mackie later wrote:

> In retrospect, I think it would have been far better to have talked about it a lot more, with demonstrations by those experts in the field, with the object of generally making pilots more gun-conscious or firing-conscious. To point out errors that could occur, and perhaps did occur. If they had talked about it a lot more on the ground I'm sure a lot of people, junior pilots in particular, would have assimilated a lot of that stuff and in turn argued about it themselves, brought forth new ideas. (quoted in Avery with Shores, *Spitfire Leader*)

Indeed, it was seen as taboo in many squadrons to talk 'shop', especially in the mess, and where the officer and NCO pilots were segregated the situation was even worse. Shared experience, good and bad, is an essential part of learning and this reticence, both official and personal, prevented such debates. This was not a universal scenario, however, and some squadrons encouraged this type of activity. Any amount of crew-room discussion could not, however, address root problems such as gunnery, tactics and leadership.

Gunnery School

The Central Gunnery School (CGS) was formed at Warmwell in November 1939 as the centre of excellence for all air-gunnery matters in order to improve standards and provide specialist training. The school operated a range of aircraft types from trainers to front-line fighters, including Spitfires of various Marks. A large number of Spitfire pilots went through the short course, the intention being that they would pass on the wisdom gained there to other members of their squadron.

By 1944 Spitfires were the main fighter type with CGS; Roy Barker was an instrument fitter when the CGS was at Catfoss:

> Two types of courses were run in my time. The Gunnery Leaders' course and the Advanced Gunnery course, the latter contained the cream of the fighter pilots. However, 'Sailor' Malan (to me an old man, being over 30) who ran the Advanced classes was not over enamoured with the appearance of his illustrious pupils and issued a directive in an attempt to stop their 'sloppy appearance, high jinks and outrageous behaviour.'

By the following year the establishment included twenty Spitfire XVIs, although the actual strength in terms of numbers and Marks varied.

A March 1943 tactical bulletin included a report by a Spitfire squadron CO in North Africa and he had this to say on training of pilots and gunnery in particular:

My opinion, which was shared by my senior pilots, was that the air firing instruction that I received at the Central Gunnery School, which was passed on to them in a very limited time, paid for itself a hundred times over. The dog-fight is coming back into its own again, and in consequence it becomes more and more important that young pilots are highly aerobatically minded before they start fighting in Tunisia. The pilots without exception agreed that they learnt more about air tactics and air fighting in three weeks in Tunisia than they had during all their previous experience in Britain.

The Middle East Central Gunnery School was located at El Ballah, by the Suez Canal. Jerry Jarrold was detached from 80 Squadron to join No 6 Course

this comprised ten pilots drawn from squadrons all over the Middle East. The Course lasted for a month and was very interesting, with flying commencing on 20th September and continuing almost daily to 15th October. I flew 32 times and logged over 30 hours in the three types used on the Course – the Harvard II, Hurricane I and Spitfire VC. It was mostly air-to-air and air-to-ground firing, interspersed with cine-camera attacks, with the Harvard being used by the CO, Sqn Ldr Lyne, or other instructors, to assess us.

My assessment at the end of the course, which was signed by Wg Cdr MacDonald, Officer Commanding, RAF Station, El Ballah on 15th October 1943 was:

1	Marksman (air-to-air)	Average
2	Marksman (air-to-ground)	Average
3	Marksman (air combat)	Above Average
4	Instructor	Average

He also recalls that he was not asked to pass on his new-found skills and wisdom to anyone else on the Squadron.

'Rosie' Mackie continued to place a great deal of importance on armament accuracy. He was convinced that the RAF gunnery courses were inadequate, and that more time and trouble should have been taken in teaching fighter pilots the finer points of deflection shooting. He would sometimes persuade a fellow pilot to fly out with him on practice sessions low over the desert, so that he could fire at the shadow cast by the other aircraft. There is no doubt that gunnery training improved during the war, from almost zero in 1940 to a structured series of basic and advanced instruction by late 1943. Nevertheless, Spitfire pilot gunnery remained an issue throughout the war. The 'solution' adopted by some pilots was in line with Malan's 'whites of the eyes' principle – get in really close and make sure. There were pros and cons to this and it was never official policy, which still taught the pilots to estimate target size to give optimum opening and closing ranges for the harmonised guns. When it came to snap shooting (fleeting targets) or deflection shooting, success was more a matter of practice and luck, although some pilots were naturally good shots (especially those who had hunted wildfowl). There was no substitute for experience, and whilst 'cine-gunning' a drogue or another aircraft was useful, the real experience came in the multi-aircraft combat arena. There was even less formal training in the art of ground attack.

Fighter Leaders

There was no specialist tactics school that dealt just with the Spitfire; they were all concerned with tactical leadership of fighter-type aircraft rather than with a specific aircraft. However, in January 1943 the Fighter Leaders School (FLS) was formed at Chedworth from part of No 52 OTU. The new organisation had an establishment of thirty-six Spitfires and its role was as stated in its title – to teach flight and squadron commanders tactical employment of fighter aircraft, for both air fighting and ground attack. The FLS was staffed by very experienced pilots and although the course was short, it was intensive with theory, a great deal of discussion, and as much flying as could be packed in.

The School continued to grow and by October 1943 its official designation was No 52 OTU (Fighter Command School of Tactics). Perhaps surprisingly, its established strength was comprised of Spitfire Is and IIs, although later Marks also made an appearance or were acquired on short-term or long-term visits. It reverted to the FLS title in January 1944, by which time it was at Millfield and had grown both in size and diversity of aircraft, with sixty-nine Spitfires, eighteen Typhoons, eleven Hurricanes and eight Masters.

In December 1944 the FLS became part of the Central Fighter Establishment's (CFE) Day Fighter Wing at Wittering. The CFE gradually acquired most of the Fighter Command specialist units that performed this type of role, such as the Day Fighter Development Squadron. Their importance as far as this book is concerned is that tactical development and instruction in tactics became increasingly well established from 1943, although it was still a moot point as to how much of this actually filtered down to the pilots on the squadrons. In theory, those who attended a specialist course not only improved their own skills, especially in leadership, but also imparted the latest tactical wisdom to the rest of the squadron. The theory was sound but it was by no means always applied.

Summary

Overall, the training given to Spitfire pilots in the first two years of the war was barely adequate and it is remarkable that there were not more accidents and that the squadrons were able to act effectively as combat units. To some extent this was a bonus granted by the Germans with the period of Phoney War from September 1939 to May 1940, which allowed squadrons precious training time. Whilst tactics might have been inadequate, it at least gave pilots flying time to gain experience with and confidence in handling their Spitfires. The real crunch came for those pilots who joined squadrons from summer 1940 when it was a case of learn quick – or else. By 1941 the training system was both better organised and more efficient, in part because some of the pressure was off and in part because of the lessons that had been hard won. From 1942 onwards the training system, including the creation of various specialist schools, was remarkably effective and it continued to improve into the last years of the war.

Training is the key to success in military operations; good equipment is vital but without training it will never be fully effective. RAF fighter-pilot training is considered to be the best in the world and the tenets of that training were laid in the Second World War.

~ 5 ~

Offensive Operations – Europe

The Battle of Britain had been won, the Spitfire legend had been born – now it was time to take the fighter battle to the enemy. This chapter looks at Fighter Command operations over Europe from 1941 to summer 1944, by which time the Tactical Air Force was also in action. During this period, four major fighter variants entered service – the Spitfire V, IX, XII and XIV – plus specialised versions such as the Mark VI. The Mark VIII also entered service during this period but as its greatest impact was in the overseas theatres it has been included in Chapter 7, 'Over the Desert and Italy'.

The first of the new Rhubarb offensive sweeps was flown by a pair of 66 Squadron Spitfires (Flt Lt G. Christie and Plt Off C. Brodie); on 20 December 1940, both strafed buildings at Le Touquet airfield. However, the first major offensive sweep was that of 9 January 1941 when five squadrons in two formations flew over the French coast hoping to provoke Luftwaffe fighter reaction. None was forthcoming. This had been partly anticipated and as a result the first Circus operation was flown the following day. If the Luftwaffe would not react to a fighter sweep then surely it would have to react if bombers were involved. The mission of 10 January saw six Spitfire squadrons escorting a Blenheim attack on targets in the Calais area. Although a few German fighters made an appearance there were no significant combats.

This combination of Rhubarbs, offensive fighter sweeps and Circus operations was to remain the standard Fighter Command tactic up until the June 1944 invasion. During this forty-month period the major changes were to be the increasing number of Spitfire squadrons and, in response to improved enemy fighters, development of more capable Spitfire Marks such as the Mk V and Mk IX to claw back advantage over the improved Bf 109s and the introduction of the Fw 190. With planning for the invasion of Europe reaching a more advanced stage, a change in the RAF's structure was brought about by the creation of 2nd Tactical Air Force in June 1943. Air Defence of Great Britain (ADGB) was re-formed in November and both

Commands began to build up and re-equip. By the late spring of 1944 2nd Tactical Air Force had thirty-four RAF Spitfire squadrons and four FAA Seafire units, whilst ADGB had twenty-two Spitfire squadrons.

New Spitfires

By spring 1941 most front-line units had re-equipped with the Spitfire II (the first unit had been 611 Squadron at Digby in August 1940), the surviving Is being transferred to OTUs. However, at around the same time, the Luftwaffe was fielding the Bf 109F, an aircraft that proved to be greatly superior to the existing Spitfires. Duncan Smith highlighted one of the concerns felt by pilots.

> Though our Spits were quite capable of fighting the '109s, we felt we were outgunned. We desperately needed more punch. The eight Browning machine-guns were devastating at close quarters but were inadequate at longer ranges against manoeuvring enemy fighters, unless a hit was registered in the engine, petrol tank or cooling system. Initial tests on 20mm cannons had proved unsuccessful, largely because of the stoppage rate. The 'powers that be' told us that this was a temporary setback and that Mk V Spitfires sporting two 20mm Hispano cannon and four Brownings were on the way. (Smith, *Spitfire into Battle*)

The first cannon-armed Spitfire IBs had in fact been tested operationally by 19 Squadron as early as spring 1940 (one trial aircraft flown by Fg Off George Proudman had actually been in combat in January 1940), but the decision had been taken to rely on the Browning-armed variants until the cannon system had been made reliable. The thin aerodynamic wing of the Spitfire was never designed to hold the bulk of a cannon mechanism and interim solutions proved ineffective.

Spitfire development, as with all aircraft types, was closely linked to the development of its engine and in this respect the Spitfire was blessed with Rolls-Royce and the Merlin. It was obvious that a new Spitfire was needed and so was born, as an 'interim', the Spitfire VA (Browning) and VB (Hispano cannon). The prototype (X4922) first flew, in the hands of Jeffrey Quill, in February 1941, with the first unit being 92 Squadron at Biggin Hill. In essence the Spitfire V was a Mark I/II fitted with a Merlin 45, but with a number of significant airframe improvements, and it provided an all-round improvement in performance, albeit not as great as some had hoped for. Indeed, the first 'production' Vs were converted Is and IIs. At this stage the Germans were continuing to develop the Bf 109 and with the F variant maintained a superiority over the Spitfire. In July a Bf 109F-1 of JG26 was captured and thus made available for comparative flight tests (it acquired the RAF serial ES906).

Specialisation in Fighters

In a memo dated 20 April 1941 the Commander-in-Chief of Fighter Command (Air Marshal Sir W. Sholto Douglas) expressed his views in answer to the debates on future Spitfire production.

> It is agreed that we are heading for specialisation in fighters and this is inevitable. Specialisation must be between the pressurised and un-pressurised fighter. In other words, the dividing line must come on the limit of altitude which can be tolerated by the human body unassisted by artificial pressure. Let us put this line at 35,000ft. Below this there can be no specialisation and our aim must be to provide all aircraft (un-pressurised) with a performance to make them reasonable for fighting machines up to 35,000ft. Another class of fighter for employment up to, say, 25,000ft, would place quite intolerable operational limitations on fighter operations and could not be accepted as policy. Although the Mk II has merged into the Mk V we must anticipate it being outclassed by 1942 when nothing below a maximum speed of 400mph will be of much use to us.

Much of this statement was reasonable and the comment about the new Mark V being outclassed by 1942 was certainly valid; the split of the combat zone into three heights (up to 25,000ft, 25–35,000ft and above 35,000ft) was also valid and was to cause various problems, although a tactical switch to lower levels for air combat both eased and complicated the problem – as we shall see.

Spitfire V – Interim but Effective

The Battle of Britain had been fought by the Spitfire Is, and in the later stages by the Spitfire IIA, but it was realised that further improvements in performance would be needed to overcome the limitations shown up during the Battle and to cater for new operational tactics, including the need to engage targets at higher altitudes. Airframe development and engine development were inextricably linked and in the case of the Spitfire V it was the lack of Merlin XX production capacity, the preferred engine for the intended follow-on Spitfire III, and the subsequent development of the Merlin 45 that gave the impetus for the Spitfire V. The Merlin 45 was essentially a Merlin XX but without the low-altitude blower and in December 1940 production of the Spitfire V with this engine was authorised – as an interim measure. This interim Mark went on to be produced in three major variants, two of which were produced in significant numbers and were used by large numbers of RAF squadrons. The Mark V dominated RAF fighter operations in Europe from late 1941 to 1943.

As with its predecessor variants, the Mark V was initially produced in a machine-gun (eight 0.303-in) variant (VA) and a mixed armament (two 20-mm and four 0.303-in) variant (VB). However, perhaps the most significant development was the adoption of what became known as the 'Universal Wing' (as featured on the Spitfire VC), which could be fitted with either four 20-mm cannon or two cannon plus four machine guns. In addition to the useful armament option it was also all-round a better wing, being stronger and with improved aerodynamics.

The Air Ministry's interrogators took every opportunity to record the views of captured German aircrew and from time to time the results of such interrogations were circulated. One such document was Tactical Bulletin No 1, issued in July 1941, which outlined the view of a Bf 109F pilot of the comparative performances of the Bf 109F and the Spitfire. 'This pilot believes the Me 109F is superior in every respect – except that the new Spitfire (the Mark V) might, when handled by an equally good pilot, be superior to the 109F in steep turns at high speed. This difference, however, can be more than counter-balanced if the German pilot is better.'

The report also included other related comments.

> The outstanding disadvantage of the Me 109 is that the wings are not as stable as they might be. At least two German pilots have been killed within the last three weeks by tearing the wings off their 109s when trying to follow Spitfires in a snaking dive. After a fast dive pilots have to pull out fairly gradually. The new arrangement of guns in the nose of the 109F enables pilots to fire very accurately whilst in a turn and to open fire at a greater range. This pilot, however, usually opens fire at 100 yards, closing to 50 yards.

One of the key tactical lessons from the Battle of Britain was that the fighters with height advantage at the start of a combat were well-placed; this was expressed by a senior pilot at Hornchurch in July 1941: 'diving attacks are always the most effective as the element of surprise is achieved' – but he also stated that the ability to get higher should not be at the expense of other performance elements.

> ... but turning radius and acceleration are equally important. At all heights a Spitfire can turn inside a Me 109, but the 109 appears to have quicker initial acceleration in a dive and also in climbing ... Reserve of power and manoeuvrability are the foremost requirements for efficient fighting at great heights. The superiority in this respect of the Me 109, particularly the Me 109F, must, to a large extent, be due to its light weight. At present the Spitfire V has insufficient reserves of power to stay in combat with the Me 109 at 35,000ft. The latter definitely has greater speed at that height on the level, climb or dive.

A few months later, in October 1941, Tactical Bulletin No 5 summarised a recent comparative trial between the Spitfire V and the Bf 109F:

Me 109F v Spitfire V

1 The results of some recent comparative performance trials between a captured Me 109F and a Spitfire V are of interest.

2 Up to 21,000ft the Spitfire V at a loading of 6450lbs is nearly 8mph faster than the Me 109F at an all-up weight of 6090lbs. This difference is however reduced to 2mph at 22,000ft but increases to nearly 4mph at 26,000ft.

3 At 5,000ft with the Spitfire V at 2,850 engine rpm and the Me 109F at 2,600 rpm the Me 109F climbs about 500ft/min faster than the Spitfire, but at 20,000ft under the same engine conditions, this Me 109 has only about 100ft/min in hand.

4 The engine used in the Me 109F was not functioning properly and it is possible therefore that the rate of climb might be higher and thereby greater in comparison to the Spitfire.

5 Trials of the Me 109F by itself showed that with the radiator flaps fully closed, its maximum level speed was 371mph at about 22,000ft.

This was pretty inconclusive and although it was the result of a number of flights – as indeed were all such tactical trials – by more than one pilot, and often with pilots swapping aircraft, there were many variables that could affect the overall conclusion. It would have been interesting if the report had included the scores from any mock dogfights rather than simple performance data. The general impression was that there was little to choose between the two aircraft and that combat results would depend on other factors, such as experience and tactics. The same report also gave initial details of the German aircraft that was about to make the Spitfire V outdated; the short brief on the Fw 190 gave an estimated performance of 380mph at 20,000ft and a ceiling of 32–34,000ft.

By this time the Spitfire V had been in front-line service for eight months, the first unit, 92 Squadron having taken delivery of the variant at Biggin Hill in February to replace its Spitfire Is. By May a further seven squadrons of Fighter Command had been re-equipped and early combats indicated that the type was on a par with the latest Bf 109s.

The Spitfire V was now in quantity production and was destined to become the most common mark of Spitfire (with 6,479 built), seeing service in all the operational theatres. Total Fighter Command operational strength in April 1941 was seventy-seven and a half squadrons, which included the twenty-three Spitfire and thirty-eight and a half Hurricane squadrons, so the Spitfire was still by no means the dominant type. By July the statistics were eighty-two squadrons, including twenty-nine Hurricane and thirty-two and a half Spitfire, with a further seven and a half Spitfire units non-operational, a remarkable change in the space of a few months. The detailed breakdown for Spitfire units, by Mark is shown in Table 7.

Table 7: *Summary of Fighter Command Spitfire Squadrons, 1941*

	8 April 1941			1 July 1941		
	Op	Non-Op	Total	Op	Non-Op	Total
Spitfire I	4	2	6	5½	6½	12
Spitfire II	18	0	18	20	1	21
Spitfire V	1	0	1	7	0	7
Total	23	2	25	32½	7½	40

'Sammy' Sampson was flying Spitfire VBs with 602 Squadron and his early experience of combat was typical of most 'new boys'.

> I had survived these first two actions more by luck than judgement and soon came to realise what men like Johnny Niven and Eric Bocock had been telling us junior pilots – the fact that as the Spitfire VB could always outturn the 109F and 190 there was no reason to be defeated in combat. The Huns usually relied on the jump or bounce and if they saw a Spitfire break at 5–600 yards they immediately half-rolled and quickly disappeared. (Sampson, *Spitfire Offensive*)

The point about surviving the first few combats is a very valid one and luck certainly played a part, as did the guidance and leadership of the more experience pilots. It is an established view that the greatest danger to a new pilot is during his first combats and it is this rationale that is the basis of much of the RAF's current training, whereby exercises attempt to simulate the combat scenario as closely as possible. That luxury was not usually available in the early years of the Second World War and pilots had to learn 'on the job'. The situation improved as the war progressed and there was less pressure on aircrew training, as outlined in Chapter 4.

Miroslav Liskutin had flown a tour on Spitfire IIs with 145 Squadron and in December 1941 joined 312 Squadron at Ayr, where Hurricanes were being replaced by Mark VB Spitfires.

> This was nearly identical in most respects to the IIB I flew at Catterick, the main difference being the Merlin 45 or 46 engine, which produced 1,500hp at 19,000ft. The early VB only had 60 rounds per gun in the usual drums. A little later, when our Spitfires acquired the universal wing the Hispano cannon were each provided with 120 rounds of ammunition in belts; that of course increased the available firing time to approximately 16 seconds. (Liskutin, *Challenge in the Air*)

It appeared, therefore, that the Spitfire V was on a par with or even slightly better than its main opponent, the Bf 109E and 109F, with pilot experience and tactics of more importance than aircraft performance.

New Threat – The Fw 190

Combat-aircraft development was rapid on both sides of the Channel and by late summer 1941 there was sufficient evidence of a new, superior German fighter to give cause for concern. The Fw 190A was being operated by JG26 and had the edge over the Spitfire V in a number of crucial performance areas.

Operating out of Bolt Head with 312 Squadron, Miroslav Liskutin recalled his first brush with the 190:

> We were directed to intercept four Focke Wulfs in the Torbay area . . . I spotted three aircraft low over the sea, but already heading back towards France after a hit and run attack against Torquay. We were some 5 miles from the enemy formation. After 'cutting the corner' on them the distance was quickly reduced to under one mile. My engine was at full power with the boost over-ride beyond the gate and the propeller set at maximum revolutions. My Spitfire was gradually closing to about 700 yards when they spotted us. Until then we had no idea how the Spitfire VB would compare in a real-life race with a Fw 190. Our pilots knew that there was no great difference in the performance between these two aircraft, although the Fw 190 would have to be regarded as a marginal favourite. This occasion gave us proof that at sea level we were absolutely equal . . . Despite my earlier optimism, my distance behind the No 3 Fw 190 became stabilised at about 650 yards. Joe (Pipa) tried some shots from this distance. It looked like the only effect of Joe's firing was a temporary slight slowing down of his aircraft, due to the recoil of his cannons. I was still hoping to close to at least 100 yards, to get a better chance with shooting.

Both formations were going all out, as evidenced by the black smoke from the German fighters. 'In these conditions my airspeed indicator was showing a steady 330mph. There is no doubt that this was the true maximum speed of the Spitfire VB and the Fw 190 at sea level, in the summer of 1942' (Liskutin, *Challenge in the Air*). With the range still not closing, Miroslav attempted to sight on the German fighter and let loose with all guns, but there was no evident result and with the enemy coast looming up, the pursuit was abandoned.

In July 1942 the AFDU was able to evaluate 'a Spitfire from an operational squadron' against an Fw 190 that had landed at Pembrey 'in error' the previous month. Acquiring an intact operational enemy fighter straight from a war sortie was a fantastic opportunity – but it soon confirmed the superiority that Allied pilots had already discovered. The report concluded that:

> The manoeuvrability of the Fw 190 is better than that of the Spitfire VB except in turning circles, when the Spitfire can quite easily out-turn it. The Fw 190 has better acceleration under all conditions of flight and this must obviously be most useful during combat.
>
> When the Fw 190 was in a turn and was attacked by the Spitfire, the superior rate of roll enabled it to flick into a diving turn in the opposite direction. The pilot of the Spitfire found great difficulty in following this manoeuvre and even when prepared for it, was seldom able to allow the correct deflection. A dive from this manoeuvre enabled the Fw 190 to draw away from the Spitfire which was then forced to break off the attack.
>
> Several flights were carried out to ascertain the best evasive manoeuvres to adopt if 'bounced'. It was found that if the Spitfire was cruising at low speed and was 'bounced' by the Fw 190, it was easily caught even if the Fw 190 was sighted when well out of range, and the Spitfire was then forced to take avoiding action by using its superiority in turning circles. If on the other hand the Spitfire was flying at maximum continuous cruising and was 'bounced' under the same conditions, it had a reasonable chance of avoiding being caught by opening the throttle and going into a shallow dive, providing the Fw 190 was seen in time . . .
>
> If the Spitfire VB is 'bounced' it is thought unwise to evade by diving steeply, as the Fw 190 will have little difficulty in catching up owing to its superiority in the dive.
>
> The above trials have shown that the Spitfire VB must cruise at high speed when in an area where enemy fighters can be expected. It will then, in addition to lessening the chances of being successfully 'bounced', have a better chance of catching the Fw 190, particularly if it has the advantage of surprise. (the complete report is at Annexe D)

These comments were not at all promising at a time when combats with the new German fighter were on the increase. A typical mission was that recorded by 602 Squadron, as part of the Kenley Wing on 24 April 1942.

> The Wing took off again at 1635 as Draw Wing on Circus 123. S/L Wells was leading. Tangmere Wing was met over Beachy Head and the French coast crossed near Hardelot. The Wing then turned south climbing to 18–23,000 feet, and over the Hesdin area 485 Sqn came out of the sun to attack four Fw 190s which were taken completely by surprise. Three were destroyed and one claimed as probable. About six other enemy aircraft came in sight, one of these was damaged by P/O Watson of 457 Sqn. The Wing was broken up and it re-crossed the French coast at various places south of Le Touquet, landing safely at Kenley and Redhill by 1800 hours. (602 Squadron ORB)

With the classic fighter advantage of speed and surprise, this combat had gone well, but this set-up was increasingly rare.

American and Russian Spitfires

June 1942 was very significant in the Spitfire story with the arrival of the first American fighter unit in England – the 31st Fighter Group. The unit's original equipment of P-39s was considered to be inadequate for the European war and so they were issued with Spitfires. It was a similar story for the 52nd Fighter Group and, in September, the famous Eagle squadrons were, reluctantly, incorporated into the USAAF at Debden to become the 4th Fighter Group – keeping their Spitfires. The initial agreement with the USAAF was for up to 600 Spitfires under what was referred to as 'reverse lease-lend'. However, this was not the only Allied air force seeking to obtain Britain's premier fighter, as in October the Russian ambassador requested a large consignment of Spitfires as part of the reinforcement package. Churchill had little choice but to agree as it was essential to keep Russia an active member of the Allied cause. It was, therefore, planned to deliver an initial 150 aircraft via the Middle East; the first batch of 143 Spitfire Vs was handed over to the Russian Mission at Basra, Iraq, in March the following year. In Russian service the Spitfires were initially allocated to the air defence of Moscow; other than this brief mention, Russian and American use of the Spitfire is not featured in this book. Mid-1942 was, however, also very significant for Fighter Command as it, and especially the Spitfire squadrons, was about to take part in a major air battle.

Dieppe, August 1942 – Operation Jubilee

At 0445 hours on 19 August 1942 the first assault waves of Canadian troops went ashore at Dieppe under Operation Jubilee, a 'reconnaissance in force' that turned out to be a disaster for the troops but provided valuable lessons for the planners involved with the later D-Day operation. Air support was a vital element of Jubilee and forty-eight Spitfire squadrons (forty-two with Mark Vs and four with Mark IXs) were involved with close air support – 129 Squadron for example strafed ground targets in advance of the first landings – or providing fighter cover to prevent German aircraft interfering with the operation, or escort for Allied bombers. It was the busiest day for many squadrons since the height of the Battle of Britain and some units flew four sorties during the day. Don Morrison was operating with 401 Squadron over Dieppe,

> Just as we in Yellow Section arrived over the Dieppe area, I spotted a single '190 some 1,000–1,500 feet below and heading in the same direction. I did a wide, slipping barrel roll to lose height and levelled out about 150 yards behind him. As I closed up I opened fire with a two second burst of cannon fire. I saw strikes all along the starboard side of the fuselage and several pieces

blew off from around the cowling. Just as we both went into a very thin layer of cloud he exploded with a terrific flash of flame and black smoke.

'Sammy' Sampson saw action twice in the Dieppe area. On one sortie he engaged a Dornier of KG2:

> As I started to overhaul it I was completely put-off by the rear-gunner opening up on me and what looked like red tomatoes passed by me on either side. The result of this was that I opened-up far too early. However, I saw hits on the port wing and petrol started to pour out of the port wing tank. Then Johnny warned me of two 190s above and behind so I quickly broke off and rejoined him.

He attacked a second Dornier but with similar results and the exhaustion of his cannon ammunition. A sortie later in the day resulted in the destruction of a Fw 190 courtesy of the ideal set-up of sneak up and shoot without being seen. 'I don't think the Hun pilot saw me for very conveniently he turned to starboard, which enabled me to give him a 3-second burst from 150 yards and he went down on fire into the sea' (Ralph Sampson, *Spitfire Offensive*).

The air element was the only truly successful aspect of the entire operation. Although Spitfire losses amounted to eighty-eight aircraft, the squadrons had performed all that had been asked of them and the amphibious assault had taken place 'unmolested by enemy air activity'. There was, though, still nagging concern over the Spitfire V's ability to handle the latest German fighters.

Losing the Edge?

In August 1942 the Air Ministry Air Tactics Section issued a memo on 'how to make best use of the performance of the Spitfire V, VI and IX'. This is an interesting document, although the inclusion of the Mark VI and Mark IX in this appraisal could be considered premature, as both were just entering service and therefore had no real combat basis; indeed, the performance graphs only covered the VB and VC. However, the memo does provide an excellent insight into the overall tactical picture and is therefore quoted in full below.

How to make best use of the performance of the Spitfire V, VI and IX

1 This memorandum, which is based on Fighter Command Tactical Memo No. 18, is intended to bring to the notice of all concerned the necessity of making full use of the power available in our Spitfire aircraft. It applies equally, in principle, to all our fighter aircraft when operating against an enemy whose performance is equal or superior to our own.

2 At the present stage of the war, the enemy in France is equipped with the Fw 190, a fighter with an excellent rate of climb and good acceleration. To defeat this aircraft and to avoid casualties on our side, our aircraft must fly as fast as possible whenever they are in the combat zone.

3 In the past, pilots have been told to fly at low rpm and high boost to economise in petrol. All pilots must know the correct rpm and boost at which to fly to obtain the longest duration of flight or range.

4 Wings must still fly at the most economical rpm when they are flying under the enemy RDF screens, but it is essential, as soon as they are liable to be detected, that they open up to maximum power for formation flying.

5 The acceleration of the Spitfire is relatively poor. It is therefore dangerous to cruise at, say, +2 boost and 1900rpm when the Hun is about, because the time taken in accelerating to maximum speed will allow him quickly to draw into firing range.

6 It is fully realised that the speed of formations depends on the ability of the worst pilots to keep up. This is only a question of training and practice. At present, +5 boost and 2650rpm are the maximum boost and rpm settings known to be used successfully by a wing. On this occasion, the pilots said that they could have gone faster, and this is definitely a step in the right direction.

7 It is recommended that when planning operations it should be decided at what speed the aircraft should fly and at what point in the operation wings should open up to maximum speed. After opening up to maximum speed, they should not throttle back to economical cruising speed until they are well clear of the area in which they may be attacked.

8 Spitfires are now modified to give +16 emergency boost. It must be impressed on pilots that this gives a great increase of speed under 21,500ft and 18,500ft for the Merlin 46 and 45 engines respectively, and that if used for combat only, there is no risk of engine failure.

Safety Fast – or Prune's Guide for Living

(i) Don't loiter. When you can't keep up don't blame your leader; pull your finger out and cut the corners.

(ii) Low revs and high boost will bring you safely back to roost.

(iii) Don't wait until you see the Hun before you decide to get a move on. It will take a couple of minutes for your Spitfire to respond after you open up, and by that time whatever you do will be irrelevant. When you are liable to meet the enemy fly always at maximum cruising speed.

(iv) If you want to live on the other side, you must move fast, but equally, if you want to come back again you must save petrol. You will find your engine happier at, say, +4lbs and 1700rpm than at +1lb and 2650rpm. Both these adjustments give the same ASI but if you fly at +4lbs and 1700rpm you will save seven gallons of petrol an hour. It is possible to get full throttle and +4lbs above 10,000ft by reducing the revs until the boost falls to +4lbs. Use full throttle and minimum revs above full throttle height for any desired ASI. This gives the best combination of fast cruising and minimum consumption.

(v) When you are travelling at full throttle, and full power is suddenly wanted, it is only necessary to push the constant speed lever fully forward to get full revs and boost. To return to high speed cruising at best economical conditions, reduce your *revs* and not your boost.

(vi) When being briefed, always ask what revs and boost you should fly. This will naturally depend upon the length of the sweep, but don't forget that:

   a   When hard pressed you can fly +16 boost and 3,000 revs without any danger of blowing up, but

   b   Your consumption will be 150 gallons per hour.

(vii) Finally, when unlikely to be engaged always fly minimum revs and under 4lbs boost, but when in the vicinity of Huns, fly maximum everything and in good time.

In many respects this was a pessimistic appraisal and almost implied that the RAF was on the defensive whilst on the 'other side'. Did this reflect the true situation? We have seen from the Spitfire V reports that the Fw 190 had the upper hand in terms of combat performance, the German squadrons had the advantage of being over 'home' territory and the quality of the pilots on the squadrons was still high, with a high percentage of combat veterans not simply in terms of hours flown but actual air fighting. So in overall terms it seems valid, but it is not a view reflected in the RAF fighter squadron records, where an aggressive ethos remained dominant and where morale was still high despite frustration with the evident limitations of their aircraft. In combat these are vital factors; higher morale is an element in achieving air superiority. The RAF had also settled into a policy of posting young, aggressive, experienced pilots to command Spitfire squadrons, often from having been a flight commander on a different squadron. It didn't always work but generally it was an excellent 'system'.

Total production of Spitfire Vs was in the region of 6,500, with a further 180 being created by conversion of Mark Is and IIs. There were numerous sub-variants, not just with the A, B and C wings but also a number of Merlin engine options, and clipped wings, which created sub-variants such as the LF.VB, a successful method of improving performance at lower altitudes (below 25,000ft). In a trial conducted by the AFDU a standard Mark VB was marginally faster in level speed and quicker in the climb than the clipped-wing VB but when it came to manoeuvrability:

At all heights to 25,000 feet the rate of roll is considerably improved by removal of the wing tips. The response to aileron movements is very quick and very crisp. Four dog-fights were carried out, starting with the standard Spitfire on the tail of the clipped wing Spitfire. On two occasions the clipped wing Spitfire evaded so rapidly in the rolling plane that it was able to lose the standard Spitfire and reverse the positions in about 20 seconds. On the third occasion the clipped wing Spitfire was also able to lose the standard Spitfire. The fourth occasion was at 25,000 feet and the standard Spitfire was able to keep the clipped wing Spitfire in sight. ('Spitfire VB Clipped-wing versus Standard Version', the full report is at Annexe E)

Countering High-Altitude Raiders – Spitfire VI and Modified Mark IXs

The appearance of German high-flying raiders (both bombers and recce aircraft) caused a major problem, and one that was beyond the performance capability of the standard Spitfires. Two things were needed for such an aircraft: an improved engine with high-altitude performance and a pressure cabin. Whilst consideration of both aspects was in hand from late 1940 it was only on 29 April 1941 that an Air Ministry memo recognised the need for two streams of future fighter (this was dated a few days after the memo from the Commander-in-Chief of Fighter Command mentioned above). The memo identified the need for:

a   A pressure-cabin aircraft with a ceiling of 41,000ft at first, later increasing to 45,000ft.
b   An unpressurised fighter able to operate at up to 35,000ft with a maximum speed of over 400mph at 20–25,000ft, and a service ceiling of 38–40,000ft.

For Rolls-Royce this gave added impetus to Merlin development in respect of two-stage supercharging and for Supermarine it confirmed the need for a pressure-cabin variant, with associated systems such as cockpit heating. The engine was in fact already running in test-bed version and it was not long before it was fitted to a Spitfire, as the Merlin 61. When fitted in Spitfire III N3297 it produced a startling increase in performance in both speed (422mph) and ceiling (43,000ft) when trialled at Boscombe Down in October 1941. This showed the way forward in terms of improving the performance of the standard Mark Vs – but that development is moving ahead of our look at the high-altitude Spitfire, which matured as the Mark VI, and later the Mark VII.

The prototype Spitfire VI for high-altitude fighting was a modified Mark V (X4942) and first flew on 5 July 1941. In addition to some airframe modification it was given a pressure cabin and cockpit heating; in May 1942 the AFDU evaluated Spitfire VI BR289 and concluded that: 'the pressure cabin adds greatly to the pilot's comfort at high altitude. He is kept warmer and needs less oxygen, but on a hot day below 15,000ft the cabin is unbearably hot.' Only 100 were built and the Mark entered service with

616 Squadron at Kings Cliffe in April 1942. Pilots went to Boscombe Down to learn about the new aircraft and the specific problems of operating at the notional engagement heights, although their initial impressions were not good – 10mph less than a Mark V and a locked-on canopy because of the pressurisation. The entire Squadron had re-equipped by early June and the comment made by the AFDU pilots on cockpit overheating was supported by 616, who recorded that 'the major problem was that of excessive heating below 20,000ft with the pilots gently frying and being unable to do anything about it. As an interim solution a ban was placed on operational flying below 20,000ft' (616 Squadron ORB). On 28 July Flt Lt Tony Gaze claimed the Squadron's first success with the Mark VI, claiming a Fw 190. The Squadron was still flying wing sweeps, and finding it difficult because of the poorer performance of their aircraft. Indeed, on one sweep they were held down at 500ft until half-way over the Channel before being cleared to climb – at which point they were bounced by more than fifty Bf 109s and promptly lost four aircraft.

The Squadron spent a great deal of time holding standby to scramble after high-flyers and to give them more time to climb to height they were moved to Great Sampford, not that there was much trade. Even when tasked to provide high cover during the Dieppe operation, the usual patrol height was down at 12,000ft. There were also still a number of problems with the aircraft, one of the most disconcerting for a fighter pilot being the tendency of the engine to cut out during tight turns! This carburettor problem kept them grounded for four days but Rolls-Royce soon came up with a fix. It was not the end of the engine problems and the Squadron suffered a higher than average rate of engine failure, with the ORB recording that 'most patrols were notable only for their boredom, although continuing problems with the reliability of the engines kept pilots on their toes – and ditching was a well-practised art.'

The Spitfire VII entered service with the High-Altitude Flight in September 1942, this being followed in March 1943 by 124 Squadron at North Weald and 616 Squadron in September. The latter flew its first operational scramble with the new aircraft on 14 September, but like the vast majority of such scrambles it turned out to be a 'friendly'. The Squadron considered the Mark VII to have a significant all-round improvement in performance, being 40mph faster and with a better ceiling and rate of climb. The bread-and-butter routine became patrols at 20,000ft to 25,000ft to prevent hit-and-run raids; this produced little result other than a signal complementing 'the efficient patrols kept up by the Squadron which deterred any enemy aircraft from reaching the SW coast.' It was not all boring, however, and the Squadron was able to make some contact with the enemy – at low level over France. On 21 April, Black Section (Plt Off Clerc and Fg Off Jennings) were scrambled and vectored towards Cherbourg and once in the area they spotted a Fw 190 going in to land at Maupertus; not quite the target they were after but too tempting to resist. 'Clerc came astern of the now taxiing aircraft and opened fire at about 300 yards, upon which the 190 promptly blew up; following up, Jennings fired into the debris.'

The problem of high-flying enemy aircraft was also addressed using modified Mark IXs. The Special Service Flight at Northolt was given a number of aircraft (the first one being BF273) that had been lightened by up to 450lb through removal of armour plate and all armament except the two cannons. On 9 September Plt Off Galitzine intercepted one of the raiders near Southampton.

> I took off from Northolt at 0930 hours to intercept Raid 55 . . . I was told that the E/A was to port at 42,000ft, my own height then being 38,000ft. Almost immediately I saw black trails and made off in that direction quickly overhauling the aircraft. I turned to starboard to maintain climbing speed and avoid overhauling and came level at 42,000ft with the aircraft – which I recognised as a Ju 86P. The E/A jettisoned a medium bomb and I jettisoned my reserve fuel tank so that I could gain height . . . dead astern I opened fire with a three second burst, observing that his starboard wing was hit, my port gun then jammed . . .

Galitzine made a number of other attacks but with no luck as the aircraft yawed whenever the single cannon was fired.

Spitfire IX – Regaining the Performance Edge (Just)

As mentioned above, the Spitfire V had proved an effective interim (and mass-produced) solution in the drive for increased performance and firepower but up against the Fw 190 it was outclassed and a new quantum jump was needed; it came in the form of the Spitfire IX. Although the first Spitfire IXs had joined 64 Squadron in June 1942, it would be some time before this Mark replaced significant numbers of units equipped with Vs.

Like the Mark V, the Spitfire IX appeared in a number of variants, primarily with HF or LF designation to indicate the airframe/engine optimisation for high-level or low-level, a designation concept that followed with most of the late fighter versions. During its combat career it underwent numerous modifications to airframe, such as cut-back rear fuselage or bubble canopy, or equipment, such as a new gyro gun-sight. Without doubt the Spitfire IX was one of the great fighter aircraft, and this was largely down to the higher performance of the new Merlin, coupled with the aerodynamic excellence that had been a feature of the Spitfire from its earliest days. A total of 5,665 Spitfire IXs were built, the majority at the large production (and flight-testing) works at Castle Bromwich.

The first Mark IX was actually a modified VC (AB505) and it was tested by the AFDU in April 1942, with a general conclusion that:

> The performance of the Spitfire IX is outstandingly better than the Spitfire V especially at heights above 20,000 feet. On the level the Spitfire is considerably faster and its climb is exceptionally good. It will climb easily to 38,000 feet and when levelled off there can be made to climb in stages to above 40,000 feet by building up speed on the level and a slight zoom. Its manoeuvrability is as good as a Spitfire V up to 30,000 feet and above that is very much better. At 38,000 feet it is capable of a true speed of 368mph and is still able to manoeuvre well for fighting.

The complete AFDU trials report is at Annexe I. A subsequent evaluation against the Fw 190 concluded that: 'the general impression gained by pilots taking part in the trials is that the Spitfire IX compares favourably with the Fw 190 and that provided the Spitfire has the initiative, it has undoubtedly a good chance of shooting it down.'

The words 'compares favourably' show that the new Spitfire was not superior but simply more or less even, and no doubt the Germans were continuing to develop the 190. Indeed, the report noted that in some situations, the Mark IX was inferior: 'The Spitfire IX's worst heights for fighting the Fw 190 were between 18,000 and 22,000 feet and below 3,000 feet. At these heights the Fw 190 is a little faster.' It was evident that further work needed to be done to improve the overall performance. The complete AFDU trials report for this comparative evaluation is at Annexe J.

Rolls-Royce and the Merlin soon responded and the Merlin 66 appeared with re-scheduled blower gear ratios, essentially a 'simple' method of providing extra power in the critical altitude band, most combats now taking place between 15,000ft and 25,000ft. Fitted with the new engine, and available from early 1943, the Spitfire became known as the IXB, although it was officially the LF Mk IX.

By January 1943 Fighter Command had seventy squadrons operational, forty-seven of these being equipped with Spitfires (see Table 8), with an average daily availability of aircraft with pilots of 1,063 fighters, of which 633 were Spitfires, the majority still being Mark Vs but with a steadily increasing strength of Mark IXs.

Clipped wings to improve manoeuvrability at lower altitudes had been introduced with the Mark V and this trend was continued with the Mark IX, several squadrons choosing to remove the wing-tips to give an improved lateral control. Whilst it is true that this did increase manoeuvrability, it also increased wing loading, which in some combat circumstances produced a poorer performance. This main disadvantage, of aerodynamic penalty, was not really apparent in the normal operating heights.

Table 8: War Room Summary of Fighter Command Ops, January 1943
Operational Squadrons

Aircraft	Squadrons	Establishment	Available with Crew
Hurricane	1 flt	4	30
Spitfire	47 sqns	752	633
Typhoon	8 sqns	128	80
Whirlwind	2 sqns	32	26
Beaufighter	12 sqns	192	151
Mosquito	8 sqns	128	84
Boston	2 sqns	32	19
Boston/Havoc			20
Totals	79 sqns, 1 flt	1,268	1,063

In early 1943 the AFDU tested the Spitfire IX against the Mustang X, an interesting comparison with the leading American fighter in the European Theatre of Operations (ETO). Both aircraft were fitted with Merlin 60 series engines and the results were somewhat mixed, with each aircraft having some performance advantages over the other. The conclusions were that the

two high performance low-altitude fighters can be compared as follows:

(i) In level speed the Mustang is 12–22mph faster than the Spitfire up to 30,000ft.
(ii) In rate of climb the Spitfire is better than the Mustang by about 800ft/min up to 20,000ft, the operational ceiling of 1,000ft/min being 37,000ft for the Spitfire and 34,000 for the Mustang.
(iii) In the dive the Mustang is able to out-pace the Spitfire without difficulty.
(iv) In turning and rolling manoeuvres the Spitfire is better, save that at 400mph IAS, with standard wing it was a little inferior to the Mustang in rate of roll. With the Spitfire wing tips clipped their roll is identical at this speed. At altitude the Mustang's aileron control does not appear sufficient.
(v) The Mustang suffers badly from lack of directional stability and adequate rudder control, both of which detract seriously from its fighting capabilities. Modifications are in hand to improve these qualities.
(vi) The view for fighting and search generally from the Mustang is inferior to that from the Spitfire.
(vii) The Mustang carries 150 gallons as compared with the Spitfire's 85 gallons. The latter can be increased by 30 gallons in a jettison tank.

The last comment would later be particularly pertinent and probably encapsulates one of the major differences between what were undoubtedly two great fighters – the P-51 Mustang would be able to fight over Berlin from bases in the UK whereas the Spitfire was barely able to reach Paris. This is a subject that we will return to later. The complete trials report is at Annexe K.

The Spitfire IX is considered by many to have been the best Spitfire; indeed some squadron commanders or wing leaders continued to fly their IXBs instead of the later models with which their Squadron was equipped.

Fighter Sweeps

One of Fighter Command's main roles from mid-1943 was fighter sweeps over Occupied Europe to keep up the pressure on the Luftwaffe as part of the overall preparation for the future invasion of the European battlefield, and to prevent resources being despatched to other theatres of the war. Typical of the new Fighter Command formations charged with this work was No 127 Wing, which formed at Kenley on 11 July 1943, with an initial strength of two Canadian squadrons equipped with Spitfire IXs. 'Fighter leadership consists not in scoring personal victories but in the achievement of success with the whole Wing. My job would be to lead and to fight.' So wrote that great air combat pilot and leader of No 127, Wg Cdr Johnnie Johnson.

Airfields were amongst the most heavily defended targets in Occupied Europe, bristling with quadruple 20-mm anti-aircraft guns. The gun positions were usually arranged to give murderous crossfire kill zones, and 'flak traps' were set up on the most likely lines of attack. In the face of such opposition it was very difficult for pilots to target aircraft on the ground, a fleeting pass with a burst or two being all that could be achieved. To stay in the area and make a second or third pass was to court disaster. 'Johnnie' Johnson recalled one such hairy occasion:

I led a section of Spitfires down to the deck to sweep the numerous airfields scattered around the circumference of the French capital. After 20 minutes at low level I was lost, although I knew we were a few miles south of Paris. I put the map away and concentrated on flying the various courses I had worked out before leaving base. About another five minutes on this leg and then turn to the west to avoid getting too close to Paris.

We crossed the complicated mass of railway lines which indicated that we were close to Paris. We sped across a wide river and ahead of us was a heavily wooded slope, perhaps rising 200ft above the river. We raced up this slope, only a few feet above the topmost branches, and found ourselves looking straight across a large grass airfield with several large hangars on the far side.

The gunners were ready and waiting. The shot and shell came from all angles, for some of the gun positions were on the hangar roofs and they fired down on us. I had never seen the like of this barrage. Enemy aircraft were parked here and there, but our only thought was to get out of this inferno. There was no time for radio orders. It was every man for himself. It seemed that all our exits were blocked with a concentrated criss-cross pattern of fire from a hundred guns.

My only hope of a getaway lay in a small gap between two hangars. I pointed the Spitfire at this gap, hurtled through it and caught sight of the multiple barrels of a light flak gun swinging on to me from one of the parapets. Beyond lay a long, straight road with tall poplars on either side and I belted the Spitfire down the road with the trees forming some sort of screen. Tracer was still bursting over the cockpit. Half a dozen cyclists were making their way up the road towards the airfield. They flung themselves and their bicycles in all directions. I pulled up above the light flak and called the other pilots. Miraculously, they had all come through the barrage. (Johnson, *Wing Leader*)

With the creation on 15 November 1943, of the Allied Expeditionary Air Force (AEAF) the structure of Allied air operations strategy changed – Fighter Command was now confined to defensive operations over the UK. To reflect this new defensive stance, the Command reverted to its old name of Air Defence of Great Britain (ADGB), much to the chagrin of many within it. The offensive arm became 2nd Tactical Air Force and it too was a major operator of the Spitfire. With fewer and fewer air combats, the Spitfire's main future lay in attacking ground targets, initially strafing with cannon and machine gun but later with bombs and rockets. It was a whole new ball game and one that we will look at in detail later.

More Range

One of the problems with the Spitfire was its lack of combat radius because the internal fuel tankage was limited, despite attempts to squeeze in extra tanks, which had met with some success in the PR variants (with no guns). The only true long-legged Spitfires in terms of range were the reconnaissance variants (see Chapter 10, 'Reconnaissance Operations'), but, as with all fighter aircraft, there was a need for increased range and endurance, especially with the RAF increasingly taking the offensive. The problem increased as more powerful – and thirsty – engines were used, particularly with the Griffon engines. There was little that could be done with the general airframe, although the internal fuel fraction did increase during the Spitfire's life. The only realistic solution was the use of external tanks. As far as this story is concerned we will ignore the attempts at what would now be known as conformal tanks that were essentially airframe bulges, as none of the experiments saw significant use. It was the bolt-on fuel tank, that could also be jettisoned when extra performance was required, that was adopted, with the forty-five-gallon and ninety-gallon tanks being the two main ones used operationally by the Spitfire. The data tables in Annexe A (Spitfire Variants) show the tankage and range of the various Spitfire Marks.

A memo from General Arnold (Commander USAAF) to ACM Portal (British Chief of Air Staff) queried the Spitfire's combat range and the British 'reluctance' to make best use of their substantial fighter force (the bulk of which was Spitfire based).

> Overlord hangs directly on the success of our combined aerial offensive and I am sure that our failure to decisively cripple both sources of German air power and the GAF itself is causing you and me concern. I am afraid that we are not sufficiently alert to changes in the overall course of the air war. In particular I refer to the fact that we are not employing our forces in adequate numbers against the *GAF in being*, as well as his facilities and sources. On my part I am pressing Eaker to get a much higher proportion of his forces off the ground and put them where they will hurt the enemy.

One of the General's main points was the lack of fighter support for the daylight bombers:

> as presently employed it would appear that your thousands of fighters are not making use of their full capabilities. Our transition from the defensive to the offensive should surely carry with it the application of your large fighter force offensively. Is it not true that we have a staggering air superiority over the Germans and we are not using it.

Arnold also made the point that the P-47's basic design had a shorter range than that of the Spitfire but when fitted with long-range tanks it was working well as an escort. The implication was that the American daylight offensive could be far more effective (and less costly) if the RAF's fighters were used as escorts and employed in an offensive way to destroy the Luftwaffe's remaining combat power. The RAF comment was that attempts were being made to improve the range of the Spitfire but that an external tank only gave an extra fifty miles and, besides, 'our fighter force has been designed to obtain air superiority over northern France, for which it is eminently suitable.' It could have been added, however, that on short-range penetrations and offensive fighter sweeps the Luftwaffe seldom made an appearance.

Perversely there was a Spitfire in which extra internal fuel had been incorporated, the Mark VIII with its 124 gallons, but this was destined for service overseas. This left the 'short-range' Spitfires operating over Europe and if no more fuel could be squeezed into the airframe the only alternative was to hang it underneath. The Spitfire had first used external tanks in late 1941, with ninety-gallon slipper tanks fitted for ferry purposes, the first significant use being in March 1942 when fifteen Tropical VBs flew 660 miles from the carrier HMS *Eagle* to Malta under Operation Spotter. External tanks were a great way of providing extra fuel for ferry flights and even for routine combat ops – as long as they could be dropped when contact was made with the enemy. Two main combat tanks were eventually used by the Spitfire, the forty-five-gallon and the ninety-gallon, although the latter was to prove troublesome.

First Griffon – Spitfire XII

The Griffon engine has never attracted the same reputation as the Merlin and is often ignored in the popular image concerning the Spitfire, but yet it was the major power plant for all the later versions of the fighter. A modified Spitfire IV, DP845, was the first to carry a Griffon and it flew on 27 November 1941, making an immediate impression on Jeffrey Quill, who later said that 'DP845 was my favourite Spitfire. It had a wonderful performance at low altitude.' By early 1942 a Griffon Spitfire was being developed as the Mark XII, although it was a lengthy gestation and the first unit, 41 Squadron at High Ercall, did not receive the type until February 1943.

The AFDU evaluated EN223 in December 1942, the report concluding that:

> The Spitfire XII handles in general better than the previous marks of Spitfire. Its longitudinal stability has been improved, but the rudder control is not at present completely satisfactory, as it needs constant re-trimming and is rather heavy. The aircraft fills the category of a low-altitude fighter extremely well, being capable of speeds of 372mph at 5,700ft and 397mph at 18,000ft. The climb is not as good as the rest of the performance in general, being inferior to the Spitfire IX and similar to the Spitfire V at 16lb boost up to 10,000ft. The operational ceiling (with clipped wings) is about 28,500ft. Modifications already in hand should improve the rate of climb, especially at low altitudes. The aircraft dives well and benefits from having its wing tips clipped. Manoeuvrability is excellent particularly in its rate of roll. (AFDU, 'Report No 61. Tactical Trials: Spitfire XII', the full report is at Annexe L)

The other debate underway during this period concerned armament, with various views being expressed that ranged from six 20-mm cannon to twelve 0.303-in machine guns or even the 0.5-in guns favoured by the Americans and used in the Mustang. One thing that all agreed on was that greater fire-power was necessary and by this stage of the war the vote tended to be in favour of cannon, although this was generally resisted by the Americans. However, the standard fit for Spitfires remained two 20-mm cannon and four Brownings and it was only later with the Spitfire F.21 that four cannon were introduced. Only 100 Mark XIIs were produced and only three RAF squadrons flew the type, but it introduced the Griffon to operational service and as such played a significant part in the development of the final series of Griffon-powered Spitfires. It also impressed the Navy when in February 1943 two aircraft were fitted with hooks and evaluated by the Fleet Air Arm Service Trials Unit at Arbroath. This led to the development of the Seafire XV and XVII, as detailed in Chapter 9, 'Carrier Operations'.

Increased Performance – Spitfire XIV

Having proved itself in the Mark XII the next development for the Griffon engine was the addition of a two-stage supercharger, in due course leading to the Spitfire XIV, which in Jeffrey Quill's opinion was the best of the fighter variants. He first flew the prototype (JF316), then referred to as the VIIIG, on 20 January 1943 and recorded that:

> it had a spectacular performance, doing 445mph at 25,000ft with a sea-level rate of climb of over 5,000 feet per minute, and I remember being greatly delighted with the aircraft. It seemed to me that from this relatively simple conversion had come something quite outstanding – another quantum jump, almost on a par with the jump from the Mk V to the Mk IX. (Quill, *Spitfire, a Test Pilot's Story*)

The first production Mark XIVs appeared in October 1943 and in January 1944 Spitfire Mk XIV RB141 was delivered to the Air Fighting Development Unit at Duxford for tactical trials, although in the same month it was also issued to the first operational unit, 610 Squadron at Exeter. The general conclusions were that 'the Spitfire XIV is superior to the Spitfire IX in all respects. It has the best all-round performance of any present-day fighter, apart from range.' One of the trials was flown against a Bf 109G: 'The Spitfire XIV is 40mph faster at all heights except near 16,000ft where it is only 10mph faster. Climbing at full throttle it draws away from the Me 109G quite easily. The Spitfire XIV easily out-turns the Me 109G in either direction; it is superior to it in every respect.' The Fw 190 was more of a problem; the trials involved flight against a 190 with a BMW 801D engine and concluded that:

> In defence, the Spitfire XIV should use its remarkable maximum climb and turning circle against any enemy aircraft. In the attack it can afford to 'mix it' but should beware the quick roll and dive. If this manoeuvre is used by an Fw 190 and the Spitfire XIV follows, it will probably not be able to close the range

until the Fw 190 has pulled out of its dive. (AFDU, 'Report No 117. Tactical Trials: Spitfire XIV', the full report is at Annexe M)

A later Tactical Air Force tactical paper stated that

> The better known German fighters, the Me 109 and Fw 190, presented little difficulty to the versatile Spitfire IXB, and the Spitfire XIV was vastly superior to either of them as it was faster and could out-turn and out-climb them with ease. The Me 262 was quite a different problem as it was very fast and quite impossible to catch even when the Spitfire possessed a good height advantage.

Although the trials quoted above mentioned that no bomb racks were fitted to the Spitfire XIV, the fighter-bomber role occupied much of this variant's operational career, especially with the Tactical Air Force, where it essentially took over from the Spitfire IX. The Mark XIV was able to carry the same assortment of bombs as its predecessor but it also suffered from the same limitations in respect of ground-attack operations. Likewise, the Spitfire XIV appeared in a number of variants amongst its production total of 957 aircraft, including the FR.XIV, a fighter-reconnaissance variant that first went to 2 Squadron in November 1944. The performance of this variant also made it one of the few fighters able to catch the V-1 flying bombs (see Chapter 6, 'D-Day and Beyond').

Sweeping the skies clear of enemy aircraft, bombing and strafing ground targets and escorting medium bombers kept the tactical squadrons very busy in the first half of 1944 as all efforts were directed to preparing the way for the invasion of Europe. The last great air battles of the war were about to begin.

More Ground Attack

The whole of the Allies' tactical and strategic air power was thrown into preparing the battlefield and thousands of sorties were flown against all manner of military installations and the transportation network. Whilst the Spitfires were by no means a leading element in this, when weighed against the US 8th and 9th Air Forces, Bomber Command and tactical types such as the Typhoon, they did play their part. The following accounts indicate the type of actions.

On 21 May Spitfires of 222 Squadron were airborne on Ramrod 905:

> train busting in the Somme–Seine area. The squadron led by Squadron Leader Innes proceeded to Freiston with 30-gallon slipper tanks to refuel and to be briefed. Take off was at 1030 hours. The squadron crossed in at Ault at 10,000 feet and then split up into three sections. Cloud was 10/10ths

with base at 2,500 feet. Blue Section proceeded to the Amiens area and Red Section went to Gourney, Yellow Section to the Forges area: Blue Section destroyed one loco and two trains damaged, two lorries destroyed and troops strafed. Red Section encountered flak but located no targets. Yellow Section fired at a signal box and some goods wagons. Yellow Section had two aircraft damaged by flak. Warrant Officer Lenehan (MK833) lost most of his rudder. Pilot Officer Reid (MK830) had to make a belly landing as his wheels would not come down. (222 Squadron ORB)

Not all damage to the enemy communications network was intentional; on May 21 Spitfire BL646 of 234 Squadron had a 'small problem': 'Lieutenant Bernard was successful in being able to tear away a good few feet of telephone communications in Belgium after having made his attack on a train, and retained the wire for use in this country by bringing it back wrapped around his kite' (234 Squadron ORB). This was but one of many hazards faced by aircraft operating at ultra low level; this Spitfire came back, many other Allied aircraft were not so lucky.

In addition to the offensive work of the 2nd Tactical Air Force Spitfires, the aircraft of ADGB, primarily Spitfires, was kept busy in the build-up phase, flying 18,639 sorties between 1 April and 5 June, claiming 111 victories for forty-six losses.

~ 6 ~

D-Day and Beyond

The air plan for D-Day was the most complex ever devised and called for thousands of Allied aircraft, including the US 8th and 9th Air Forces, to act in concert to achieve air supremacy and provide support for ground and naval forces. One of the major roles on 6 June for the Spitfire units was combat air patrols (CAPs) providing low cover over the assault beaches, the more distant 'stopper' patrols being flown by American P-51 Wings. Although a number of combats took place over the next few days, air activity was generally fairly light and once units had been relieved from their CAP positions they invariably went free-ranging after ground targets, including enemy airfields. Within days of the invasion, Spitfire squadrons were operating from landing grounds in Normandy. Ground attack, especially hunting for enemy motor transport (MT), became the norm and it may well have been a Spitfire of 602 Squadron that attacked the staff car of Erwin Rommel on 17 June and put that great general out of the battle. This was, in essence, to be the story of the remaining months of the war. The Spitfire units advanced with the ground forces and provided invaluable support, as well as air escort for other aircraft types. The photographic reconnaissance (PR) role continued to be a vital one and such reconnaissance was essential in the battle against the German V-weapons. The Spitfire tactical Wings continued to move forward with the advancing Allied troops, taking over airfields recently vacated by the Luftwaffe. Ground attack remained the primary role, both bombing and strafing, and losses were not insignificant in the face of effective German anti-aircraft fire. These activities took the Tactical Air Force Spitfire squadrons into Germany and the end of the war.

Invasion

At last the long-awaited invasion had arrived and it brought a sense of satisfaction: 'This morning at 4am when the boys were getting ready for their first patrol, the groundcrew were told and they cheered. The uplift in morale was good to see. All pilots and ground-crew realised the big day had arrived and they seemed to take a new lease of life, and went about their work with renewed keenness' (402 Squadron RCAF ORB; the Squadron was operating Spitfire Vs out of Horne).

It was the same story at most bases, the aircrew knew by late on the 5th and the groundcrew – those who had not already guessed – by early morning the following day. All knew that it would be the prelude to days of intense effort, that there would be losses, but they all also knew that the war was a step nearer ending.

After the first waves of heavy and medium bombers cleared their targets it was the turn of naval gunfire and the fighter-bombers to batter the defenders. The bombardment ships were to be on station at 0500 hours, having moved into position under the cover of a smoke-screen laid by RAF Bostons. These ships were capable of laying down a massive amount of firepower, the accuracy and effectiveness of which was assisted by the aircraft of the Air Spotting Pool (ASP), based at Lee-on-Solent and comprising four Fleet Air Arm Seafire squadrons of No 3 Naval Wing (808, 885, 886, 897), five RAF squadrons (26, 63, 2, 268, 144 – although the last three of these were only available up to midday) plus a number of Spitfires operated by US Naval Squadron VCS-7. As this was mainly a Seafire operation it is covered in Chapter 9, 'Carrier Operations'.

For the fighter squadrons D-Day was hectic but fairly unproductive (as shown in Table 9), the day's events being summarised in the Fighter Command intelligence summary: 'No major encounters took place throughout the first day of the launching of the invasion of Normandy. Enemy air activity was negligible. It is estimated that both escorting and protective fighters over the assault areas and defensive fighters over France did not exceed 50 to 70 [enemy] sorties.'

The Allied expectation had been somewhat different, the directive issued to the fighter forces stating that: 'the intention of the British and American fighter forces is to attain and maintain an air situation which will assure freedom of action for our forces without effective interference by the German Air Force, and to render maximum air protection to the land and naval forces in the common object of assaulting, securing and developing the bridgehead'. SHAEF anticipated a major German air reaction along the lines of that encountered over Dieppe in 1942 and, although the air campaign had spent much effort on attacking German airfields and the fighter control system, the fighter plan for D-Day was complex and comprehensive. The all-important task of preventing German reconnaissance was given to the Spitfire XIVs of 91 and 322 squadrons, along with the Spitfire VIIs of 124 Squadron.

In his book, *The Big Show*, Pierre Clostermann, then with 602 Squadron, records an evening patrol:

We flew along the Cotentin peninsula. There were fires all along the coast and a destroyer surrounded by small boats was sinking near a little island. Our patrol zone was the area between Montebourg and Carentan. We were covering the 101st and 82nd American Airborne Divisions while the 4th Division, which had just landed, marched on Ste Mere-Eglise. We couldn't see much. A few houses were in flames. A few jeeps on the roads. The sky was full of American fighters, in pairs. They were wandering about rather haphazard, and showed a tendency to come and sniff at us from very close to, when they seemed too aggressive we showed our teeth and faced them. One Mustang coming out of a cloud actually fired a burst at Graham. Graham, whose shooting was as good as his temper was bad, opened fire on him, but luckily for the Mustang, he missed.

Miroslav Liskutin flew a number of sorties in Spitfire IXs over the D-Day period and recorded that on one occasion Ota Smik:

gave a demonstration of his superior talent in front of the whole Wing. Shortly after the usual radar warning about approaching enemy aircraft, he spotted two Fw 190s some 3,000ft above the patrolling Spitfires. In a most spectacular manner, before the rest of the pilots even realised what was going on, he attacked alone and shot down both enemy aircraft. Ota Smik's use of the true maximum power in this action, beyond the normally available boost override, had shown that he learned more than was expected during the usual Rolls-Royce engine handling course. Just the same as everybody else who attended this course, I regarded the lecture on boost capsule failure purely as advice on how to cope and what is the correct emergency drill. Not so Ota Smik! He realised the potential. This situation can be created at will, deliberately, for a purpose. He worked out the technique for breaking the capsule, when wanted, at a moment's notice. The purpose was to obtain a brief burst of 32lbs of boost. He also evaluated the chances of the engine surviving and how long it could last before exploding. Ota Smik had learned this technical secret and applied it in action, taking a chance on his engine's survival after such treatment. (Liskutin, *Challenge in the Air*)

German air activity continued to increase and more Allied fighter squadrons reported combats; 222 Squadron's Spitfire flew four missions on 8 June, the final one taking off at 1850 hours to patrol Sword beach. Some thirty minutes after commencing the patrol the Spitfires were warned of enemy aircraft in the area and soon visually acquired a gaggle of Fw 190s. Battle was joined and in the space of a few minutes the Squadron claimed three enemy aircraft shot down, one probable and a further four damaged – all for no loss. The Spitfires of 222 Squadron, having completed their patrol of Sword beach on 10 June, landed at 1630 hours,

*Table 9: Spitfire Operations Flown between 2100 hours 5 June
and 1900 hours 6 June 1944*

Type of mission	Aircraft	Squadrons	Target	ToT
2100 5 June to sunrise 6 June: 2nd TAF				
Convoy patrol	72	401, 416, 441, 443, 453		1742–2305
2100 5 June to sunrise 6 June: ADGB				
Convoy patrol	40		No 10 Gp area	1935–2316
	26		No 11 Gp area	1505–2310
Defensive	52		No 11 Gp area	0120–0505
Recce	6	56, 611	shipping	2015–2256
ASR	6	277		2100–2225
Sunrise to 1900 6 June: 2nd TAF				
Offensive patrol	36	403, 416, 421	Cherbourg area	0624–0815
Beachhead	109			0715–1010
	216			1020–1533
	36	329, 340, 341	eastern area	0904–1110
	36	132, 453, 602	western area	1309–1510
	36	302, 308, 317	western area	1545–1727
	108		eastern area	1314–1742
Convoy escort	35	302, 308, 317	western area	0523–0755
	36	441, 442, 443	eastern area	0633–0832
	36	132, 453, 602	western area	0809–1010
	36	222, 349, 485		1445–1645
Recce	17	16	Battle area	0645–1900
	3	400		0830–1922
Air spotting	344	ASP		all day
2100 5 June to sunrise 6 June: ADGB				
Offensive patrol	48			0532–0645
Beachhead patrol	280			
Convoy escort	132			
Defensive	74			
Notes: ToT = Time on Target ASP = Air Spotting Pool				

at airfield B3 (Ste-Croix-sur-Mer), the first time that this Squadron had landed in Europe. The servicing commandos refuelled and re-armed the aircraft whilst the pilots went on a quick souvenir hunt, and the Spitfires were back on patrol at 1800 hours. These quick turnrounds on airfields in Normandy meant that greater use could be made of the available tactical aircraft. On the same day, Pilot Officer Bavis of 402 Squadron had to force-land, his Spitfire having been damaged in a tangle with enemy fighters; however, he had no time to admire the French countryside as he was whisked away to the beach, taken by motor torpedo boat (MTB) to England, caught a train to Horley and was back on the Squadron the day following his incident. However, not all pilots made it back.

> At the time, I recall, we were experiencing quite a number of problems with our rather ancient Spitfire IXs, and that on 10 June, whilst on a beachhead patrol, two of our pilots, Fg Off 'Jerry' Bush and Fg Off Larry Foubert RCAF, had to bale out into the sea, because of engine failure due to glycol leaks. Both pilots were picked up OK and uninjured. I noted that Fg Off Bush's aircraft, BS462, had been air tested by me twice on 28th May after engine trouble. Then on 19 June, Flt Lt Aylott from 274 Squadron, also based at Detling, went into the sea south of Beachy Head following a glycol leak. He was on beachhead patrol, but was sadly killed. Despite this apparent problem with the aircraft, I do not recall anything being said or anything being done. (Jerry Jarrold, 80 Squadron)

However, something must have been done, as the Squadron records had this to say: 'both pilots baled-out off Beachy Head because of glycol leaks possibly caused by the strain set-up by the 90-gallon long-range tanks.' The entry for 11 June said: 'most aircraft unserviceable whilst tests take place on the re-occurring problem of glycol leaks. The 90-gallon tanks are being replaced by 45-gallon tanks, which have proved adequate for beachhead patrols.'

> 14th June: We actually came across enemy fighters! The Squadron had 12 Spitfires on a controlled sweep between Dieppe and Paris, and we were vectored by *Snackbar* to a group of bogeys half-way between Paris and Beauvais. We picked up seven or eight 109's and a single Fw 190 and having jettisoned tanks, tipped over and dived at them. The enemy had seen us, and they half-rolled and spiralled down into the 6/10ths cloud layer at 12,000 feet before we could really get at them. I spent all of the time trying to keep up with the fellow in front of me, eventually losing him, and found myself going round in huge circles trying to get on the tail of one of the 109's. One flashed across in front of me. I gave it a quick burst with no effect, and then everyone seemed to disappear. I appeared to be on my own, so I put the nose down and returned to the U.K. at sea level, eventually catching up with another

one of our Squadron, and together we landed at Detling. (Jerry Jarrold, 80 Squadron)

The Second Blitz

In the morning on 13 June 1944, at 0418, the peace at Swanscombe, near Gravesend, Kent, was shattered by a fierce explosion. The first of Hitler's new 'terror' weapons had landed on English soil. Within an hour, three more of these V-1 flying bombs had come to earth – one crashing into a railway bridge at Grove Road, Bethnal Green, in London, and causing six deaths and a substantial amount of damage.

This missile assault had been anticipated and, as recounted above, a great deal of air effort had been expended on delaying or negating its effectiveness. In the twenty-four-hour period from 2230 on 15 June to 16 June 1944, British records show 151 reported launches, with 144 V-1s crossing the English coast. Of those, seventy-three reached the London area. The defences notched up only a modest score, seven falling to the fighters, fourteen to the guns and one shared, whilst a further eleven were shot down by the guns of the Inner Artillery Zone.

The V-1, spanning a little over 17ft 6in, was a very small target, and it flew fast (300–400mph) and low. Pilots first had to find this small target and then came the challenge of actually shooting it down. The official RAF account of the campaign summarised the speed problem: 'as for the fighters, the short time in which interception had to be made, demanded that they should be quickly and accurately directed on to the course of the bomb.' The Tempest has frequently been quoted as the most successful of the anti-Diver fighters, but the Spitfire XIIs and XIVs also played their part, whilst other Spitfire units were somewhat less successful. A number of Mark XIVs were given extra low-level performance by being modified to operate with 150 octane fuel and +25lbs boost, giving them a top speed of around 400mph (an increase of 30mph or so) at 2,000ft. By late September seven RAF squadrons had re-equipped with the Mark XIV, which, despite its modification for low-level ops against the V-1, was primarily optimised at this stage for high-level fighting, although this soon changed. It was also one of the few Spitfires with 0.5-in guns, the 'E Wing' being equipped with two 20-mm cannon and two machine guns.

Fighter-Bombers

In the months after the landings in Normandy the Tactical Air Force Spitfire squadrons were increasingly used as fighter-bombers, partly because of the seemingly endless requirement for this role and partly because the decline of the German fighter force meant that ground attack kept the Spitfires far more gainfully employed. It was not, however, an ideal role for the aircraft, not because of a lack of firepower – the combined cannon and bomb armament was potent enough – but because the aircraft was vulnerable to self-damage and to ground fire. Like its fighter cousin the P-51 Mustang, the Spitfire was more prone to fatal damage, unlike the more rugged types such as the Typhoon and P-47 Thunderbolt. Ricochets from machine-gun and cannon fire, and fragmentation splinters from exploding bombs were frequent causes of damage to aircraft. As the RAF entered its last year of the war the Spitfire IX was still operational in large numbers but it was being joined by the Marks XIV and XVI.

The Mark XVI was to all intents and purposes a Mark IX with a Packard Merlin 266 and it appeared in two main variants, the F.XVI and the LF.XVI, the primary aim being to create a fighter optimised for the lower altitudes in which most combats were taking place by 1944. The new Mark number was perhaps unnecessary and it was more a question of paperwork rather than significant variation of the actual aircraft. The Spitfire XVI looked almost identical to the IX and they were built alongside each other at Castle Bromwich, with 1,055 Mark XVIs being produced. Standard wings were of C or E Type (the latter might therefore be an LF.XVIE to denote clipped wing and E Type wing). The first five squadrons re-equipped in November 1944, with four more the following month.

'We can assert that pilots who took part in sorties in T.A.F. had to possess all the characteristics required of a fighter pilot and had to display great courage, speed of decision and speed of action' (2nd TAF, Tactical Notes). The following extract is taken from a briefing paper entitled 'Tactical Paper No 4: Tactics used by Spitfire Day Fighter/Bomber Squadrons of 2nd T.A.F.' and it encapsulates the main roles of the Spitfire during this latter phase of the war in Europe. The complete briefing paper is included at Annexe O.

1 The Tactical Air Force, which was created for the invasion of the Continent was based mainly on the fighter force which was then existing in Great Britain.

2 The aircraft deployed by the new force were the same fighter aircraft modified so as to carry bombs and rocket-projectiles. In their role in 2nd T.A.F. the aircraft of the Spitfire XVI Squadrons normally carried the following armament:

(a) Two 20-mm cannons with 260 rounds of ammunition.

(b) Two 0.5-in machine-guns with 500 rounds of ammunition.

    (c) One 500-lb bomb plus two 250lb (fully loaded) or
    (d) Two 250-lb plus drop tank (45 gallons).
The bombs were of two types, high explosive and incendiary. The high explosive bombs were either instantaneous or had delayed-action fuses from 0.025 second to 72 hours, depending on the kind of target. The bombing was carried out from low-level or from a dive. In the case of low level bombing the normal fuse was of at least 11 seconds delay in order that it should not endanger the bombing aircraft.

3 The first trials of using fighter aircraft for new purposes were the 'Rhubarb' operations. From the experience gained in these operations and in mass exercises of the fighter squadrons in Great Britain in the years 1943–1944, the basis of the formation of a Tactical Air Force was formed. The employment of fighter aircraft in the Tactical Air Force necessitated new tactics being evolved because of:
    (a) Flying at lower altitude in the reach of enemy flak defences.
    (b) The employment of fighter aircraft in attacks on ground targets.
    (c) The arming of fighter aircraft so that they could carry bombs and rocket projectiles.

4 The creation of a Tactical Air Force did not change the main tasks of the Fighter Force. It only added new tasks and the personnel and material had to carry out a more varied programme.

5 The general tactics of the Fighter Force were only changed in as much as the technical improvements of the material allowed it. We will limit ourselves in the review of the Tactical Air Force to the experience of certain Units who had Spitfires Mk XVI at their disposal. These Squadrons had the following tasks to carry out:
    (a) Direct co-operation with our own first-line troops.
    (b) Attacks on the enemy's front line and rear.
    (c) Normal fighter force tasks.

Ralph Sampson, an experienced Spitfire pilot – and quoted in the previous chapter as a fan of the Spitfire IXB – was posted to take command of 127 Squadron after its previous CO, Otto Smik had, along with another Squadron pilot, been shot down by ground fire during a bombing mission, 'I was pleased finally to have my command, but apprehensive as to the missions the Squadron was engaged in.' Sampson was told by the airfield commander at Brussels, Gp Capt Douglas Morris, that the Squadron's morale was low because of the losses caused by the ground-attack role and his predecessor's seeming willingness to attack heavily defended targets. Morris told him: 'the object in attacking a definite strategic but heavily defended target is to try and avoid the flak or, at least, the worst of it with skill and speed.' In other words, he was not to make risky attacks on targets that were not of sufficient strategic value.

Table 10: *Spitfire – Schedule of Bomb Loads*

Bomb Type	Port	Centre	Starboard
GP 250lb Mk IV	1	1	1
GP 500lb	1	x	1
MC 250lb Mk I, II	1	1	1
MC 500lb Mk I–III (L), Mk VI-VIII (S)	x	1	x
MC 500lb Mk IV, IX (L) (S)	x	1	x
MC 500lb Mk V (S)	x	1	x
SAP 250lb Mk II–V	1	1	1
SAP 500lb Mk II–V	x	1	x
AS 100lb Mk IV	1	1	1
AS 100lb Mk VI	1	1	1
AS 250lb Mk IV	1	1	1
AS 500lb Mk IV	x	1	x
LC 250lb Mk I–II	1	1	1
LC 500lb Mk I–II	x	1	x
Smoke 200lb No 2 Mk 2	x	1	x
Depth Charge 250lb Mk IV	x	1	x
Notes: S = Shortened L = Long x = not fitted			

Our dive-bombing sorties usually commenced at 10,000ft and the bombs were released at 4,000ft, the aircraft pulling away to either side as quickly as possible. As bombing operations attracted flak there were differing opinions as to the best way to avoid flak if possible. Peter Hillwood, my senior Flight Commander, said that the Huns, being short of shells, were conserving them so would only open fire when Spitfires approached in a straight line to the target. It therefore seemed more sensible to fly some 100 to 200 yards either to left or right of the target as if we were on our way elsewhere, and then at the very last moment, scream down. There were then two alternatives; the target could either be attacked from the side or the Squadron could proceed further and then turn and attack on a reciprocal course. With instantaneous bombs the dive commenced almost directly over the target, pulling out as the bombs were released, at approximately 4,000ft. With delay bombs the leader had to arrive at ground level abut 100 yards from the target. In either case the leader would be spraying the target area from side to side with cannon and machine-gun fire, hopefully to nullify some of the ack-ack, or at least to encourage the gunners to keep their heads down. (Sampson, *Spitfire Offensive*)

The 2nd TAF Tactical Notes had this to say about attacking trains:

> In reconnaissance and attacks on targets in defined regions, the fighter force
> had to reconnoitre a defined region and find its own targets for attack. This
> kind of operation was called 'Armed Recce' and was mainly directed against
> enemy's lines of communication (road and rail transport) . . . After steadying
> the aircraft and getting the target in the sights, the pilot would open fire at a
> height of about 700ft from a distance of about 500 yards and at an angle of 25
> to 30 degrees. The angle of attack in relation to the direction of the moving
> target used to vary from 0 to 90 degrees and dependent mainly on the nature
> of the target, its position and the outlines of the terrain. The attacks on motor
> transport and locomotives were normally carried out as far as possible at an
> angle of 30 degrees from the front.

Ralph Sampson was flying No 2 to Rolf Berg on 25 December 1944, a
period when the 2nd TAF was very much focused on armed recces, with
reports of a large goods train near the airfield at Twente promising a
valuable target.

> Sure enough as we reached the airfield we could see the train and he decided
> to attack, with the airfield [and its defences] literally about 100 yards on our
> left. Just before starting his attack he warned us of potential flak from the left.
> As we started our run I could see shell bursts behind his Spitfire and just in
> front of mine. Apart from being very frightened indeed, my thoughts were
> that I wouldn't survive to enjoy the Christmas dinner which I knew had been
> promised us. In the event I was lucky and only received some light flak near
> the tail of my Spit, causing small damage. However, we severely damaged
> this train and then two others we found elsewhere, one of which was seen
> to blow up. When we found the one with a flak wagon Berg, as was to be
> expected, attacked it while we concentrated on the train itself. It was a sweaty
> business but we did get back for our dinner. (Sampson, *Spitfire Offensive*)

Flak wagons were a serious threat and the Germans had for some time been
setting traps for unwary pilots, with seemingly vulnerable and tempting
trains suddenly sprouting barrages of flak, with inevitable losses amongst
the attackers.

Progress Through Europe

By July 1944 the AEAF included thirty-four Spitfire squadrons, the majority
in No 84 and No 85 Groups; their primary role was support of the ground
offensive. As the 2nd TAF paper outlined above indicated, the squadrons
were tasked with ground attack, and strafing and dive bombing occupied
them to the end of the war, moving forward from airfield to airfield to stay
close to the battlefield. As such there is little more to add, except for the

problem of the German jet fighters. None of the Allied fighters had the performance to catch aircraft such as the Me 262 unless they started from a very advantageous position; the best way to catch the jets was to lurk near their airfields and hit them on take-off or landing. Air combat was an increasingly rare occurrence and the era of the birth of the Spitfire legend in a mass aerial melée of turning and twisting fighters (Battle of Britain) was long gone. Such was the confidence in the Spitfire as a breed that continued efforts were made to develop the type – and to preserve the name.

A Backward Step – Spitfire 21

A major re-design was required for the Griffon 61 series but that was only one of the considerations in what was virtually a new aircraft, albeit one whose basic concepts could be traced back to the Mark IV and a whole string of 'desired' changes to the Spitfire airframe. Higher speed and performance meant that a new wing was needed, and as part of this design, and in addition to the basic requirement for added stiffness (all to do with aileron control and high-speed effects) consideration was given to heavier armament (four 20-mm cannon) and extra fuel. It all took time and it was nearly three years before the aircraft became a reality, and it was to prove problematic.

The interim Mark 21 (DP851) was followed by PP139 as the first fully modified aircraft and then LA187 as the first production aircraft, which flew in March 1944. The initial thoughts were that there were a few faults but that it showed great promise. However, the AFDU report of November 1944 on LA201 was damning.

> The instability in the yawing plane and the critical trimming characteristics of this aircraft make it difficult to fly accurately under the easiest conditions. As a sighting platform it is unsatisfactory both for air-to-air gunnery and ground-attack. Its handling qualities compare unfavourably with all earlier Marks of Spitfire ... The Spitfire XIV is a better all-round fighter than the Spitfire 21. The handling qualities of successive Marks of the basic Spitfire have gradually deteriorated until as exemplified in the Spitfire 21, they prejudice the pilot's ability to exploit the increased performance.

Various airframe modifications were made, including rudder and elevator, and a contra-rotating prop was eventually fitted. In March 1945 a second report by the AFDU (which had become part of the Central Fighter Establishment) seemed to confirm that the changes had worked, concluding that 'it is a satisfactory combat aircraft for the average pilot.' This was not exactly glowing praise but at least it was not entirely negative. The Mark entered service with 91 Squadron at Manston in January 1945 and only one other squadron received the type before the end of the war, so there was little opportunity to truly judge its operational performance.

The November report also contained the comment that 'no further attempt should be made to perpetuate the Spitfire family'. It had reached its logical limit of development and the future lay with new airframe and engine combinations. On this note it is worth looking at an aircraft that was *almost* a Spitfire, as the naming process rehearsed some interesting arguments.

What's in a Name? – Spitfire, Spiteful or Seafang?

The prototype Supermarine Spiteful (NN660) first flew on 30 June 1944 in response to Specification F1/43 for a new fighter with a laminar-flow wing. A Spitfire variant with such a wing was already under development as the Supermarine Type 470 – and by early 1943 the naming of this aircraft was under discussion. The Air Council Meetings for 1944 make regular mention of the discussions involved in the naming decision, the first such reference being 10 August 1943,

> The Secretary of State said that it had not been decided to style the aircraft Victor and that the question had been discussed with Chief of Air Staff and Sir Wilfred Freeman. There were objections to Victor, which suggested neither speed nor aggressiveness, and might be thought presumptuous as well as out of place in certain operational contingencies. On the other hand, no one had produced a better name and the retention of Spitfire might well appeal to pilots, although there were objections to retaining names which suggested that old aircraft were still in issue. AMT considered it a mistake to perpetuate names although there might be some point in resuscitating old names e.g. Fury.

It was the laminar wing which was prompting the desire for a completely new name for what was very much a developed Spitfire. Such a wing was desirable as speeds had now been reached at which compressibility was a significant factor; in the latter part of 1943 a Spitfire XI (EN409) flown by Sqn Ldr J. R. Tobin had recorded an indicated Mach of 0.92. The new wing form would delay the formation of shock waves and associated drag and thus improve speed performance.

A rather more detailed discussion took place at the Air Council meeting of 14 September:

> Under Secretary of State said that a good many new names had been suggested from various sources but none had any general support. He had consulted Group commanders, Commanding Officers and pilots. The feeling was universal against a change from the name Spitfire. The Secretary of State

thought that it would be a mistake to make a change unless a better name were found. It had been represented earlier that there were objections, on the score of morale, to pilots flying an aircraft with the old name of Spitfire. Now these objections appeared to have been transferred to the workmen who would construct the aircraft. The AOC-in-C Fighter Command had favoured a change but had altered his view on ascertaining the opinion of his Group Commanders. Their opinion weighed and only considerations of high importance would justify a change which was viewed with disfavour by the operational personnel concerned.

Four of the senior officers present then summarised their arguments in favour of a new name, typical of these was that of AMSO who,

> saw no reason for giving the name Spitfire to what was a different aircraft and not another Spitfire. Little about the new aircraft was interchangeable with the Spitfire, and continuance of the latter name would be a nuisance from the supply point of view. He doubted whether those pilots who had objected to a change of name appreciated that the Spitfire XXI was a different type.

The VCAS concluded that the only reason for keeping the name Spitfire was psychological in that: 'there was a natural reluctance to give up a name which was more or less synonymous with a first-class fighter'.

By the autumn of 1943 the Spitfire was serving with some fifty squadrons in Fighter Command and was also beginning to make its way to other theatres of the war; a great many senior officers, certainly at Wing and Group level, had been operational pilots with the Spitfire in the Battle of Britain; in other words, the name Spitfire certainly had a very strong 'grass roots' following, as well as a great deal of public support. The psychological effect of the name was, therefore, of great importance.

At the 12 October 1943 Air Council Meeting the 'stakes' were raised with a 'statement by the Secretary of State that the Prime Minister was interested in the choice of name and wished to discuss it with him, and of a statement by Chief of Air Staff that "Valiant" seemed, for several reasons, a far better name than "Victor", but we should need to consult the Admiralty before adopting it.' A list of possible names had been circulated after the September meeting, although this list does not appear to have survived, the name 'Valiant' must have been on that list. Consultation with the Admiralty was required as the new aircraft would almost certainly include a navalised version.

The subject was on the agenda again with the 9 November meeting,

> Secretary of State said that a decision on the naming of this aircraft could no longer be deferred. General opinion favoured 'Valiant' which CAS had suggested. AM Sorley said that there was an urgent need for a decision. We had previously given the name Valiant to an aircraft which had not, however,

been introduced into service. The Council decided that the Spitfire XXI should be named Valiant, and invited the Permanent Under-Secretary to clear the proposal with the Admiralty.

It did not take long for the Admiralty to reply; a short note being included in the 7 December minutes, 'Statement by the Permanent Under-Secretary that Admiralty had agreed that the name Valiant might be used for this aircraft'. Thus, as 1943 came to a close the situation would appear to have been resolved, and the psychological arguments brushed aside. It was, however, not that simple.

The Air Council meetings make no mention of the subject again until 7 March 1944,

> The Chief of Air Staff referred to a Minute in which Supermarine had reacted unfavourably to Valiant and considered that a name should be chosen beginning with the letter S. There was also the objection that the Americans had decided to use the name for one of their aircraft. A folder was circulating to members of the Council containing a number of alternatives. Of these, he favoured Spiteful.

Sadly, the arguments raised by Supermarine are not mentioned in any detail, although the earlier reference to 'worker discontent' may have played some part. Indeed, the general impression now is that any name would do and the Air Council did not even debate the suggestion put forward by CAS – scratch Valiant, insert Spiteful.

The second prototype, NN664, was completed to production specification (the first prototype had essentially been a Spitfire XIV that had been given a laminar-flow wing) and first flew on 8 January 1945 in the hands of Jeffrey Quill. The flight trials on these two prototypes revealed numerous elements that needed modification and in due course the first production Spiteful (RB515) took to the air in April 1945. Almost 200 were ordered but only seventeen were built as the war ended and RAF interest in this 'follow-on' Spitfire came to an end. The Admiralty were not called upon to adopt the Spiteful as under Specification N5/45 they had their own laminar-flow Spitfire follow-on – which they promptly named Seafang. Spiteful F.14 RB520 was navalised to be the prototype for the Seafang until the true prototype, VB895, was ready. An order was placed for 150 aircraft but in the event only ten Seafang F.31s were built.

Perhaps the most confusing reference is that to the Spitfire XXI as there appears to be no reason for this – definite – Spitfire Mark number to be included in this debate. Was it an accident or was it misinformation? It should not have been the latter as these were primarily classified memos!

~ 7 ~

Over the Desert and Italy

The overall story of the Spitfire and its combat development is very much linked to the European Theatre of Operations (ETO) but its role and development in the other two theatres – Mediterranean and Middle East, which also includes the Italian campaign as the bulk of the tactical air power in Italy came via the North African campaign, and the Far East, brought new tactical problems and solutions.

Malta

The island of Malta was a critical strategic base for Britain and as such its defence assumed a high priority. The Italian and German air arms had been pounding the island for many months and Malta was in dire need of fighter reinforcements. However, the shortage of Spitfires and the pressing need of other areas meant that it was spring 1942 before the first aircraft were sent to the beleaguered island.

On 7 March 1942, the carrier HMS *Eagle* steamed close enough to Malta for its cargo of fifteen Spitfires to be flown to the island. Three days later the fighters flew their first air defence sorties, accounting for a number of Bf 109s. Axis intelligence had been caught unawares, but within days the intensive air bombardment had put the Spitfires out of action. It was clear that many more were needed in order to have any impact on the air battle.

Churchill requested and was granted use of the American carrier USS *Wasp* and with its much greater capacity this ship took fifty-four Spitfires to within range of the island on 20 April. Forty-seven of the fighters made it to Malta but the Germans were ready and within hours air attacks had reduced the total to eighteen serviceable aircraft. A third reinforcement flight was arranged for 9 May with both *Wasp* and *Eagle* involved. This time sixty-four aircraft were flown off and upon arrival at Malta were immediately escorted to prepared blast pens for re-fuelling and re-arming.

A heavy German raid the following day was met by scores of RAF fighters, the Spitfires flying 110 sorties during the day for the loss of three aircraft — the attackers lost twenty-three aircraft. More reinforcement flights were flown in the subsequent weeks and never again was the air defence of Malta in any serious trouble. By August 1942 Malta had a notional strength of 163 Spitfires, of which 120 were serviceable. This enabled the island not only to defend itself but also to go on to the offensive.

However, the Luftwaffe had not finished with the George Cross island and a renewed air assault saw losses mount and serviceability of the remaining aircraft decline, so that by autumn the island was once more short of fighters. October saw the start of direct ferry flights from Gibraltar, the Spitfires carrying a 170-gallon ferry fuel tank. In a development that was anathema to purist fighter pilots but one that was made through tactical expediency, the Malta Spitfires became the first to operate as fighter-bombers. Malta's Spitfires notched up another first in August 1942 with modifications to aircraft of 126 Squadron, based at Luqa, to enable them to carry two 250-lb bombs with which to attack targets in Sicily. Malta's aircraft had been flying offensive fighter sweeps for some time, taking the war to the Axis air bases, but with little reaction. The Spitfire bombers would release their bombs from 10–15,000ft in a slight dive, thus keeping away from the main flak threat, whilst additional Spitfires provided air escort. The air commander, Sir Keith Park, of Battle of Britain fame, sent a memo to the Air Ministry in December 1942:

> The reason I introduced the Spit-bomber was that the enemy was ignoring our fighter sweeps over his aerodromes in the south of Sicily. As a result of flying trials we found that fitting 2 x 250-lb bombs to the Spitfire slightly increased the take-off run, and slowed down the rate of climb by about 10%. There was practically no difference in the speed at level flight, and in the dive the speed was increased owing to the higher wing loading.
>
> We designed the bomb gear so that there was no loss of performance when the bombs were dropped. Unlike the Hurricane bomb gear, our Spitfire throws away all external fittings with the exception of the steel rib which protrudes less than one inch from the wing. Our practice is for 50% of a Spitfire sweep to carry bombs with stick extension and to approach the target at about 20,000ft. The aircraft do a stall turn over the target diving at an angle of about 75 degrees, and release the bombs at between 7 and 12,000ft, depending on the intensity of heavy flak.

Desert Spitfires

The honour of conducting the first Spitfire operations in the Middle East and Mediterranean theatre went to the PR.IVs of No 2 Photographic Reconnaissance Unit (PRU), with four aircraft (AB312, AB421, BP883, BP904) joining the unit in March 1942 to supplement the existing Hurricanes. Photographic reconnaissance had always been a critical role within this theatre of operations and the arrival of the Spitfires added a new capability. Typical of the missions flown was one on 29 March when BP883 took off from Gambut for a four-hour fifty-five-minute sortie covering northern Greece. Two months later 145 Squadron became the first unit in the Desert Air Force to acquire the type, in the shape of the VB, flying its first CAS mission on 1 June.

However, it was the Mark V that really launched the Spitfire's career in the Western Desert theatre; indeed, it was in this theatre that the majority of VCs were employed. The problems of operating in desert conditions were well known and so aircraft were fitted with the Vokes filter to preserve engine life; however, the aerodynamics of the Spitfire were affected, resulting in a significant drop in the speed. The Maintenance Unit (MU) at Aboukir soon addressed the problem and produced a modified Vokes filter (often referred to as the Aboukir filter). The MU at Aboukir was also called upon to modify a number of Spitfires to counter the high-flying Ju 86P recce aircraft that frequently appeared over the Cairo area. One such modified aircraft was BR114 and this reached the amazing (for a VB) height of 50,000ft (15,240m). Although Fg Off Reynolds managed to damage one of the high-flying enemy on 24 August 1942, it was the 29th of the month before the first confirmed 'kill' was made.

Fighter Wing

Whilst deliveries of Spitfires to the Middle East never kept pace with demand they did increase over the ensuing months, the primary source being via the Takoradi route (shipped out to Takoradi and then flown across Africa to Egypt). The first unit of the Desert Air Force (DAF) to operate the type was 145 Squadron, which arrived at Heliopolis from the UK in April 1942 with Spitfire Vs; the unit moved into the Western Desert theatre of operations in late May and flew its first mission, escort to Hurricanes on a CAS mission, on 1 June. The build-up of Spitfire units was slow but at last the DAF had an aircraft to counter the threat posed by the Luftwaffe's fighters.

Air Fighting Committee Paper No 152 presented 'Tactical notes on operations in North-West Africa by RAF fighter squadrons December 1942 to March 1943' and this included various references to the Spitfire. The main

Spitfire element of fighter operations in this theatre comprised No 322 Wing at Bone (the Rear Wing) and No 324 Wing near Souk El Khemis (Forward Wing). The latter was comprised of four squadrons of Spitfire Vs and one of their main roles was tactical reconnaissance. The report stated that:

> The TacR Spitfires operated in pairs, aircraft flying well spaced in line astern so that both could concentrate on searching the ground, with adequate cloud cover (7/10th to 10/10th at 5,000ft) or in the early dawn, an escort of 4–6 aircraft was found to be sufficient. In clear weather a close escort of 6 and a medium/ top cover of 6 were provided.

As to ground strafing '. . . when the target is located, attack from the sun immediately, always leaving a top cover . . . open fire at maximum range, closing to zero feet and carrying on at ground level, weaving frantically.'

No 324 Wing had formed at Wilmslow in September 1942 for operations in North Africa and by November had established a mobile wing headquarters at Maison Blanche with four Spitfire squadrons on strength, plus a Beaufighter unit (255 Squadron). The Spitfire squadrons were: 72 Squadron (Spitfire VB), 92 Squadron (Spitfire VC), 111 Squadron (Spitfire VC) and152 Squadron (Spitfire VB). The Wing moved to Souk-El-Arba as part of No 242 Group on 29 November but by the middle of January were at Souk-El-Khemis. No 322 Wing had formed at West Kirby in September 1942 and moved to North Africa, establishing its mobile wing headquarters at Maison Blanche. It too had four Spitfire units: 81 Squadron (Spitfire VC), 154 Squadron (Spitfire VC), 225 Squadron (Spitfire VB) and 242 Squadron (Spitfire VB).

The El Alamein offensive was launched on 18 October under the cover of massive air support. Air superiority was soon achieved and the Allied forces advanced, Tobruk falling on 13 November. Meanwhile, the second part of the Allied blow fell with the amphibious assault (Operation Torch) on the Vichy-held Tunisia/Algeria area. Amongst the aircraft involved in tthis operation were the Seafires of 801 and 807 squadrons. Jerry Jarrold was with 80 Squadron in the Western Desert when Spitfire Vs arrived to replace the Hurricanes:

> we were overjoyed to have delivered to us Spitfire VCs – not necessarily brand new, but none the less welcome. The Spitfire was much more manoeuvrable than the Hurricane and could out-climb it and get higher, and with its reputation it was one of those aircraft that all fighter pilots wanted to fly. However, the Hurricane was a much sturdier beast, and we reckoned that in a forced-landing it would go through a house, whereas the Spitfire would simply crumple!

A March 1943 Tactical Bulletin contained 'extracts from an interesting report by the commanding officer of a British Spitfire squadron in

North Africa'. The bulletin included a number of interesting points on Spitfire operations and tactics, starting with an appraisal of the aircraft's serviceability:

The serviceability of the Spitfire V proved exceptionally good throughout the operations. The engines and airframes stood up to the unnatural conditions exceptionally well. In my squadron practically no cases of damaged undercarriages occurred, although aerodrome surfaces were by no means satisfactory.

In the preliminary stages of the campaign, difficulty was found with the sighting of the guns and I suggest that all aircraft should be marked with a harmonising spot upon the airscrew blades as a quick check for harmonisation. The cannons and machine guns had no more than the normal amount of stoppages.

The bulletin went on to comment on tactics – German and British.

Once the Me 109G or the Focke-Wulf 190 had lost its initial advantage of speed from a dive and had been caught, it is powerless to shake you off at low altitudes, due to poor manoeuvrability. The 109G has proved itself very manoeuvrable in the looping plane and even a small rate of turn will produce very noticeable vapour trails from its wing tips. It was very noticeable that Ju 88s seemed to get away far too often from attacking Spitfires. This was due either to bad harmonisation of sights or bad marksmanship.

In search formation we adopted the No. 11 Group three sections of four, sections keeping line abreast, travelling fast and relying on perfect cross-cover with section leaders level and slightly above squadron leaders. Squadrons would always break, i.e. 180 degree turns instead of cross-over turns. Widely spread formations were found impracticable because sections would lose each other due to the perfect camouflage conditions. In Wing formation, squadrons would fly in line abreast. When attacked, the squadrons split into strict pairs using diving and climbing, thereby getting depth. Depth (by which the writer means dispersion in height) was found to be the answer to Hun fighter tactics. Individual pairs note their position from the ground when attacked and attempt to remain over the same spot. This results in the squadron keeping together, although in individual pairs. By breaking the squadron into small units in depth, the enemy aircraft could never position each pair in the sky, and would invariably attack aircraft that he thought were the top pair, only to find that another pair was above him still. Once he had lost his height and had been drawn down so that he was unable to pull out altogether, he was sunk, so to speak.

To escape superior odds it was found that by flying at ground level and making use of the mountainous country one could invariably shake-off ones adversary who would lose you due to the good camouflage of the Spitfire. While carrying out standing patrols over the Army it was found that the German fighters knew exactly where you were and how long you could maintain your patrol, and invariably came into attack the squadron as it was on its way back short of fuel, or to attack the Army when our fighter cover had returned to its base.

A good deflection shot was worth its weight in gold.

Air-to-air combats were infrequent, although the threat was always there and the CO expressed the opinion that 'even the most experienced "sweeper" is a babe for his first few weeks in North Africa'.

Ground attack was becoming the usual routine and he had this to say on ground strafing:

> When the target is located, attack from the sun immediately, always leaving a top cover. If your first run up on the target is bad, carry on and let the Hun think you are going on to another job and that you have not spotted his position. Return a few minutes later, making sure of your position, and make a quick dart down before he realises that he has been spotted. He will not give his position away by AA fire unless he thinks that he has been spotted, i.e. if he sees Spitfire circling round overhead and he is pretty certain they are going to attack and will open up. Never attack the same target twice on one patrol. Open fire at maximum range and closing to zero feet and carrying on at ground level, weaving frantically.

The comment on not attacking the same target twice has been an adage of ground attack ever since the 'art' was developed and yet it was seldom adhered to and all too often pilots paid the penalty. Its comments concerning the apparent ease with which the Mark V could deal with the 109G and Fw 190 is perhaps surprising considering the impression gained from the European theatre.

Tunisia finally fell in May 1943 and the next obvious move was the invasion of Italy. Air power built up massively on Malta and aircraft, including a veritable armada of Spitfires, roamed the skies looking for 'customers'. The assault on Sicily was launched on 10 July, supported by a massive air umbrella, Spitfires operating from Malta and Seafires off various carriers. On this first day an aircraft of 72 Squadron had to land at Pachino, the first Allied aircraft to touch down in Sicily. Summer 1943 had also brought a new Spitfire variant to the theatre – the Mark VIII.

Spitfire VIII

The Spitfire VIII first flew in April 1942, the initial flights being by the first production aircraft (JF299). However, it was over a year before the first operational unit, 145 Squadron, re-equipped. When 145 Squadron received its first Mk VIIIs in June 1943 it was based at Luqa, Malta and had been a Spitfire squadron since January 1941, first in the UK and since early 1942 in the Middle East/Mediterranean theatre. The Squadron had been operating

Mk IXs since March 1943 (and continued to do so until September); the new variant was a Mark number lower but a significant improvement.

The Spitfire VIII appeared with the Merlin 66 (LF.VIII) or Merlin 70 (HF. VIII), both had the 'C' wing; a total of 1,658 of the variant were built. 'When I am asked which Mark of Spitfire I consider the best from a pure flying point of view, I usually reply "the Mark VIII with standard wing tips"' (Quill, *Spitfire, a Test Pilot's Story*). It is strange, then, that it is one of the less well-known versions of the Spitfire; a reflection perhaps of its combat career being outside the European theatre. In July 1943 the Air Fighting Development Unit undertook a comparative trial between the Spitfire VIII and the Spitfire IX, the latter being the best variant then in service. The report included a number of interesting points in respect of performance and manoeuvrability: first, that the Mk VIII was generally, albeit marginally, superior to the Mk IX in both climb to height and speed above 30,000ft; second, that the AFDU considered that the small ailerons with the extended wing caused problems of manoeuvrability at high speed. According to RAF performance records the original Merlin 63-powered Mk VIII had a maximum emergency speed of 352kts at 27,500ft and an economical cruise of 191kts at 20,000ft. The comparative figures for a Spitfire IX were 353kts and 198kts, which on paper would make the IX a better performer; unfortunately, the AFDU report does not include the actual performance figures. In its developed version, the HF.VIII – powered by a Packard-built Merlin 70 – the notional maximum speed increased to 361kts at 27,000ft and the time to 20,000ft improved from eight minutes to 6.7 minutes. The complete report on this trial is included at Annexe G.

'Experience has shown that the Spitfire IX with Merlin 66 engine at low altitude, say 0–10,000ft, can overtake or out-climb a Me 109 or Fw 190.' Headquarters Mediterranean Allied Air Forces (MAAF) issued a bulletin on 29 April 1944 outlining the 'tactics of the Desert Air Force during the spring 1944'. The bulletin contained two main references to Spitfire usage:

> The technique of intercepting hostile raids has entirely altered since the days of massed hostile raids when a system of close vectoring or close control of our own fighters was employed. Now, with little opposition, and seldom more than one or two hostile formations in one area, it is found much better for the controller to give a running commentary describing to all aircraft in the area the information he has in front of him regarding movements, heights, speeds, etc of the enemy aircraft. In this way, successful interceptions have been brought about by aircraft engaged on duties other than fighter defence who happen to be in the area. For example, a squadron of fighter-bombers airborne on a strafing mission have made use of this information and intercepted hostile raids in their area. The controller gives his information in relation to well-known features along the coastline, big towns or other prominent landmarks.

This was one of the advantages of having a 'swing-role' (to use modern parlance) aircraft such as the fighter-bomber Spitfire IX – with its bombs gone it was once more an aggressive, potent fighter. This was also reflected in the way the aircraft were employed: 'the system of providing close escort for light-bombers has, to a large extent, given way to the provision of area cover over the target or places where bombers are liable to be intercepted. This system can only be employed when fighter opposition is weak and targets are not too distant from the bomb-line.'

The bulletin also highlighted the increasing use of the Spitfire in the fighter-bomber role:

> the Spitfire VIII and IX are now being converted into fighter/bombers, and experiments have already proved that they can carry 1,000lb of bombs; viz. 1 x 500-lb under the belly and 1 x 250-lb bomb under each wing. They have not as yet been used operationally with this load. The present intention is to convert all Spitfire VIIIs and IXs into fighter/bombers, and if the present light scale of opposition continues they will probably be employed on the basis of three squadrons as fighter/bombers to one squadron as pure fighters.

Italian Campaign

The pace of operations did not slacken and September brought landings on the mainland of Italy and at Salerno in October, in an attempt to break a strategic stalemate. The latter operation was at the extreme range of Malta-based Spitfires but the Seafires of Force V operated from five of the so-called 'baby flat-tops'; Force H and Force V combined had a total of 130 Seafires available at the start of the operation. Having spent the first few days of January carrying-out practice bombing with live 500-lb GP bombs, or 11½-lb practice bombs for high-level bombing, the Spitfires of 80 Squadron left the Middle East for Italy, arriving at Madna on 19 January. An offensive sweep was flown by six aircraft at first light on 22 January in the Korcula area; although a number of small ships were seen there were no suitable targets, but 'moderately accurate light flak damaged one aircraft'. This was the start of what would be an intensive period of operations for the Squadron on either sweeps of escort for fighter-bombers, primarily Kittyhawks, or medium-bombers such as the Baltimore. Sweeps involved attacking any suitable target in the assigned area and ultra low-level was the order of the day, as evidenced when one Spitfire came back damaged having struck the machine-gun post it was strafing whilst another struck a tree when attacking a group of vehicles.

Jerry Jarrold wrote in February 1944:

I flew again on the 8th of February, strafing in the Rieti and Sora area. On this op Flying Officer Holdsworth was hit by flak, but he baled out and although safe, was injured. The Squadron ORB recorded the mission: 'Six aircraft offensive patrol Avezzano–Arsoli–Frosimone with one M/T destroyed (flamer) and one damaged. Flak – intense inaccurate HAA at Alatri, moderate inaccurate LAA near Lake Cambrino, slight inaccurate HAA from Sora. Haze and low cloud met on outward journey had cleared by the time the aircraft returned. Fg Off R. S. Holdsworth (EP968) was seen to strafe the Frosimone–Ferrentine road but did not rejoin the formation. Some 10 minutes later he called ground station on Channel B saying that he was baling out. Nothing further was heard from him, he is presumed to have landed behind enemy lines.

On the 10th of February – there was more strafing in Rieti area. I was one of four aircraft on the sortie and the Flight shot up motor transport, resulting in six flamers and five others damaged. Again plenty of flak but nobody hit. The ORB recorded: 'four aircraft searched for MT reported snowbound at B9905 but nothing found. Continued on offensive patrol to Rieti–Rome road; in area Verola–Poggia two MT were attacked and damaged. A convoy of five trucks was attacked and four left flaming and one smoking. A second convoy of six 3-ton trucks was attacked; one left flaming, one smoking and one damaged. A large truck towing a trailer was set on fire.' (Jarrold with Delve, *Did You Survive the War?*)

This general routine was followed throughout February and March, but at the end of March the Squadron was one of a number of units in Italy to be given warning notice for a move to the UK to join the build-up of air strength for D-Day. As the Order of Battle for July 1944 shows (see Annexe B) there were twenty Spitfire squadrons in Italy, comprising No 232 Wing at Foggia (72 and 253 squadrons) in the fighter-bomber role, and 682 Squadron at San Severo with No 336 Wing with Spitfire XIs in the reconnaissance role, but with the other thirteen under the command of MAAF but based in Italy, the majority in wings of three squadrons. These were stationed at Piombino (43, 72, 93, 111 squadrons), Calenzana (154, 232, 242 squadrons), Calvi (237, 238, 451 squadrons), Fermo (241, 318 squadrons) and Venafro (92, 208, 417 squadrons), with single squadrons at Follonica (225 Squadron) and Perugia (145 Squadron).

Some thirty Spitfire squadrons were operating with the various air forces in Italy, although the number was reduced when squadrons were returned to the UK for the D-Day preparation. However, the type remained an important element of tactical air power for the rest of the campaign in Italy – a slow and at times hard slog up Italy in the face of dogged German resistance.

~ 8 ~

Jungle Operations

By January 1942 the British bastion at Singapore had fallen to the Japanese and the situation in the Far East was critical. Although the RAF had attempted to implement expansion and re-equipment programmes these had borne little fruit in the face of 'higher priorities' elsewhere and in terms of aircraft the Far East theatre was always seen as a backwater. The first Spitfires to make it to the theatre were two PR.IVs of No 2 PRU, their first operation being flown over Burma on 19 October 1942. By August 1942 the Japanese expansion was at its furthest point, Burma had fallen, India and Australia were threatened. The RAF's Hurricane squadrons did a superb job, along with other antiquated types such as the Blenheim, but there was no chance of achieving even air parity until reinforcements, and preferably superior types such as the Spitfire, arrived. However, it was September 1943 before the first such units were operational in the Far East (136, 607, 615 squadrons), all equipped with Spitfire Vs. The aircraft not only flew fighter and escort missions but were also involved with ground-attack work. The build-up accelerated in the early part of 1944 and by spring the number of units had doubled and the Spitfire VIII was the primary type. The second Battle of Arakan was launched on 4 February 1944 with the aim of achieving air superiority and re-conquering Burma (the Arakan area was particularly important because of its series of airfields). Despite minor setbacks the Allied advance continued through Burma; meanwhile, American forces were 'island-hopping' towards the Japanese home islands, a campaign that also involved FAA Seafire units and only came to an end with the Japanese surrender in August 1945.

So what tactics were applied in this theatre and what difference did the Spitfire make?

Although this chapter is titled 'Jungle Operations', and although the majority of Spitfire operations were indeed flown over the jungle, the first Spitfires were actually despatched to help defend Northern Australia from Japanese attack. Following a bombing raid on Darwin (19 February 1942) there was pressure for RAAF units, or pilots serving with the RAF, to return home to defend Australia. Churchill's response that summer was to order three Spitfire squadrons to move to Australia. These eventually became No 1 RAAF (Fighter) Wing and by January 1943 they were operational out of various strips in the Darwin area.

The Spitfires scored their first victory on 6 February and a few weeks later, 2 March, the first engagements with the Zero took place. The Wing was led by Wing Command Clive Caldwell, like many of his pilots he was already a successful fighter pilot, and in the engagement they shot down two Japanese fighters for no loss.

A South-West Pacific Area (SWPA) Intelligence Summary included a debrief by one of the Wing's Spitfire leaders; the following extract focused on the performance and tactics of the Zeke.

... A diving head-on attack was refused by a Zeke, which broke downwards before coming to range. This was repeated in the case of another Zeke a few minutes later. I observed several other Zekes fire on me and took necessary action; others, not seen, may have fired, but the shooting was bad, despite liberal use of tracer, and the attempts at correcting aim were poor. Engaging in turns with a Zeke at about 160mph IAS, I pulled my aircraft as tight as possible. The Zeke did not get dangerously close, until the speed began to drop at about the completion of the second turn. Breaking severely downwards to the inside of the turn, I experienced no difficulty in losing the Zeke. My engine cut momentarily in this manoeuvre. I observed Zekes looping, half rolling and firing whilst on their backs, which though interesting as a spectacle, seemed profitless in dogfighting.

During the engagement I saw a Spitfire diving away with a Zeke at its tail. The Spitfire appeared to be gaining distance. When leaving the combat area, I dived steeply away and was followed down in the dive by a Zeke. At a speed in excess of 400mph IAS, the Zeke did not close the distance and gave up quickly, though supported by several of his kind. The Zekes appeared to be armed with M/G and 20-mm cannon.

To summarise, in view of the whole circumstances surrounding the brief engagement, and despite the fact that both height and numbers favoured the Zekes, I regard the Spitfire as a superior aircraft generally, though less manoeuvrable at low speeds. In straight and level flight and in the dive the Spitfire appears faster. Though the angle of climb of the Zeke is steeper, the actual gaining of height seems much the same, the Spitfire going up at a lesser angle but at greater forward speed – an advantage. No difficulty was experienced in keeping height with the Zekes during the combat. I believe that at altitudes above 20,000ft the Spitfire, in relation to the Zeke, will prove an even better aircraft in general performance. It must be remembered, however, that the Japanese pilots had been airborne for a very long period and their efficiency must necessarily have been impaired by considerations of fuel conservation and fatigue.

Spitfire versus Zeke

Tactical Memo No 42 was issued by RAF India and provided a guide to the approved tactics for use by Spitfire pilots when engaging Japanese fighters, primarily the Navy 'O' Mk 1 – the Zeke. It also included, as an annexe, the SWPA summary referred to above.

1 The tactics which Spitfire pilots in this area have been instructed to employ against Jap fighters are set out briefly below. They have been decided upon after close study of the somewhat meagre experience of combats, and the characteristics of the types obtained from intelligence sources. Tactics naturally are not hard and fast but are subject to review from time to time in the light of additional operational experience.

2 Points favouring the Spitfire are:
    a Maximum level speed at all heights.
    b Manoeuvrability at high speeds.
    c Diving speed.
    Zekes on the other hand are more manoeuvrable at low speeds. Characteristics giving no appreciable advantage to either type over the other are:
    a Service ceiling.
    b Rate of climb.
    Although the rate of climb is approximately the same, the Spitfire appears to climb and zoom at a slightly shallower angle and higher speed than the Zeke, thus opening the range by covering a greater plan distance.

3 Factors primarily affecting 'dogfighting' are:
    a Speed of the aircraft engaged.
    b Stalling characteristics.
    Where speeds are in excess of 250mph the 'g' which a pilot can impose without 'blacking out' is the limiting factor so that no advantage can be expected on either side. At speeds below 250mph however, due to the higher wing loading of the Spitfire, a high-speed stall will occur if the pilot attempts to turn with a Zeke at progressively lower speeds and smaller radii of the turning circle. The conclusion drawn is that in a sustained 'dogfight', irrespective of the speed at which it commenced, the advantage must pass ultimately to the Zeke.

4 Tactics in these circumstances are:
    a Endeavour to take station at least 1,000 to 2,000ft above and up sun of fighter(s) to be attacked.
    b Attacks may be carried out from any angle from head on to dead astern, but where a no-deflection or small-deflection shot is possible it should be taken.
    c Break should be a zoom away to one side to retain height advantage, up sun if possible, care being taken not to overrun the aircraft being attacked.
    d Each deliberate attack should be separate and undertaken only with the advantage of height.

e DO NOT ATTEMPT TO REMAIN AND DOGFIGHT.

f When being attacked or attack is imminent and complementary attack is not possible, pilot should open range by quickest possible method, i.e. diving, turning under and away from attack, etc.

g When hard pressed 'everything into one corner' i.e. violent break preferably under the attacking aircraft and into a vertical dive. Follow this by an aileron turn as speed builds up. Until speed builds up take violent evasive action as necessary, i.e. rudder and or elevator to throw attacking pilots aim off the aircraft.

h Favourite 'break' by Zekes when attacked from rear is a steep zoom combined with turn away to one side. Another frequently used is the full loop with the object of reversing the relative positions of attacked and attacked. Spitfire break at sub para c above is designed to counter either of these manoeuvres.

i Zeke pilots air discipline when acting as bomber escort is good. Defensive action only sufficient to protect bombers is taken normally and they reform immediately attack ceases. Zekes do not willingly 'dogfight' and will not follow up an advantage if it takes them away from the bombers or from their track home.

j Short range engagements are likely to favour the Spitfire, due to its sturdier construction and armour. Hence it is advisable to 'get in' and 'get out'.

5 Basic element of tactical formation is the 'loose pair'. Two or three pairs comprise each Section and two more Sections make up the squadron. Battle formation is usually as shown below:

3 ▲	▲		5 ▲	1 ▲	3 ▲		1 ▲	3 ▲
BLUE				RED			WHITE	
▲ 4	2 ▲		▲ 6	2 ▲	4 ▲		▲ 2	4 ▲

When not in the vicinity of the enemy, squadron may climb either in battle formation, or Sections in line astern as below:

BLUE	RED	WHITE
	1 ▲	
1 ▲	2 ▲	1 ▲
2 ▲	3 ▲	2 ▲
3 ▲	4 ▲	3 ▲
4 ▲		4 ▲

Major changes of direction are by 'cross-over' turns by Sections, or individual aircraft turn about in the same direction after squadron is line abreast.

6 Movement of the Wing can be affected in the same manner. In meeting raids the object is to rendezvous the Wing and make contact with full

numbers. The Wing Leader allots specific tasks to squadrons immediately after giving 'Tally Ho.' Positioning of the squadron to carry out its tasks is at the discretion of the Squadron Leader.

The Tactical Paper was all very well and good but at this time the Spitfire was still to be introduced to the Bengal theatre, the main area of operations. It was not until September 1943 that the Alipore Wing was able to send pilots to collect Spitfires from the depot at Drigh Road, Karachi. No 607 Squadron, which had been operating Hurricanes in this theatre since May 1942, was the first to re-equip, taking on Mark VCs in September, and spending the next few months training with their 'new' aircraft. Of the pilots on the three Alipore squadrons (136, 607, 615) only six had previous Spitfire experience and it fell to them to do most of the ferrying work. The first combat scramble was made on 4 October when Flt Lt Paul Louis of 615 Squadron was sent after a high-flying Dinah reconnaissance aircraft, although without result (it was actually intercepted and hit by a pair of Hurricanes, the first successful interception for a long time). By this stage of the war the RAF had appreciated the need for air-gunnery and tactical training for fighter pilots and the new Spitfire squadrons were sent to the Air Fighting Training Unit (AFTU) to sharpen their skills (see Chapter 4, '"There I Was" – Training').

There were concerns over the Spitfire's reputation for engine overheating and for a weak (and narrow track) undercarriage that might not stand up to the poor airfield conditions; indeed, these were reasons that had been cited in 1942 for refusing Spitfires and remaining with Hurricanes.

Arakan Campaign

The Spitfire opened its score in this campaign on 8 November 1943 when Flt Lt Paul Louis and Fg Off S. Weggerty of 615 Squadron scrambled from Chittagong to intercept the Japanese early-morning reconnaissance over-flight. Whilst Louis closed on the Dinah, his No 2 acted as cover against any escorting fighters. Despite a starboard cannon failure, the attack from 250 yards to fifty yards was lethal to the Japanese aircraft. A few days later Flight Sergeant 'Willie' Hyde sent a second recce Dinah down, the initial engagement having taken place at 30,000ft. The Japanese got the message and despite the importance of these sorties there was a lull in activity for a week, after which 615 sent a third Dinah to earth on 16 November. Despite the lack of recent reconnaissance information, the Japanese were ready to launch a new offensive and in late November the Arakan campaign got underway. For the first few weeks the fighter strength was primarily that of five Hurricane squadrons plus 615 Squadron's Spitfires, the other Spitfire units still being at Alipore under training. The first incursion, a fighter sweep, took place on 23 November and amongst the fighters scrambled to intercept the enemy formation were ten Spitfires. No successful intercepts were made by 615 Squadron but on a second scramble a few hours later they lost their first Spitfire in air combat with Japanese fighters, Plt Off Leonard being shot down (but safe).

There was still much to learn for both the pilots and the ground controllers; the 29th was another frustrating day with poor positioning of the fighters causing ineffectual interception, as recorded by Plt Off 'Nappy' Carroll of 615 Squadron:

The height was all wrong. Our controller had got us in position and then we found the Japs were well below us; they were just specks in the distance. We dived like crazy and everybody got split up. I was really travelling and they rapidly got larger. I realised these were the boys we were after. As I remember it there were about eight fighters on each side and about 12 bombers – Army 99s.

I took a shot at two of the fighters. One from astern and I hit it but I was travelling at such speed that I just saw strikes, then it was gone. Then another fighter came right across me which I had a go at but my chances of hitting it were pretty nil. Then I pulled up and round with my speed, to get at the bombers, which was a piece of cake as I must have been going twice as fast as they were. But I couldn't pull the Spitfire round in a tight sweep to get into the nearest bombers and I came right out on the far side of the formation. I got behind one of them and by that time I was beginning to slow up so was able to give a much better and longer burst of cannon and machine gun. There were little sparkles on it from where I was hitting it and a plume of smoke or fuel came from one engine as the aircraft started to drop out of formation. By that time I was now past it and had lost all my speed. (Franks, *Spitfires over the Arakan* – this is the best single account of Spitfire operations in this theatre)

The other two Spitfire squadrons became operational at the end of November, but just as the Spitfires moved from Alipore (near Calcutta) to the Arakan, the Japanese attention moved to the Indian city. The route from the Japanese bases across the Bay of Bengal to Calcutta would put them in range of interception from the Chittagong areas as long as the controllers made the right calls. In early December this was not the case and all too often the fighters were scrambled but not put in a position to intercept.

A major Japanese raid on 26 December was intercepted by only a handful of fighters despite the fact that most squadrons had been scrambled and what should have been the first major air battle was a haphazard affair in which only a few Spitfires made contact, although those few did achieve some success for the loss of one aircraft. There was an inquiry at Group, but it was really a simple question of more experience and coordination with the ground controllers. Although December was frustrating for the RAF squadrons, and had cost the Hurricane unit a higher than average number of losses, the overall air capability of the Allies in this theatre was on the turn as the situation in Europe had reached a point whereby more and better aircraft could be released to the 'Forgotten War'. In addition to a number of organisational changes in command, including the formation of the 3rd Tactical Air Force, the number of Spitfire squadrons was in the process of doubling. The last day of 1943 ended with proof that when things went right the prospects were indeed very good. Twelve aircraft of 136 Squadron were scrambled to patrol base with a large raid inbound to Chittagong. The Squadron was airborne at 1051 hours and by the time they landed an hour or so later they had claimed thirteen destroyed (eight Sally bombers and five Oscar fighters) plus a further four probables and nine damaged. The cost was one Spitfire destroyed and two damaged; it was also virtually a swan song for the Mark Vs as the Spitfire Mark VIII was already in the Far East.

Enter the Mark VIII

By 1 January 1944 the RAF had six Spitfire squadrons operational in this theatre, comprising:

No 165 Wing: 136, 607 squadrons with Spitfire VCs at Ramu
No 166 Wing: 615 Squadron with Spitfire VCs at Dohazari
No 293 Wing: 152, 155 squadrons with Spitfire VIIIs at Baigachi and Alipore
Imphal: 81 Squadron with Spitfire VIIIs at Tulihal

The first Spitfire VIIIs had been taken on by 81 Squadron in November 1943, followed by 152 Squadron in November and 155 Squadron in January. The other squadrons re-equipped in the first months of 1944, the last being 615 Squadron, which did not give up its VCs until July 1944.

'This is the first occasion on this front when Spitfires met the Japanese fighters – mistakes were made and profited by – types of attack were experimented with and the results have been reproduced for the information of all concerned.' These were amongst the introductory comments to Tactical Memorandum No 9 issued by Air Command South-East Asia relating to Spitfire operations in the Arakan between December 1943 and March 1944.

Perhaps the most notable feature of the fighter versus fighter operation is the reversal of tactics in this theatre as opposed to the Western War, where our fighter squadrons used their superior manoeuvrability to tactical advantage. The lesson is obvious. DO NOT ATTEMPT TO DOG FIGHT WITH THE JAP. Keep your speed and use the superior dive and climb of the Spitfire then the Jap fighters cannot use their manoeuvrability.'

Japanese fighter escorts during this period have shown excellent air discipline. They stuck to their bombers and afforded maximum cover. The fighter escort (for shipping attacks) was composed of conventional Oscars, which are no match for Spitfires in speed or climb. The tactics adopted by the Spitfires, who had 6,000ft over the enemy in the initial attack, were to dive, attack and climb steeply, which manoeuvre the Oscars could not follow and they fell off in the climb.

The Japanese also flew fighter sweeps to cover the land offensive they launched in February. 'The Jap prefers to fight at his best performance height – 15,000–20,000ft. He expects to be jumped and is usually well prepared for the attack from above.' In response to the Japanese operations the Spitfire squadrons operated 'independently so that just as one squadron was running out of petrol the second squadron engaged the fighters. This was very much appreciated by the first squadron who were getting into a "tough spot", being outnumbered and wanting to break away from the Japs who were not so keen that our fighters should break off the engagement.'

Although the conventional Oscar was considered little of a threat there was one fighter starting to make its appearance that caused more concern – the Tojo. 'The performance of the Tojo may be, in some aspects, such as climb and dive, considered comparable to that of the Spitfire. It is believed that only a few were used as few pilots reported seeing them. One said that he was held in a climb by one of the fighters – he was in a Spit VIII too, at about 20,000ft!'

The first two months of 1944 had witnessed a battle for air superiority over the battlefield and it was largely due to the Spitfire squadrons that the Allies won this fight, enabling effective ground-support missions to be flown. In part this success stemmed from the blinding of the Japanese reconnaissance with the Spitfires' destruction of the Dinah missions. The previous Japanese tactic of pinpointing active airfields and mounting effective strafing raids was not attempted this time and with the improved radar and control, combined with the Spitfire VIII's performance, including climb to height, meant that the RAF fighters could frequently be put into an advantageous tactical position. The first major battles took place on 16 January and both 136 and 607 were in the thick of it – and doing well, but not without loss. The extreme agility of the Japanese fighters was witnessed by many pilots; Dudley Barnett was airborne with 136 Squadron:

Climbed up orbiting, found a single fighter below, again dived but had hardly opened fire when he flicked incredibly quickly out of my sights . . . Dived down again and headed for base. About 1,200 feet, had difficulty opening the canopy, finally got it back, re-adjusted mirror and found a Jap some 400 yards astern. Vicious turn starboard and down, with everything wide. He must have had closing speed for he got well within 100 yards. Jinked as hard as I dared at that height, feeling pretty warm too. Gradually drew away – whew

– and he gave it up when I was about 3–400 yards ahead. (Franks, *Spitfires over the Arakan*)

The other point noted by pilots was that most of the Japanese that they hit turned into flamers with little chance of survival for the crew; the lack of protective systems for fuel tanks and cockpits was to cause the Japanese heavy losses now that they were facing fighters of equal performance. As the battle progressed the Spitfire squadrons continued to add to their scores.

The Japanese tried various tactics.

The enemy made use of decoys with different camouflage. These would fly straight and level about 15,000ft whilst higher up a patrol of well camouflaged aircraft would be waiting. Our fighters on two occasions patrolling above the whole lot saw the decoys first – dived to lose height and were set upon by another 'bunch' whilst positioning for attack on what turned out to be the decoys.

Perhaps the most important factor for pilots to remember when intercepting these sweeps is the low speed at which the Japanese fly. Normally they fly in the battle area quite slowly, possibly about 150mph and so are extremely manoeuvrable and do not get split up when they fly in all directions. The Spits normally had a high overtaking speed, which ensured a good getaway but also left little time for shooting when the Jap once saw the attack develop and did a quick turn in evasion. It is quite possible that in many cases deflection has been too great and aircraft have not been hit when attacked because their speed was assumed to be too great. This is a point to be borne in mind when Japanese tactics are being explained to new pilots to this theatre of war. In one case a pilot did not obtain strikes in what was practically a full deflection shot until he reduced the deflection to just a ring; i.e. the Jap was flying at little more than 100mph. The Japanese are not speed merchants in air fighting and rely on their very superior manoeuvrability at low speeds to keep them out of trouble. One seldom sees a Jap diving at high speed unless he has been hit. They seem to prefer to be jumped – execute a quick turn, thus getting on their opponent's tail. They are not frightened of elaborate aerobatics as a means of evasion or positioning for attack.

It was a very different scenario to that being played in the air battles over Europe and the report concluded:

The Japs most probably have a healthy respect for our Spitfires, which is as it should be. Things can be very unpleasant when the Spits are outnumbered if the Japs decide to hang around. An aircraft short of petrol is a very easy target if one is prepared to bide one's time. We must always try and keep the enemy engaged all the time and not just for the first ten minutes. To achieve this all our eggs should not be kept in the same basket. We should always have something up our sleeve for Japanese who like the like the look of our side of the line and are prepared to stay and admire the scenery. (This and all of the

above extracts, unless stated otherwise, are from ACSEA Tactical Memo No 9
dated 7 April 1944)

The first six weeks of the battle had involved only three of the Spitfire
units and it was 9 February when 81 Squadron arrived at Ramu to join in,
their first scramble taking place the following morning. Alan Peart was in
action with 81 Squadron on 13 February:

> we had discussed at length what tactics we needed to adopt against Japanese
> fighters with our Spitfire VIIIs and were keen to try them out. The outcome of
> the combat was rather unexpected in that structural weaknesses were exposed
> in the VIII and hasty modifications had to be made. Our tactics were to use
> height to five and attack after which we were to disengage by climbing to a
> further attack position using our assumed superiority in speed and climb . . .
> Later discussion of our first encounter highlighted a Japanese willingness to
> stick around and an aggressiveness which we thought applied only to us.
> (Franks, *Spitfires over the Arakan*)

Meanwhile, the Japanese were making progress with their ground offensive
and from time to time the Spitfires flew ground-support missions to strafe
targets marked by coloured smoke laid down by mortars.

The problem referred to above was connected with excessive G being
pulled by pilots, either in air combat trying to avoid or chase the Japanese
fighters, or when manoeuvring at low level. The result was that the wings
were rippling, with 'impressive' ridges up to an inch high. A temporary
grounding of all Mark VIIIs gave the ground-crew time to replace the wings
with the more suitable standard elliptical wing-tip.

From mid-February the air battles were virtually over and the Spitfires
increasingly took an ground-support role, as well as escorting bombers
and transports. The Allies went on to the offensive on 5 March, although
this was soon disrupted and reversed when the Japanese attacked again in
the Kohima and Imphal areas. There were more air battles to be flown but
increasingly it was support of the Army that became the main occupation
for air power.

Army Cooperation

No 155 Squadron had reformed in India in April 1942 and for nearly two
years had operated with Mohawk IVs before receiving Spitfire VIIIs in
January 1944, which they retained to the end of the war. Jack Woollett joined
the Squadron in November 1944 – as the only sergeant pilot and therefore
known as 'the General' – and he recalled that cooperation with British-led
guerrillas was a typical mission:

we would attack specific targets arranged by an Army Intelligence officer, known as 'Captain Mac' to us. We would go to a certain map reference to find a white circle with an arrow pointing in a certain direction with a 3 or 5 by the side, indicating a target 3 or 5 miles in that direction. We would follow this and find a thicket which we assumed harboured either supplies or troops, which we strafed.

The CO, Sqn Ldr Gordon Conway, wrote a press report on the Squadron's operations in the last major campaign, providing ground support for the Battle of the Sittang River Bend.

On the 20th of June we were told that there were 9,000 Japanese west of us, 10 miles away in the jungle-covered hills along the Pegu–Toungoo road. Every now and then a good target would come in, usually from the guerrillas, and we would take-off despite the soggy condition of the runway and have a crack at them. As we went over to strafe we could see the guerrillas quite clearly on a very close hill, watching with obvious enjoyment the large explosions and fires starting in the middle of frantically running Japs.

During this period we ran what was called a 'private war'. We were the only squadron at Toungoo for quite some time and the war for us consisted of 155 Squadron and the 19th Division against the 'rest'. The Japs had built up a strength of 17,000 and were preparing for a mass breakout to the East, across the road and the Sittang River into Siam. The 17th and 19th Division who we were now supporting were on the road waiting for them. We now started real work and in the next 10 days each pilot on my squadron flew an average of two or three bombing and strafing sorties each day, answering urgent priority calls for direct support from the Army.

We were now carrying in addition to our cannon and machine guns, beautiful 500-lb bombs under the fuselage. We were very pleased to get these bombs and had been waiting some time for them. They came just in time. The weather now was not exactly good flying weather. It was sometimes so bad that it was impossible to see the aircraft in front of you during a strafing attack. When we approached the target in these conditions we would go into long line astern about 800 yards behind each other and as each pilot went in and bombed he would call out over the radio 'RED One bombed', 'RED Two bombed' and so on. Everyone would break-away from the target in the same direction and climb to roughly the same height so that in the blinding rain as we made our attacks, each pilot relied on everyone else attacking the right thing.

Fortunately this usually worked out alright in nearly every case, although there were some fraught occasions when someone would be a little stupid and go round the other way. Two of three would be converging on the same target firing at the same time, whereupon there would be frantic yells on the RT and everyone would sort themselves out again.

Generally we would fly low down to the target in an endeavour to catch the Japs by surprise, hoping that the first thing they would see would be the first bomb falling. When all our bombs were gone, we went in strafing with cannon and machine-guns, starting fires where we could until all our ammunition was used up.

Jungle XIVs

The Mark XIV arrived in the Far East in June 1945, re-equipping established Spitfire units such as 11 Squadron at Chettinad and 17 Squadron at Madura. The pilots of 17 Squadron at Madura found their new F.XIVs somewhat different to their VIIIs. Don Healey commented that:

The Mk XIV was a hairy beast to fly, and took some getting used to. Fortunately, Madura boasted a concrete runway that was over 3,000 yards long, having been an important base for RAF Liberator units bombing Burma and Malaya in 1944/45 – it was just the ticket for a squadron coming to grips for the first time with the vicious torque swing of the Griffon engine.

We were told to open the throttle very slowly at the start of our take-off, with full opposite rudder applied to offset the five-bladed prop, which was driven by the Griffon in the opposite direction to the Merlin – this took some getting used to! Even with full aileron, elevator and rudder, this brute of a fighter still took off slightly sideways. However, once you picked up flying speed, and trimmed the rudder and elevator, this torque pull became bearable.

One aspect you always had to bear in mind with the Mk XIV that no flying surface trimming could allow for was its considerable weight – it tipped the scales at 8,475lbs when fuelled and armed, which made it over 2,000lbs heavier than the Mk VIII. Therefore, extra height had to be allowed for rolls and loops, as it tended to 'wash out' when being flown in this way (Holmes, 'Jungle Fighter')

Colonial Problems

The end of the war did not mean the end of active operations in the Far East; the old colonial powers – England, France and Holland – attempted to re-impose their authority in the region. The Spitfires of 273 Squadron were part of the RAF force involved with operations in French Indo-China whilst other units participated in operations over the Dutch East Indies. However, these were both small-scale affairs and the major post-war campaign for the RAF was to the anti-terrorist war in Malaya. This was to be the RAF's last Spitfire campaign and is covered in Chapter 10, 'Reconnaissance Operations'.

~ 9 ~

Carrier Operations

If the RAF's air doctrine was flawed in the 1920s and 1930s, that of the Royal Navy was even more of a disaster, with a belief that fleet defence was best left to naval gunnery and that the primary role of aircraft should be reconnaissance, dive-bombing and, as epitomised by the Fairey Swordfish, torpedo attack. In fairness to the Navy, they had no control of the aircraft – they were an RAF asset; indeed, it was only on the verge of the Second World War that the Navy regained control of the Fleet Air Arm. This may indeed have been part of the reason for the Admiralty's doctrinal stance.

The first few weeks of war disabused the Navy of this doctrine and an urgent requirement was issued for a high-performance fighter for carrier operations. The obvious interim solution was to look at ways of adapting the Hurricane and Spitfire for carrier use. The Supermarine test pilots at Eastleigh, a Naval Air Station since the outbreak of war, had already, for fun, taken to landing on the marked-out carrier 'deck' (ADDL – aerodrome dummy deck landing); by making a slow curved approach such a 'landing' was quite possible, although a hook would be useful to guarantee that the aircraft stayed down.

In October 1939 Supermarine was asked to look at putting an arrestor hook on the Spitfire, a request that was soon followed by that other standard naval requirement of folding wings (space was limited on an aircraft carrier and folding wings were essential). Thus was born the Sea Spitfire, for which initial drawings were issued to the Admiralty in early January 1940. All parties agreed that it could be done and an initial interest was expressed in acquiring fifty aircraft by summer 1940; however, a few weeks later the request was shelved. It would be another two years before a navalised Spitfire, which was soon renamed as the Seafire; saw the light of day and in the meantime the Fleet Air Arm soldiered on with the likes of the Fulmar. Contrary to the popular belief that the Navy was a minor user of the Spitfire/Seafire, over 2,000 aircraft were taken on charge. It was not, however, to be a particularly successful marriage.

Spitfire on Floats

The Norwegian campaign of 1940 highlighted the problem caused by lack of land bases. A rush decision was made to fit floats to Spitfires during April 1940, when fifty sets of Blackburn Roc floats were to be fitted to Spitfire Mark Is. After some preliminary work had been carried out, the project was cancelled in June 1940 when it became apparent that all available Spitfires would be needed for the forthcoming Battle of Britain. However, the idea was revived in May 1941 when Supermarine developed a set of floats for the Spitfire Mark V. The result was the Type 355 Spitfire VB floatplane W3760, which made its first flight during October 1942. This aircraft, plus two other floatplanes, went on to do trials in the Middle East, but as operations proved impractical they returned to the UK. The idea was mooted once more in 1944 for use in the Far East, with Spitfire IX MJ982 being converted for evaluation and flying with floats on 18 June 1944. Once again the concept proved viable but the operational requirement was cancelled. The only valid way to put aircraft to sea was on a carrier.

Spitfires at Sea

The requirement for a navalised version of the Spitfire had been recognised before the war but it was June 1942 before the first unit, 807 Squadron, received its Seafires, acquiring a few IBs for training until it received its full complement of twelve Seafire IICs.

In January 1940 Supermarine responded to a request from the Fleet Air Arm for a Spitfire with arrestor hook and folding wings, the maximum folded wing span not to exceed 18ft; a prototype would be available thirteen months from the placing of an order. However, they also suggested a quicker route by using a standard Spitfire wing that pivoted back along the fuselage (an arrangement used by some American carrier types). The project was cancelled in March, in part due to intervention by Churchill but also because of the impact it might have had on production of ordinary Spitfires for the RAF, with an estimation that fifty folding-wing Spitfires would mean 200 less Spitfires for the RAF.

It is worth pointing out that the Fleet Air Arm were not just looking for a modern carrier-based fighter but were after something that could defend the Navy's shore installations in the UK; a German attack on Scapa Flow on 16 March 1940 confirming the need for such defences. The whole question of acquisition of fighter aircraft for the FAA was a complex one and beyond the scope of this book; all that needs be said here is that there was a general feeling that the Spitfire was both suitable and desirable. The compromise reached in 1941 was an agreement for the transfer from the RAF of a number of Spitfire Is, forty-eight Mark VBs and, under some pressure and a little later, a batch of 200 Mark VCs. Trials had been taking place with Vickers at Worthy Down, Farnborough and with the Service Trials Unit (STU) at RNAS Arbroath into catapult launches and arrestor landings.

The Spitfire VBs were contracted to Air Service Training for modification, to emerge as Seafire IBs with an arrestor hook but no catapult spools for launching. The first Seafire IB was taken on charge by the Navy on 15 June 1942, with 807 Squadron receiving a few aircraft but 801 Squadron being the first (and only) squadron to operate a full complement of Seafire IBs. The navalised version of the Mark VC, the Seafire IIC, first flew in February 1942 (AD371 a modified Mark V), with the first production aircraft (MA970) flying on 28 May 1942. Deliveries took place from 15 June, the same day as the first IBs were handed over, and by October some fifty aircraft had been delivered. The Seafire IIC had an arrestor hook and a catapult spool, along with appropriate airframe strengthening, and was armed with two 20-mm cannon and four 0.303-in machine guns. When given the Merlin 32 and optimised for low-altitude performance it was designated the LIIC. For the reconnaissance role the LIIC was given two F24 cameras (one 20-in focal-length vertical and one 14-in focal-length oblique), whilst retaining its armament, under the designation PRLIIC, although this designation was not always used.

Into Action

Within weeks of the first deliveries of Seafires to 807 Squadron in June, four other squadrons had started to receive Seafires; one of these, 801 Squadron, fully equipped with IBs, whilst the others (880, 884 and 885) were equipped with IICs. All were put on intensive work-up to be ready for the next major naval operation – Operation Torch, the invasion of North Africa. All five embarked in October, using the carriers *Argus* (880 Squadron), *Formidable* (885 Squadron), *Furious* (801 and 807 squadrons) and *Victorious* (884 Squadron) and sailed for the Mediterranean. It was the Seafires of 801 Squadron that opened the type's combat career when Lt S. J. Hall chased a Ju 88 that had attacked the carrier. The performance of his Mark IB barely enabled him to catch his quarry and despite firing all his cannon ammunition and a good part of his machine-gun ammunition he could only claim the enemy as damaged. It was not a good start and indeed it confirmed the belief that many pilots held that the Merlin Seafire was too heavy for its engine and that performance was not adequate. In fairness, the Ju 88 was a fast aircraft and most fighters had trouble catching one unless they started from an advantageous position.

The assault commenced on 8 November and the Seafires provided part of the air umbrella, although there was very little in the way of air opposition for the Algiers landings, which involved HMS *Argus*, it was somewhat more hectic for the carriers supporting the Oran landings. Seafires from this group flew sweeps against French airfields, scoring some success, including the downing of a Maryland (the first confirmed Seafire victory) by Sub-Lt A. S. Long of 885 Squadron, but also suffering the first combat loss, Lt A. B. Fraser-Harris of 807 Squadron being brought down by anti-aircraft fire. French fighters (D 520s) tangled with 807 Squadron near La Senia but the Seafires easily outmanoeuvred the enemy and claimed one shot-down and two damaged. The Seafire squadrons participated in a variety of missions during the short-lived campaign and emerged with three combat losses and a number of successes in the air and on the ground. There had, however, been a major problem.

In the air the Seafires were almost as good as land-based Spitfires, but the problem came with deck landings, and during Operation Torch six aircraft were written off in landing incidents on HMS *Argus*, plus a further three on the other carriers. *Argus* was an old carrier with a short flight-deck but the myth of Seafire landing problems was born; whilst it, like many myths and legends, has been exaggerated, there is certainly a core of truth. The main problem was that the aircraft needed a 25-kt wind component – a combination of the forward speed of the carrier and the surface wind speed – and with some carriers only able to make 15–18kts this meant that the surface wind had to be at least 10kts. Where Torch had indicated shortcomings, the operations connected with the Anzio landings in September 1943 revealed the scale of the problem. Seven British carriers were part of Force H (two fleet carriers) and Force V (five carriers), with a large number of Seafires operating from the inshore Force V. An impressive 265 Seafire sorties were flown on the first day by the 105 available aircraft, but landing incidents began straight away. It was calm weather and so the over-deck wind speed was restricted to that generated by the carrier itself, added to which it was a hot September day. By the end of Day Two the number of serviceable Seafires was down to thirty-nine, with most 'losses' down to landing accidents. However, there was one unit, No 834 Fighter Flight that operated its six Seafires throughout the period with no incident, which they put down to proper training and pilot awareness. It was almost certainly true that the main cause of the problem was lack of pilot experience and training, although it was also true that the Seafire required more careful handling in order to get the perfect set-up for landing, whereas other naval types were more forgiving.

The aircraft's reputation had, however, been born and despite all that followed it never shook this reputation. Jeffrey Quill was posted to the Fleet Air Arm to undertake the deck-landing course and to fly with an embarked squadron in order to evaluate the true nature of the problem. His autobiography noted that:

> the Seafire was not an easy aeroplane to land on the deck, partly because of its restricted view and partly because it had to be flown very carefully if the approach speed was to be kept steady and accurate. Neither was it a robust aircraft, never having been designed for deck operation in the first place, but if it was properly flown it was quite up to the job. However, if pilots were not adequately trained or practised, or if – as was obviously often the case – they returned from an operational sortie tired of otherwise a bit rattled, the Seafire was undoubtedly accident-prone. (Quill, *Spitfire, a Test Pilot's Story*)

His report of 29 February 1944 gave four main factors to be considered in making the Seafire an effective (and safe) carrier aircraft:

1 The method of approach.
2 The view from the aeroplane.
3 The speed controllability of the aeroplane.
4 The robustness of the aeroplane to withstand the degree of rough usage which may be expected on the deck under sea-going conditions.

The first point essentially meant ensuring correct training and that pilots knew, and flew, the correct approach procedure. The other three were connected with development of the actual aircraft and as a test pilot it was obvious that he would identify, comment on and seek to have remedies incorporated for such aircraft-related issues. Indeed, most of the aircraft points were addressed from the Seafire XV onwards.

Despite the mixed messages of Operation Torch, the FAA continued its planned re-equipment with Seafires and by 1 May 1943 the type had become the most numerous single aircraft in the operational inventory, equipping fourteen operational squadrons plus a number of training units. That same month saw the LIIC enter service (807 Squadron), but despite its much improved low-altitude performance it still suffered other limitations such as fixed wings. Although Seafires operated with a number of convoy escorts in 1943, the main 'outing' came with the next major amphibious operation – Husky, the Allied landings in Sicily and Avalanche, the Salerno operation. Reference has already been made above to the continued problems of losses on deck landings and in a pure balance sheet of kills to losses the Seafire record was a poor one, with very few enemy aircraft claimed. However, air cover is about more than just shooting down aircraft and an examination of the record shows that the intercepts made by the Seafire squadrons neutralised a great many enemy bombing raids – the bombers dropped their bombs and fled on seeing the fighters approach. This was a measurable success but the sad element is that the poor performance of the

1   Spitfires of 611 Squadron at Duxford in 1939; the Squadron re-equipped from Hawker
Hind biplanes in May as the RAF rushed to give its squadrons modern equipment.

2   The Spitfire lA was the first operational variant and was armed with eight 0.303-in
Brownings, usually harmonised to converge at 250 yards. Spitfire lA X4593 of 266 Squadron
was written-off in a flying accident in November 1940.

3 Sqn Ldr R.H. Leigh, Officer Commanding 66 Squadron, about to board his Spitfire at Gravesend sometime in 1940; he commanded the Squadron throughout the Battle of Britain. The Squadron claimed 531/2 kills during the Battle.

4   Teddy St Aubyn of 616 Squadron with the results of his night landing – note the second pranged Spitfire in the background; the Spitfire was used for night visual engagements but was not suited to the role, despite scoring a number of successes.

5   By 1941. the Spitfire f1 was the dominant type in Fighter Command; in April that year eighteen of the Command's twenty-three Spitfire squadrons were operating Mark IIs. Mark IIB of 91 Squadron being serviced.

6 Flt Sgt Sherk in Spitfire VB of 129 Squadron in dispersal at Debden in November 1941; the picture shows the 'snug' fit of the Spitfire cockpit, the heavy armour-plate windscreen, and the rear-view mirror. Compared with its main opponent, the bf 109, the view from the Spitfire was excellent. (Andy Thomas Collection)

7 The Spitfire V was seen as an interim Mark but was produced in very large numbers (6,487) and in a number of sub-variants, including the clipped wing as shown on this 607 Squadron aircraft. The AFDU trials on the clipped-wing Mark V stated; 'at all heights up to 25,000ft the rate of roll is considerably improved by removal of the wing tips. The response to aileron movements is very crisp.'

8   Spitfires of 64 Squadron run up at Hornchurch, May 1942; Fighter Command had gone on to the offensive in 1941 and by 1942 it was coming up against superior types such as the Fw 190 and the kill ratio was worsening.

9   Engine change at Audley End in April1943; the Merlin was a rugged and reliable engine and it was largely due to the increases in engine power that the Spitfire was able to undergo continual development, although in due course the Griffon replaced the Merlin.

10　Captain Don Willis of the 335th Fighter Squadron, 4th Fighter Group of the US 8th Air Force, April 1943. The Group was created from the Eagle Squadrons and operated Spitfires to April 1943, when it reluctantly reequipped with P-47 Thunderbolts (US National Archives).

11　Spitfire VIIIs were particularly important in the Middle East and Far East theatres, especially in the latter where the type served with distinction. Entry to service was with 145 Squadron in June 1943 and over 1,600 were produced.

12   From 1942 the Spitfire was by far the most numerous type in Fighter Command and as part of the re-organisation of air power for the invasion of Europe the Command was split. Elements were used to form Air Defence of Great Britain, whose primary task remained air combat, and part of 2nd Tactical Air Force, where ground-attack became the main role. Large numbers of Spitfires needed to be serviced and repaired to feed the ever-hungry squadrons.

13   To many commentators the Spitfire IX was the best of the bunch; it was produced in large numbers (second only to the Mark V) and it was popular with pilots. Its main significance in terms of tactics was that it was able to match the Fw 190 and thus help redress the problems being faced by Fighter Command in 1942.

14   Spitfire IXC MK264 of the Polish 308 Squadron; the aircraft is wearing D-Day recognition markings. The Spitfire squadrons provided air cover over the beach-head but also undertook strafing and bombing missions.

15   Pilots of 80 Squadron pose at West Malling in July 1944; the Squadron was one of many that had been brought back from Italy as part of the air build-up forD-Day (Jerry Jarrold).

16   Spitfire VIII MT714 of 43 Squadron being serviced, possibly at Lyons, France, September 1944; the Squadron was part of the Allied force invading Southern France, an operation often over-looked in histories of the European campaign.

above

20 Pristine Spitfire V (Trap) seen in the snow in January 1942; the addition of filters for this Tropical version of the Mark V significantly reduced performance.

facing page, from top

17 Rear-quarter view of Spitfire XIV showing the blister canopy, which provided a much-improved rear view.

18 The 'TO' codes on this aircraft identify it as probably belonging to No.61 Operational Training Unit; this training unit formed in June 1941 to train single-seat fighter pilots and continued this role into the post-war period. The training provided by the OTUs was invaluable, although in the early part of the year it was minimal and reliance was placed on squadrons to train pilots on type.

19 Spitfire LF.XVI (LF standing for Low-altitude Fighter); over 1,000 of the Packard-Merlin Mark XVI were built and although it entered the war late it did see appreciable service as a fighter-bomber in early 1945. This is a post-war shot of RW396, an aircraft that served with the Central Gunnery School.

21 Jerry Jarrold poses with a modified Spitfire IX of 80 Squadron in the Western Desert; note the screwdriver on the Mae West – this was for puncturing the jacket should it inflate in the cockpit! (Jerry Jarrold)

22 The long-suffering and all too often ignored (by historians) groundcrew service aircraft in Italy, 1944. The aircraft belong to 253 Squadron.

23 Another rough-and-ready airstrip for 111 Squadron; despite a reputation for a weak undercarriage and problems with ground manoeuvring, the Spitfire was successfully operated off diverse surface conditions.

above
26 Major work underway on an aircraft of 136 Squadron during that unit's period on the Cocos Islands from April 1945; the Squadron had been operating Spitfire Vs and VIIIs, with notable success, in the Burma area since October 1943.

facing page, from top
24 Sqn Ldr Neil Wheeler, OC 'B' Flight of 140 Squadron, one of the first Spitfire reconnaissance squadrons; his comment on reconnaissance ops was that 'there was reasonable chance that a lone Spitfire, operating at 30,000ft, could penetrate deep into enemy territory without detection.'

25 Reconnaissance Spitfire were able to carry a variety of cameras, including oblique-facing cameras with a long focal-length lens.

27 Spitfire FR.18 of 208 Squadron firing-up; the Squadron was operating in the Middle East in the post-war period and was involved in one of the few Spitfire versus Spitfire combats when intercepted by Israeli fighters.

28 The final carrier operations by Fleet Air Arm Seafires took place in 1950 during the Korean War.

29 The Mark 24 was the end of the line for the Spitfire; only eighty-one were produced and it seems to have only been used by one operational unit – 80 Squadron, from 1948 to 1951.

Seafire meant that very rarely were the frustrated fighter pilots able to close with the enemy.

A major lesson of operations to date, and not just with the Seafires, was that the tactics being employed needed improving; as part of this a new Wing organisation was instituted in autumn 1943, the intention being for a Wing of two to four squadrons, each with the same aircraft type but with squadrons specialising in particular roles. The Naval Fighter Wing concept was employed for the rest of the war and was overall a great success; all but three Seafire squadrons had been grouped into Wings by November 1943:

No 3 Wing: 808, 886, 897 squadrons.
No 4 Wing: 807, 809, 879 squadrons.
No 24 Wing: 887, 894 squadrons (re-equipped with Seafire IIIs from late
· November).

More Power – and Folding Wings

The Fleet Air Arm eventually received its folding-wing Spitfires (as Seafire IIIs) in autumn 1943. The new variant used the more powerful Merlin 55 series, plus a four-bladed propeller, and in addition to the folding wings incorporated various other changes, including the use, in the LIIIs, of the short-barrelled (and lighter) Mark V Hispano cannon. It also had the capability of carrying various under-slung weapons and fuel tanks. Like its predecessor it appeared in low-altitude and PR versions, and the Mark III was produced in large numbers, a total of 1,220 aircraft (350 by Cunliffe Owen and the rest by Westland). The first unit to re-equip was 894 Squadron in late November 1943 but they were soon followed by other Seafire units; five squadrons had re-equipped with the original FIII by mid-1944. However, it was the low-altitude LIII variant that was employed in the greatest number, a few being delivered as early as February 1944 but without the wing-fold.

In early 1944 the main carrier activity was routine 'trade protection' to guard against naval operations and maritime air operations by the Germans, with the focus of one cruise in February being an attack on German shipping off Norway. This involved a single carrier, HMS *Furious*, whose air wing included Seafires operated by 801 and 880 squadrons. In one engagement twelve Seafires tangled at low-level with Bf 109s and Fw 190s that were attempting to intercept the strike force of Barracudas. In the resulting air combat the Seafires claimed three enemy aircraft – and the Barracudas put eight torpedoes into the target ship (the 5,000-tonne MV *Ensland*), which promptly sank. Similar cruises took place throughout the spring and early summer of 1944, usually centred on *Furious* and its Barracuda/Seafire wing, but with HMS *Indefatigable* joining in from time to time, from which 887 and 894 squadrons operated Seafire IIs and IIIs to support their offensive aircraft. One of the 'favourite' targets for these operations was the *Tirpitz*, by now languishing in Altenfjord but still considered a high-priority target by the Admiralty and Prime Minister Churchill. The primary role of the Seafires was combat air patrol, to protect the carrier group but also to act as escort for the strike aircraft. However, the next major 'outing' for the Seafires came in summer 1944 with two major and distinctly different operations; D-Day over Normandy (June) and Operation Dragoon over Southern France (August).

D-Day: Air Spotting Pool

One of the main firepower elements of the D-Day assault phase was to be an intense and devastating naval bombardment. The bombardment ships were to be on station at 0500 hours on 6 June, having moved into position under the cover of a smoke screen laid by RAF Bostons. The accuracy of the naval bombardment was assisted by the Air Spotting Pool (ASP), operating from Lee-on-Solent and comprising four Fleet Air Arm Seafire squadrons, five RAF squadrons (primarily Mustangs) plus a number of Seafires/Spitfires operated by US Naval Squadron VCS-7. These last had been recruited in May from naval pilots in the UK, mostly ex-Kingfisher pilots, who were then given a rapid Spitfire conversion course at Middle Wallop followed by an even shorter course detailing shoot procedures.

Aircraft usually operated in pairs and pilots were either given details of two pre-arranged targets to engage or a specific area in which to look for targets of opportunity. The majority of sorties, certainly in the early phase, consisted of counter-battery work against coastal guns, field artillery and flak positions. Aircraft of the ASP flew over 400 sorties during the first day on 135 shoots, about 50 per cent being considered successful, many of the others being aborted due to problems with communications or, on a few instances, lack of suitable targets.

Mike Crosley was flying Seafires with No 3 Wing on D-Day:

> My first of three 'shoots' that day – with my Number 2, Don Keene – were with the Battleship *Warspite*. Cloud was rather low, which meant we had to go down well below light flak height to do our spotting. My diary says: 'Four blokes were shot down. Another managed to bail out over the Isle of Wight with only a broken arm as the damage. On our first trip we spent 45 minutes directing shot on a heavy gun position near Trouville. The shooting fairly accurate – being at short range against a vertical target – but it seemed to have no effect as I could still see the Germans firing their guns through the concrete

dust blown up by the *Warspite*'s shells hitting the emplacement at the same time.

The following day, 7 June, was livelier for the Seafires, as not only did they have to contend with errant Allied fighter pilots but the Luftwaffe too was starting to make an appearance. Mike Crosley again:

This was the most eventful day as the Germans (originally believing that the landings would be much further to the east) had begun to arrive in force. Don and I took off before sunrise in clear weather. I told Don to fly above me down-sun to keep an eye open for some Jerry Fw 190s in the area . . . The R/T was full of excited voices telling us that there were Jerries about so we kept our airspeed at about 275 knots at 6,000 feet and above light flak height in case we were jumped. Don slowed down to drop his tank and at that moment I saw what I thought were Spitfires coming from the north-east above him. One bloke fired tracer at him and he was just able to avoid it. The remainder of the 'Spits' came after me. Thanks to my G-suit I remained conscious in the steep pull-out and regained altitude astern of their ar**-end charlie. However in spite of going flat out from the word go, I still wasn't going fast enough and I could not catch up. However, he wasn't the ar**-end charlie after all, because as I flogged after him another 'spit' – recognisable this time as an Me 109 – flew past my left side about 100yds away, slowly rolling on his back as he did so. He seemed a possible target. Then others appeared from all over the place. Some might have been Spitfires of course who had joined in from somewhere and one Spit or Jerry pulled up vertically right in front of me going much faster than I was. However, I selected the bloke who was upside down, he had been going a good 30 knots faster than me as he rolled over for his dive and, having been diving for a few seconds more than I had, was getting away from me. I failed to catch this 109 in the pullout so that I expended my ammunition on him at long range without visible result and returned to Lee-on-Solent.

The second trip on this day was more eventful. Spotting for the big guns often took us about 20 miles inland. About 15 miles south-east of Caen I saw what I thought was a Mustang stooging along above cloud with not a care in the world. I could not believe it was a German as he was asking to be shot down as he stood out like a sore thumb against the white clouds. I flew by on an opposite course and up-sun As I turned round after him he disappeared into cloud. A few minutes later I saw another one heading in a straight line for Deauville. I caught him easily and got behind him very close indeed to have a look at his topsides for the black crosses. I was overtaking him much too fast, so that I could only get a two-second burst in . . . After pulling up to avoid any possible chance of his number 2 having a crack at me, I just caught sight of him, end on, before he hit the ground, 3000 or 4000 feet below, just south of Evrecy. I flew back to the French coast, fearing enemy anger at what I had done. I was relieved to be over the sea again and as I couldn't raise Don on the R/T I returned alone to Lee. Our C-Balls (Army Liason) chap said he thought that the lone Fw 109 was on a recce mission over the landing area to try to find out what the Allies were doing. (Mike Crosley, 'Seafire Diary)

The ASP disbanded as soon as the main requirement for naval bombardment ended, but Seafires were involved in another amphibious assault a few weeks later. Operation Dragoon, the invasion of Southern France, involved seven British carriers; four of these (*Attacker, Hunter, Khedive* and *Stalker*) operated Seafires of No 4 Wing, which by this time had added 899 Squadron to its strength. During a roughly two-week period of intense activity the Seafires flew over 1,000 sorties and recorded a deck-landing loss of only fourteen aircraft, a very marked difference from the Salerno operation of the previous year. It was also notable that the squadrons flew all three main air roles: fighter, fighter-bomber and tactical reconnaissance (TacR), all with some measure of success.

The next task for the carriers was participation in a series of operations in the Eastern Mediterranean and Aegean as the Allies mopped-up Axis garrisons; however, whilst these were important actions, the focus of Seafire operations had moved to the Far East.

Pacific Theatre

Even before the Seafire had truly arrived in the Far East there were warnings about the comparative performance of the Japanese fighters. In October 1944 a Seafire LIIC was evaluated against a Zeke 52 at Naval Air Station Patuxent River by Lt Cdr G. Guthrie and Lt D. Law. The general conclusion was

> Never dogfight with a Zeke 52 – it is too manoeuvrable. At low altitudes where the Seafire is at its best, it should make use of its superior rate of climb and speed to obtain a height advantage before attacking. If jumped, the Seafire should evade by using superior rate of roll. The Zeke cannot follow high speed rolls and aileron turns.

In this theatre Seafire squadrons served with the East Indies Fleet and the British Pacific Fleet.

Seafires had been present in the theatre since early 1944, a fleeting appearance of Seafire IICs aboard HMS *Battler* with 834 Squadron and Seafire IIIs aboard HMS *Atheling* with 889 Squadron. The latter saw some operational employment in the area of the Andaman Islands but by August the Squadron had disbanded, having had a less than happy experience with the Seafire. November 1944 saw HMS *Indefatigable* in the Far East as part of the Pacific Fleet, its air wing still including Seafires with 887 and 894 squadrons, as No 24 Fighter Wing. The first major operations involved the attack in January 1945 on a number of oil refineries on Sumatra. It was again a mixed result with too many landing accidents but with a good kill ratio in air-to-air combat. The operations over, or rather terminated, the fleet returned to Australia to refit prior to joining the American operations in the Pacific 'island-hopping' campaign.

Meanwhile, the East Indies Fleet had re-organised with the creation of the 21st Aircraft Carrier Squadron, whose air component included Seafires of No 4 Fighter Wing on *Hunter* (807 Squadron) and *Stalker* (809 Squadron) giving a total of fifty-four Seafire IIIs. The carriers sailed on 30 April 1945 to take part in the assault on the Rangoon area. Operations in early May included combat air patrols (CAPs), with no 'customers' and a number of fighter-bomber missions. This was followed by operations in the Bay of Bengal but on the few occasions that enemy aircraft made an appearance the Seafires were unable to score, the performance of both aircraft and pilots being below par.

The British Pacific Fleet air component included No 24 Fighter Wing's two Seafire units, 887 and 894 squadrons, with a notional strength of forty aircraft – but with only thirty-seven pilots, many of whom were inexperienced. The fleet sailed from Sydney on 10 March 1945, the Seafires aboard *Indefatigable*, for Operation Iceberg I, part of the Okinawa assault.

The squadrons flew a variety of mission types but the most important were the defensive CAPs; on 1 April these proved their worth when the Seafires managed to intercept a number of Japanese Kamikaze Zeros, although one, despite having been intercepted and damaged, managed to crash into the flight-deck of the *Indefatigable*, causing severe but not critical damage. Landing incidents, including barrier engagements, ate into the Seafire population and drastically reduced the number of available aircraft but the Wing maintained operational capability until the force was withdrawn to re-fit in late April. They sailed again for Iceberg II on 1 May and were soon in the thick of it against Kamikaze attack. This was a more successful period with a far lower incidence of accidents and a number of successful days in air combat.

Overall Seafire strength had been increased with the arrival of 801 and 880 squadrons as No 38 Wing aboard HMS *Implacable*. Mike Crosley was part of the new Wing and he recalled that during the cruise to the Far East they spent time

> practising 'downward twizzles' (an attack method from vertically above the target aircraft) and 'section drill'. This latter attack formation had been under development for some time in the Wing. It allowed strafing attacks on airfields to be carried out by up to 16 Seafires at the same time. In this way, the 200 guns firing at us would have but a few seconds of firing time shared amongst 16 targets instead of all – or most of – the guns firing at a single target as it dived in succession over a period about 16 times as long!

The first operation for the *Implacable* was an attack on the island of Truk (Operation Inmate) and at dawn on 14 June 1945 a dozen Seafires attacked airfields and harbour installations, with a second sortie being flown later in the day. The Seafires were multi-role as they were also tasked with air photography, using an F24 camera, and in an example of how well this self-contained system worked the pictures from Day One were used to determine the targets for Day Two, although it was naval bombardment with Seafire air-spotting for fall of shot. Mike Crosley was one of the spotters and he noted that the shooting was lousy due to poor radios and a problem with the gunnery system. Like the Spitfire, the Seafire was always short of fuel – not an ideal situation when operating from carriers – and whilst the standard forty-five-gallon slipper tanks were useful they still only gave about two hours of flight time. It was decided to acquire some of the eighty-nine-gallon tanks used by the Americans and according to Mike Crosley it 'was far more reliable and much easier to fit using our modified bomb racks. Although it formed half the Seafire's total fuel and therefore had to be still in use over enemy territory, it allowed Seafires to accompany strikes to the far side of the Japanese mainland, some lasting 3 hours 20 minutes.'

July saw a massive Allied fleet gathering for the invasion of the Japanese homeland, a fleet that included no less than twelve carriers and over 100 major warships. The first major Seafire operation was planned for 17 July, with forty-eight aircraft from 801 and 880 launching to attack airfields. It was a similar picture for the rest of the month and into August, with attacks on airfields, shipping and a variety of military installations, as well as CAPs and reconnaissance. The aircraft held up remarkably well, with good sortie rates, there were few landing incidents and losses were low, although a number of pilots were killed. The Armistice with Japan was signed on 2 September and the Second World War was over, but it was not quite the end of the Seafire's operational career.

Training

'Training is the key to operational success' is an age-old maxim but one that certainly holds true for aviation, although it is all too often forgotten or side-lined. The high rate of carrier landing accidents suffered by the Seafire in its first two major operations could in large part be put down to inadequate training and lack of pilot experience, a point made by Jeffrey Quill in his report into the problem. It was apparent that either no-one had determined the optimum Seafire carrier approach and landing, or that if anyone had it was either not being taught or not being used. He conclude that:

> the proper technique was to approach the ship in a gently curving left-hand turn with a thoroughly well-controlled rate of sink, sneaking in – as it were – just in front of the Seafire's blind area astern of the ship. This could be done quite safely due to the Seafire's excellent lateral stability characteristics right

down to the stall. If the circuit was properly flown and the moment of turning in correctly judged, the technique was not particularly difficult.

In his February 1944 report he outlined his:

reasonable rough rules for Seafire deck landing:

1　Circuit height – 300 to 400ft.
2　Fly ahead of the ship for 10 to 15 seconds according to windspeed before commencing circuit.
3　Keep circuit small.
4　Lower hook, undercarriage and flaps during circuit before getting abeam the ship on the downwind leg.
5　While still ahead of the beam, slow down to 80kts and watch for the moment to turn in, which can only be a matter of judgement but it will be easier to judge when you have nothing else to concentrate on.
6　When on the port quarter during your turn, settle down to your correct approach speed (70 to 75kts); keep steady rate of descent; watch the DLCO and your speed; make up your mind that you are going to arrive from the port quarter and not the starboard quarter.
7　If you have difficulty seeing the batsman, lean your head over the port side of the cockpit.

The basic instructional technique for teaching pilots carrier landings was for a course using aerodrome dummy deck landings (ADDLs), followed by landings on a training carrier, such as HMS *Ravager*, an American Ruler-class escort carrier that had been acquired by the Navy in April 1943 and spent most of its wartime career as a deck-landing training (DLT) ship. Having a training system was all very well but it was vital that the pupil pilots spent at least part of this training flying Seafires and that they were taught the correct procedures.

As with the RAF requirement, there was a need to convert pilots to type, and deck landing, train them in use of weapons and tactics, and provide specialist training. As with the RAF this organisation continued to develop and evolve throughout the war; the Fleet Air Arm made frequent, and often confusing, changes to its training system, using squadron numbers (in the 700 series) as components of a training unit. The following 'snippets' provide an indication of training units and roles; to provide a complete analysis would take too much space.

One of the largest training users of the Spitfire/Seafire was 761 Squadron, a fleet fighter school that first received Spitfire Is in September 1942 and by April 1943 was established at Henstridge as No 2 Naval Air Fighting School. The establishment of eighteen Spitfire/Seafire (plus a few Masters) eventually grew to sixty-eight aircraft by summer 1944.

Seafires equipped a number of FAA training units and one of the first such units was 748 Squadron, which formed at St Merryn in October 1942 as a fighter pool squadron with a mixed establishment of fighter types that included four Spitfire Is. The following March it had become No 10 Naval Operational Training Unit and added Spitfire Vs and, from late March, Seafire IIs.

Long-established as the fleet fighter school, 759 Squadron changed roles in April 1943 to become the advanced flying school within No 1 Naval Air Fighter School at Yeovilton. Although its establishment at this time included a small number of Spitfires, and later Seafires, its main fighter type was the Sea Hurricane, although by late 1943 the Spitfire/Seafire had increased in importance.

Reformed at Henstridge in early June 1944, No 718 Squadron acted as the Army Co-operation Naval Operational Training Unit and was equipped with nine Seafire IIIs; however, it also had six Spitfire PR.XIIIs for training photo-reconnaissance pilots. The Squadron also operated an air combat course.

On 15 June 1944 an air firing training unit – 719 Squadron – formed to give pilots training in air firing and weapon delivery. It was equipped with Masters, Wildcats and Spitfire VBs, some of which were the 'navalised' version with a hook. By the latter part of the year a number of Seafires had also been taken on charge.

In August 1944 Seafires and Corsairs were used to equip the reformed 715 Squadron at St Merryn, the unit's task being to operate a fighter air combat course and a fighter leaders' course.

Post-1945

The final Seafire variants to enter service during the war were the Mark XV and Mark XVII. The Seafire XV was the first of the Griffon-powered Seafires – yet another navalised version that had been proposed much earlier than it actually materialised. Indeed, the earliest naval bids for a Griffon-powered single-seat fighter dates back to 1939 but it was only with the appearance of the Spitfire IV that progress was made. The Seafire XV was essentially a navalised but heavily modified Spitfire XII. The prototype (NS487) was ready by November 1943 and probably made its first flight early in 1944, although it was autumn 1944 before the first production aircraft (SR446) was flying. First unit to re-equip was 802 Squadron in May 1945 but the first operational unit to receive Seafire XVs was 801 Squadron in September, then part of the 8th Carrier Group with HMS *Implacable* as their designated carrier. It was, of course, too late for active service as the war with Japan had ended. Indeed, the Squadron only kept its XVs for a short period of time, disposing of them in February 1946 prior to returning to the UK.

The continued development of the Spitfire influenced the Seafire, and the Mark XV was modified to incorporate features such as the tear-drop canopy and cut-down rear fuselage, plus a significant improvement in undercarriage strength. Under the designation Seafire XVII this aircraft certainly gave the pilot a better all-round view in combat but, as with the Spitfire, it created stability problems, although on balance pilots preferred the advantages of the better visibility. Like its predecessor it was powered by the Griffon VI engine and its all-round performance was excellent. The first production aircraft (SX232) flew in early summer 1945 and 883 Squadron was the first to receive the variant. It was not produced in large numbers and it had a short life with the operational squadrons, being relegated to reserve and training units.

The squadrons themselves had undergone changes in the immediate post-war period and by autumn 1946 had been re-organised into carrier air groups, a Seafire squadron (with XVs or XVIIs) being allocated to:

No 13 CAG (*Triumph*)
No 14 CAG (*Theseus*)
No 15 CAG (*Venerable*)
No 16 CAG (*Glory*)
No 20 CAG (*Ocean*)

The Royal Naval Volunteer Reserve (RNVR) had formed in summer 1947 and a number of its squadrons (in the 1800 series) acquired Seafires. Overall it was a very difficult period and Seafires remained operational largely because of delays in replacement types such as the Sea Fury.

Seafire 40 Series

To avoid confusion in the numbering sequence of aircraft, further naval versions were allocated numbers from 40 upwards, the first number actually allocated being Seafire 45, which was a navalised version of the Spitfire 21 with a Griffon 61. Although prototype TM379 (a converted Mark XXI) was ready by autumn 1944 the variant suffered the same problems as its RAF counterpart in terms of stability. Nevertheless, an order was placed in early 1945 for 600 of this series (Seafire 45, 46 and 47), with the Director of Naval Air Organisation stating that:

it is considered that the newer marks of Seafire, owing to their exceptional rate of climb and manoeuvrability, will be useful as interceptor fighters, particularly against the suicide dive-bombers. For at least the past 2½ years efforts have been put into the evolution of a first class, highly bred, British carrier fighter. The Seafire is the answer in its later marks with which we are planning to equip the majority of carriers to fight the Pacific war.

Carrier trials revealed no significant problems and the Seafire F.45 duly entered service but only in a support role, no aircraft being allocated to operational squadrons.

Likewise, only twenty-four of F.46 variant (prototype TM383, first flight 8 September 1944) were built and none served with a carrier-based unit, but they provided useful airframes for development of the main variant, the F.47. The first production aircraft (PS944) was fitted with a Griffon 87 but the majority of production Seafire 47s had the Griffon 88. It is generally agreed that this was the best of all the Seafires despite the fact that its maximum speed was slightly lower than the other 40-series Seafires. It was also the only one of this series to see active service – over Malaysia and Korea.

Malaysia

No 13 CAG, including 800 Squadron with Seafire FR.47s, was in Singapore in late 1949, based ashore at RNAS Sembawang, and it was from there on 21 October that the Squadron mounted a number of ground-attack (rockets and guns) sorties in the Negri Sembilan area in support of ground troops hunting terrorist camps. This type of action continued on and off to May 1950, when the outbreak of the Korean War meant a change of priorities.

Korea

Although none of the RAF's Spitfire squadrons were involved in the Korean War, which had broken out in June 1950, Fleet Air Arm Seafires did form part of the United Nations force. Aircraft of 800 Squadron operated off HMS *Triumph* in the period 3 July to 20 September 1950, flying 360 operational sorties. The aircraft flew CAP as well as ground attack, including rocket projectile against bridges and military installations. Anti-shipping work usually was comprised of the sinking of suspect junks. By the third week in September only one serviceable Seafire was left! One aircraft had earlier been shot down by a B-29, but most 'losses' were due to accidents and, more particularly, lack of spares. Nevertheless, the Seafire had acquitted itself reasonably well on this its last operational outing. In 1951 all Seafires were withdrawn from front-line service and passed to the Royal Naval Volunteer Reserve, where they served into the mid-1950s.

Carrier-Based Seafire Squadrons

(Source: Sturtivant and Balance, *The Squadrons of the Fleet Air Arm.*)

HMS *Battler*
808 Sqn	Apr 1943–Sep 1943
807 Sqn	Aug 1943–Oct 1943
834 Sqn	Sep 1943–Oct 1944

HMS *Chaser*
899 Sqn	Jan 1945–Apr 1945

HMS *Formidable*
885 Sqn	Oct 1942–Nov 1943

HMS *Furious*
807 Sqn	Aug 1942–Feb 1943
801 Sqn	Oct 1942–Sep 1944

HMS *Glory*
806 Sqn	Sep 1946–Oct 1947

HMS *Hunter*
808 Sqn	Aug 1943–Feb 1944
807 Sqn	Jan 1944–Jun 1944
	Oct 1944–Dec 1944
	Mar 1945–Oct 1945

HMS *Illustrious*
894 Sqn	Jul 1943–Oct 1943

HMS *Implacable*
887 Sqn	Oct 1944
894 Sqn	Oct 1944–Nov 1944
880 Sqn	Oct 1944–Sep 1945
801 Sqn	Nov 1944–Jun 1946

HMS *Indefatigable*
894 Sqn	May 1944–Mar 1946
887 Sqn	Jul 1944–Mar 1946

HMS *Indomitable*
880 Sqn	Mar 1943–Jul 1943
899 Sqn	Mar 1943–Jul 1943
807 Sqn	Jun 1943–Jul 1943

HMS *Khedive*
899 Sqn	Apr 1944–Oct 1944

HMS *Ocean*
805 Sqn	Jun 1946–Aug 1946
	Apr 1947–Jul 1948
804 Sqn	Aug 1948–Dec 1948
	Apr 1949–Jul 1949

HMS *Stalker*
880 Sqn	Aug 1943 –Oct 1943
897 Sqn	Dec 1943 –Feb 1944
809 Sqn	Dec 1943–Feb 1944
	May 1945–Oct 1945

HMS *Theseus*
804 Sqn	Feb 1947–Dec 1947

HMS *Tracker*
816 Sqn	Aug 1943–Dec 1943

HMS *Triumph*
827 Sqn	Jan 1947–Nov 1950

HMS *Unicorn*
887 Sqn	Apr 1943–Oct 1943
885 Sqn	Sep 1943–Oct 1943

HMS *Venerable*
802 Sqn	Sep 1946–Mar 1947

HMS *Vengeance*
807 Sqn	May 1947–Jul 1947
802 Sqn	Sep 1947–Nov 1947

HMS *Victorious*
884 Sqn	Jul 1942–Nov 1942
	Spitfire V

HMS *Warrior*
803 Sqn	Mar 1946–Aug 1947
883 Sqn	Nov 1947

~ 10 ~

Reconnaissance Operations

In the last sixty years strategic reconnaissance (SR), especially clandestine over-flight, has been based upon the capability of the reconnaissance aircraft to avoid engagement by air or ground defences; so, unarmed (better performance), high-flying, small size and stealth are usually seen as key attributes. It was these very attributes and tactics that made the Spitfire suitable for this role – but the 'powers that be' needed some persuading that this was the case.

The Second World War brought major advances in air reconnaissance, with the Spitfire involved from the start. The Heston Flight, under the command of Wg Cdr Sydney Cotton, was tasked to continue the strategic reconnaissance (this is a post-war term and at the time it was simply photographic reconnaissance) work that Cotton had been undertaking before war was formally declared. As a Fighter Command unit it had access to the Command's inventories and whilst the Blenheim was adopted as a standard type, a pair of Spitfires (N3069 and N3071) was also acquired. One of the unit's pilots, 'Shorty' Longbottom had presented a memo suggesting that stripped-down fighter-types would make ideal long-range SR aircraft – a novel and not well-received concept. His memo included the prescient comment that: 'This type of reconnaissance [strategic] must be done in such a manner as to avoid the enemy fighter and aerial defences as completely as possible. The best method of doing this appears to be the use of a single small machine relying solely on its speed, climb and ceiling to avoid detection.'

The two Spitfire Is acquired by the Heston unit were duly modified, with all excess weight, such as armament, removed. Two five-inch-lens F24 cameras were fitted in a split vertical arrangement, in the gun bays, and the airframe was given the cleanest possible aerodynamic finish to reduce drag. The PR aircraft were not intended to fight – the idea was to keep out of the way – and to make the small aircraft even less visible it was given a special camouflage scheme of pale duck-egg green (some later PR Spitfires appeared in pale pink!)

The first operational sortie by a recce Spitfire was on 18 November 1939 when Flt Lt Longbottom, flying N3071, departed Seclin in Northern France to photograph the city of Aachen. Flying at 30,000ft his navigation was slightly awry and the photographic coverage just missed his intended target. However, the principle was sound and a number of German cities were photographed over the next few months by what had now become No 2 Camouflage Unit, a cover name for this very secret unit, although this soon gave way to a more appropriate name of the Photographic Development Unit – PDU (this changed again in July 1940 to the Photographic Reconnaissance Unit – PRU).

There was a continual emphasis on increasing the radius of action for the recce Spitfires and various combinations of extra internal fuel tankage were tried; with ops being flown from France by 212 Squadron, effectively a sub-unit of the PDU. The PR.1B appeared with an extra twenty-nine-gallon fuel tank just behind the pilot, whilst the PR.1C was also given a thirty-gallon tank in a wing blister. The total of fifty-nine gallons of extra fuel gave the aircraft an appreciable additional range. However, the longest-range version, the PR.1D, required more extensive modification for the incorporation of fuel tanks in the leading edge of the wings, each tank holding fifty-seven gallons. On 29 October 1940 Fg Off Millen flew a PR.1D on a five-hour-and-twenty-minute mission to photograph Stettin. Not surprisingly, the PR.1D flown by Millen was reported as being 'tricky to handle, especially on take-off'.

There were numerous problems to be overcome but most of these centred on the cameras and their operation as the airframe proved adaptable, although there was never enough internal space to make modifications simple. The initial camera problem was that for strategic reconnaissance from 30,000ft a focal length of five inches was totally inadequate for ground scale. An eight-inch focal length became standard but even that was not really adequate from these heights.

The high-flying PR work continued throughout 1940, as did development of the Spitfire's range and camera capability, such as longer focal-length lenses and the introduction of oblique facing cameras. As a demonstration of the PR Spitfires' long-range, Berlin was reached by a PR.1F with an extra eighty-nine gallons of fuel – if only fighter Spitfires had the same range the concept of an effective escort fighter for the bombers would not have had to wait for the arrival of the 8th Air Force's P-51s.

The fighter-type performance of the Spitfire also made it suitable for an even more dangerous type of PR – low level. Vertical or even oblique images from on high were all very well for the 'big picture' but a low oblique image provided greater detail of point targets. The first aircraft modified for this role was the Spitfire PR.1E with underwing bulges, each holding an F24 facing out along the wing and with a 15-degree depression – this kept sighting simple as it was pretty much a case of point the wing at the target. The major problem with this type of imagery was blurring because of the forward speed of the aircraft. Very fast shutter speeds helped, as did slightly slower passes, although the latter 'tactic' was highly risky as if a target was worth photographing it was worth defending with anti-aircraft guns! The first such Spitfire mission was flown on 3 July 1940 by Wg Cdr Geoffrey Tuttle but was aborted because of bad weather; Fg Off Alistair Taylor was more successful on 7 July, bringing back pictures of Boulogne harbour.

Without the protection of height the recce Spitfire had put itself back in an environment where it could be intercepted and this led to the retention of the standard armament in the PR.1G. Having guns meant that the pilot had the opportunity of fighting back, although as most of the aircraft were painted pale pink (almost dull white) there was always the hope that any German fighter pilot would have a double-take at seeing a pink aircraft! The camera fit was also improved with two near-vertical F24s (split verts as they were later known), one with a five-inch lens and one with a fourteen-inch lens, and a single F24 (fourteen-inch lens) mounted at an oblique angle in the fuselage behind the pilot. This provided excellent flexibility for the pilot in terms of getting his target images in a variety of weather conditions.

Warren Middleton encapsulated the woes of the Spitfire recce pilot:

> Imagine being strapped in a Spitfire for 5 hours, freezing your tail, having to stay alert while at the same time doing pinpoint navigation and precision flying. I have seen pilots who had to be lifted out of the cockpit by the groundcrew after a mission. For special low-level missions the aircraft had two oblique cameras mounted in a 90-gallon drop tank under the belly of the aircraft. Most of our missions were between 1,000ft and 2,000ft, an altitude known to most as the light-flak alley.

Whilst these words were written about operations later in the war, the problems had been there from the early days; indeed, most of the later PR Spitfires had some form of cockpit heating whereas for the pioneers of 1940 there was no such luxury. Gordon Green was one of those pioneers: 'during those early missions there was no such thing as cockpit heating in our Spitfires. For the high altitude missions we wore thick suits with electrical heating. Trussed up in our Mae West and parachute, one could scarcely move in the narrow cockpit of the Spitfire' (quoted in Price, *The Spitfire Story*).

The same general feelings were expressed by Neil Wheeler:

> Because we did not appear to be experienced in flying in low temperatures nobody seemed to think of harnessing the hot air from the coolant radiator, until 1942 when, at long last, cockpit heating was provided. I found the extreme

cold most uncomfortable. On my feet I wore a pair of ladies' silk stockings, a pair of football stockings, a pair of oiled Scandinavian ski socks and RAF fur-lined boots. On my hands I wore two pairs of RAF silk gloves and some special fur-backed and lined gauntlets which I had to buy for myself. It was essential to retain some fingertip control, particularly for the camera control box. Otherwise, I wore normal uniform, with a thick vest, roll-neck sweater and a thing called a Tropal lining which was stuffed with a form of kapok. (Wheeler, 'Unarmed and Unafraid')

The main tactic for the high-level sorties was that of staying as high as possible – and at 30,000ft plus there was little danger of interception and none from flak – and also staying invisible. The problem with the latter was the formation of contrails, a nice streak of white at the front end of which would be the aircraft. Pilots were briefed on the problem, although the met officer rarely briefed pilots on likely contrail levels, and the standard instruction was watch for contrails forming and then get out of the contrail level as soon as possible. Some pilot fitted mirrors on the aircraft and at the first tell-tale signs tried to climb out of the level; however, this was often not possible for the early Spitfires and the only alternative was to descend below the level – and into the engagement range of any fighters that might be hunting for the aircraft that had made the contrails. There was no second aircraft to help with mutual lookout on these high-flying missions so recce pilots had to look after themselves.

Neil Wheeler wrote

Most people commenting on unarmed photographic 'recce' concentrate on the fear of deep penetration of enemy territory in an unarmed aircraft. The fact is that one simply could not fight it out once intercepted. The only thing to do was to go flat out for home . . . and pray – forward firing guns certainly would not have helped. Fortunately, for most of the war, we did out-perform the enemy, although there were periods when the reverse was true. Our greatest problem as regards the enemy was the condensation trails. Radar was still in its infancy and, on the whole, there was a reasonable chance that a lone Spitfire, operating at around 30,000ft, could penetrate deep into enemy territory without detection. Indeed the deeper you penetrated, the less likely the detection. A typical example was one in summer 1941 . . . When flying over north Germany I suffered trouble with my oxygen supply. At about 28,000ft I passed out and did not recover until about 1,500ft over the entrance to Kiel Harbour. It was about 1100 hours on a brilliantly clear morning and nobody seemed to take the slightest notice. The comments of a *Luftwaffe* general after the war was that nobody would have expected a lone enemy aircraft in daylight a few miles from Kiel at a few thousand feet! It would, however, have been a different story had I, before my oxygen troubles started, been leaving a condensation trail or even operating above the level where trails had been created.

To me the most serious shortcomings that the lack of high altitude flying experience brought, were the use of oxygen and the almost total ignorance about condensation trails. Before the war it was mandatory to turn on the oxygen above 10,000ft on the rare occasions that you went to that great height, but the supply system was primitive. We had a crude, very leaky cloth mask and a form of continuous supply – once you turned it on, you got it whether you were breathing in or out, a wasteful system. We had to change things since we were using oxygen for about four-plus hours. We had our own doctor and, with the RAE's help and the use of other masks – including a captured German one – we designed a good rubber mask. In November 1940 the oxygen economiser was introduced which worked with a form of bellows and only gave you oxygen when you inhaled. Inevitably we called it 'Puffing Billy'. Even here we had low temperature problems with the fabric used in the construction of the early economisers. (Wheeler, 'Unarmed and Unafraid')

At the other end of the recce spectrum – low level PR – it was essential to have at least some cloud cover in which to hide and the absence of cloud was a tactical reason for aborting a mission. There was no point taking a photograph of the target if you were then shot down, as the film would be lost with you! This, of course, also depended on the target in terms of its defences (flak and fighter) and the geographic position (using terrain or obstacles to shield an approach) and the only 'hard and fast' tactic was to avoid trouble and get back home. This type of sortie was usually referred to as 'dicing' – as the pilot was dicing with disaster.

The various interim PR Spitfires had been developed throughout 1940, mainly concentrating on squeezing ever more fuel into the aircraft – and they had certainly proved the aircraft's value in this essential but dangerous role. The value of this work and the suitability of the Spitfire had been proven and with some further development the PR.1D became the standard recce version, as the Spitfire PR.IV. Although the Spitfire PR.1D, or even just Type D as it was often known, officially became the Spitfire PR.IV it was still frequently referred to by its former title both in official records and by pilots. This has led to some confusion as the 'true' Spitfire Mark IV was the first Griffon-engined aircraft, with prototype DP845 flying on 27 November 1941. However, a few months later the new Griffon variant was re-designated the Mark XX, although destined to enter service as the Mark XII!

In September 1941, the first squadron to receive the PR.IV was 140 Squadron, which had formed on the 17 September by renumbering No 1416 Flight at Benson, which was notionally an army cooperation unit. The flight had been operating from Hendon since March but it was the increased requirement for photography, often to support bomber or coastal operations that prompted the expansion of the unit and indeed the creation of further PR units.

Goodbye PRU

The Photographic Reconnaissance Unit had grown so large and its work so diverse that in autumn 1942 the decision was taken to disband the unit and create five squadrons. With the exception of 540 Squadron, which was primarily equipped with Mosquitoes, the squadrons were long-term operators of recce Spitfires:

540 Sqn from H and L flights	Spitfire IV	Oct 1942–Dec 1942
541 Sqn from B and F flights	Spitfire D	Oct 1942–Jan 1943
	Spitfire IV	Oct 1942–Sep 1944
	Spitfire IX	Nov 1942–Dec 1942
	Spitfire XI	Dec 1942–Mar 1946
	Spitfire X	May 1944–Apr 1945
	Spitfire XIX	Jun 1944–Oct 1946
	Spitfire 19	Nov 1947–May 1951
542 Sqn from A and E flights	Spitfire IV	Oct 1942 – Jul 1943
	Spitfire XI	Mar 1943–Aug 1945
	Spitfire X	May 1944–Aug 1945
	Spitfire XIX	Jun 1944–Aug 1945
543 Sqn	Spitfire IV	Oct 1942–Oct 1943
	Spitfire XI	Apr 1943–Oct 1943
544 Sqn	Spitfire IV	Oct 1942–Oct 1943
	Spitfire XI	Aug 1943–Oct 1943

More Performance – Spitfire PR.X, PR.XI and PR.XIII

The more powerful PR.XI entered service with 541 Squadron in December 1942, the unit having been in the recce game since it formed, from the Photographic Reconnaissance Unit, with Spitfire PR.1Ds at Benson in October. The Merlin 61 provided an all-round increase in performance, which was also aided by aerodynamic improvements such as a retractable tailwheel and having the cameras in flush fittings in the rear fuselage. Standard camera fit was two F24s (later, F52s) as split verticals plus, in some aircraft, an oblique F24. In the tactical reconnaissance role, as the low-level PR was now often called, the camera fit was enhanced by the addition of two five-inch-lens F8 cameras in a blister under each wing, which had only a minimal effect on the aerodynamics. A total of 471 Mk XIs were produced, many having been converted on the Mk IX production line, with seventeen RAF squadrons using the variant, the majority re-equipping in 1943.

A small number of Spitfire PR.Xs were produced and were operated as high-flying PR aircraft by 541 and 542 squadrons from May 1944 to the end of the war. The Mk X was essentially similar in appearance and performance to the Mk XI, but it had a pressurised cockpit and a sliding Lobelle hood. According to one set of RAF figures this was the longest range of all the PR Spitfires as with 318 gallons of fuel (internal plus a ninety-gallon tank) it had a still air range of 1,690 miles at most economical cruise speed of 260mph at 30,000ft.

The PR.XIII was given the Merlin 32, rated for low-altitude, as its primary role was low-level PR; in addition to its three F24 cameras it carried four .303-in Brownings for self-defence. Only twenty-six of the Mark were produced, all conversions of other Marks, and they served with a number of squadrons in mid-1943.

Definitive Recce Bird? – Spitfire PR.XIX

By the middle years of the war the Spitfire had entered its second phase of development courtesy of the Griffon engine and all three of the main Griffon variants – XIV, XVIII and XIX – appeared in reconnaissance versions. However, the first two were primarily dual-role in the fighter-reconnaissance role. For the FR.XIV this meant a single oblique F24 camera in the rear fuselage, along with additional fuel, and the retention of the basic armament. Initial deliveries took place in late 1944 to squadrons of the 2nd Tactical Air Force, 2 Squadron and 430 Squadron being amongst the first recipients. The FR.XVIII was given a more comprehensive camera suite, comprising two vertical and one oblique camera, a fit that could have given a PR.XVIII tag. As part of the later (post-war) renumbering to lose the cumbersome Latin numerals it became the FR.18.

Although not produced in large numbers by Spitfire standards (225 aircraft) the PR.XIX (later PR.19) was in many respects the definitive, or rather, the ultimate PR Spitfire. In essence it combined the basic airframe and engine of the Mk XIV with the camera fit and wing fuel-tank capacity of the Mk XI. This provided a superb combination of performance and range, the ideal requirements of a recce bird. Initial deliveries were to 542 Squadron in May 1944 and it soon came to dominate the RAF's Spitfire PR force. It was also the last operational Spitfire Mark with the RAF, with 81 Squadron in the Far East not giving up their aircraft until summer 1954. This later period of the type's career, including operations over Malaysia is covered in Chapter 11, 'Post-1945 Operations'.

~ 11 ~

Post-1945 Operations

The Spitfire had undergone tremendous development during the Second World War and had remained combat effective from the first to last day; indeed, that combat effectiveness had increased as the war progressed, as the RAF's fighter tactics evolved and improved. However, by 1944 the RAF had determined that the future lay with jet fighters as further development of piston-engined types was limited. The post-1945 period was, therefore, one of rapid decline for the Spitfire and in terms of combat tactics there was nothing new, although there was quick, sharp shock in the Middle East in one of the only Spitfire versus Spitfire engagements. The combat future of the Spitfire continued into the 1950s and in this chapter we look at Malaysia, where the RAF's last operational Spitfire sorties took place, and the Middle East. For the Fleet Air Arm's Seafires the last major operations took place in the Far East, culminating with the Korean War. The FAA operations were covered in Chapter 9, 'Carrier Operations'.

Final Spitfires

Before looking at the operational use of the Spitfire after the Second World War, a few words must be said about the final two Marks, the F.22 and F.24, although both were derivatives of the F.21. Both were powered by Griffon series 60 engines and had four 20-mm cannon. The F.22 entered service with 73 Squadron in July 1947 and eventually equipped fourteen RAF squadrons, albeit only for a few years as the last had gone out of service by November 1951. It is also noteworthy that only 73 Squadron was a 'Regular' RAF unit, all the other belonged to the newly organised post-war Auxiliary Air Force. The most distinctive features were the tear-drop canopy and the cut-down rear fuselage, both good features that had already proved their tactical value during the war. During late April and May 1945 Shea-Simmonds flew the initial trials and he was not happy with the brakes or the lateral stability: 'Brakes are feeble to the point of being virtually useless', and more seriously 'the rear-view modification has a detrimental effect on directional stability, and although I do not consider it by any means unacceptable I anticipate trouble when carrying any form of drop-tank or bomb.'

One unique feature of the Mark 22 and 24 was the capability to fit rockets to the wings (60-lb, 100-lb or 180-lb RPs), although trials on this weapon fit had taken place on earlier variants it had not been adopted as standard – quite rightly as the Spitfire was not a good RP platform. The Mark saw no combat with the RAF and, having been phased out of service, it was taken on by 'second-hand' users in Egypt, Rhodesia and Syria.

Only one unit, 80 Squadron, flew the F.24, from January 1948 to December 1951, for the latter part of that period in Hong Kong, with the local 'branch' of the Auxiliary Air Force taking on some of the aircraft from the RAF and keeping them in service to 1955. The initial weapon trials in late 1946 showed numerous problems both with cannon stoppages and vibration; despite a few minor airframe changes, primarily to the elevators the problems were still evident in the summer 1947 trials, although the guns had been cleared for operational use.

When the last Spitfire F.24 (VN496) rolled out of the South Marston works at Swindon in February 1948 it was the last of the long line of Spitfires; it was delivered to No 6 MU at Brize Norton on 4 April 1949 and eventually made its way to 80 Squadron in August but lasted just over a year, being declared Cat. 5 and struck off charge on 15 December 1950. A somewhat sad and short history for the last Spitfire to be built.

Malayan Emergency

A state of emergency was declared in Malaya in June 1948; at that time only sixteen Spitfire FR.18s of 60 Squadron were available for offensive support (OS) and three of these were sent to Kuala Lumpur as part of the task force, where they were soon joined by the rest of the Squadron. The first air strike was made by 60 Squadron against a Communist terrorist (CT) base in Perak on 6th July when two aircraft destroyed the camp near Ayer Korah. Further strikes were made on the 15th and 16th and in the latter at least ten CTs were killed. These early missions proved the value of such air strikes and from then on attempts were made to increase the weight of available air power and the FR.18s of 28 Squadron were soon added to the task force. The third Spitfire unit involved was 81 Squadron, a unit destined to have the longest operational period of the campaign, operating in the PR role from April 1948 (when one aircraft was detached to Taiping) to 1 April 1954, when the unit flew the RAF's last operational Spitfire sortie. One of the largest strikes of the early period was that of 28 February 1949, by eight

Spitfires and four Beaufighters against Mengkuang, southern Pahang. It was also one of the most successful such attacks of the campaign; demands for air strikes, either as part of a ground-force operation or a 'stand alone' mission continued to increase and the Spitfires began to suffer problems with serviceability. The run down of the Spitfire element began in May 1949 with 28 Squadron moving to Hong Kong (part of an air reinforcement in response to the civil war in China). In December 1950, 60 Squadron re-equipped with Vampires, bringing to an end the offensive-support role for the Spitfire. The PR task continued and 81 Squadron remained as busy as ever with Firedog missions. Indeed, 1953 was one of the busiest years and the Squadron averaged 100 operational sorties a month.

As a side note to operational use on the Far East after the war, the Dutch (322 Squadron) had used Spitfires as part of their post-war attempt to re-establish colonial authority in the Dutch East Indies; the last sorties probably taking place as late as 1948. Seafires operated with the French Aéronavale in French Indo-China during the latter part of 1948, including operations from the *Arromanches* cruising in the Gulf of Tonkin during December (shades of later US Navy operations!).

Korea

Although none of the RAF's Spitfire squadrons were involved in the Korean War, which had broken out in June 1950, Fleet Air Arm Seafires did form part of the United Nations force – see Chapter 9, 'Carrier Operations'.

Middle East

In February 1945 the Royal Egyptian Air Force (REAF) had been gifted twenty ex-RAF Spitfire Vs, joined by a number of IXs in early 1946. Two RAF squadrons, 32 and 208, were operating IXs out of Petah Tiqva, Palestine, and with the British forces attempting to impose their mandate in the area there was growing tension with certain Jewish elements, for whom an independent Jewish state was the avowed intent. In what appeared to be an increasingly hopeless situation, the British announced that they would depart in 1948, and the Arab–Israeli conflict was born – a situation that brought three Spitfire users into conflict: the RAF, Israeli Air Force (IAF) and Egyptian Air Force.

For the RAF the primary missions flown during this period were TacR in support of the Army, as the latter attempted to maintain peace before the final British withdrawal. During April 1948 the RAF squadrons, now based at Ramat David, flew formations over areas of Arab–Jewish tension as a 'show of force' but later in the month had to undertake CAS missions against Jewish strong points around Jaffa. However, during these final days of the British mandate most ops were convoy escort. On 22 May 1948, two REAF Spitfires attacked Ramat David, destroying a number of aircraft. Three RAF Spitfires gave chase but without result. A short time later another REAF Spitfire attack was intercepted by the CAP and two were shot down, the third falling to ground gunners. Two hours later it was the same story, with both attackers being shot down.

The British withdrawal went ahead as planned and Ramat David was handed to the Israelis on 25 May. The nascent Israeli Air Force soon acquired Spitfires, the first of which were rebuilt out of scrap aircraft left behind by the RAF. A deal with the Czechs provided a somewhat better source and agreement was reached to purchase fifty Spitfire IXs; the first arrived in September and went to equip 101 and 105 squadrons, IAF. Reconnaissance ops commenced in August and with the end of the ceasefire the War of Independence began in October. The first Spitfire mission took place on 15 October, an attack on El Arish airfield. First air combat was 21 October with Israeli Spitfire pilots claiming one Egyptian Spitfire destroyed and two damaged. Many of the Israeli pilots were highly experienced and their combat experience was put to good use, the Spitfires flying the same range of missions that the type had flown in the Second World War; indeed, the general tactics were similar at this stage. The ground offensive was brief and a ceasefire was declared on 7 January. The Spitfires had played a significant role, having quickly established air dominance. Indeed that air dominance created a major incident when an Israeli patrol intercepted a formation of RAF Spitfires from 208 Squadron on a recce mission. Three of the RAF aircraft, operating from the Canal Zone in Egypt, were shot down by the Israeli Spitfires, two falling to McElroy and one to 'Slick' Goodlin, with the fourth being shot down by ground fire. Later in the day an RAF search mission was also intercepted, with one Tempest being shot down, the last aerial victory by the Israeli Spitfires as the type was soon replaced as the front-line fighter.

The conflict could have become more complex as there were many on the British side that were in favour of mounting attacks on the Israeli bases. Spitfires continued to fly PR missions as the borders of Israel remained tense. Border skirmishes were not infrequent and the IAF was often called on to support ground forces; the last Spitfire missions of this type took place in April and May 1951 on the Syrian front.

Last Ops?

There is always debate as to when the Spitfire flew its last combat sorties, a discussion made difficult by the fact that they probably took place as counter-insurgency in Burma, where the Burmese Air Force used ex-Israeli Spitfire IXs against dissidents. Details of these ops in the 1950s are sketchy, as is the date at which the Spitfire ceased to be used. The RAF's PR operations over Malaya may have run the last sortie but these were reconnaissance missions.

Final Comment

Gordon Levett flew Spitfires and Bf 109s with 101 Squadron of the Israeli Air Force in the 1948 conflict and in an article published in *Air Pictorial* (January 1989) he summarised his thoughts on fighter tactics; whilst these do not solely apply to the Spitfire they neatly encapsulate the 'fighter game'.

> I believe that success or failure in air combat given reasonably similar mounts depends upon the man not the machine. Not necessarily flying skill, or tactical skill but, simply, general flying experience – hours in the log book. In the shambles of a dog-fight it is the instinct of self-preservation and the experience to sustain that instinct that matters. The one thing we all learn as our hours build up is to be aware, to expect the worst, to be a cynic, to look both ways in a one-way street and, eventually, to be able to fly without thinking about it, like breathing, so that one can concentrate on staying alive, peacetime or wartime.
>
> The more experience, the easier it becomes . . . I was moderately successful with my first experience of combat in Israel because I had logged over 3,000 hours and I could forget about flying the aircraft and concentrate exclusively on tactics and the imperatives of air combat; both offensive and defensive: where's the sun, watch the mirror, eyes everywhere, never straight and level, height is precious, etc. The only hope of survival is survival, the more you survive the more you will survive. You cannot fight effectively unless you can fly effectively.

These words applied to 1948, less than a decade after the Spitfire had entered service, but in that decade the aircraft had earned a reputation that has survived another sixty years – and looks set to continue.

~ 12 ~

Spitfire Warbird

By the late 1940s the era of the piston-engined fighter was essentially at and end and although a number of types – including Spitfires – remained in operational use into the 1950s, their place as the cutting-edge of combat ops, and especially fighter ops, had been taken by the jets. With some air forces the Spitfire soldiered on into the late 1950s but it was increasingly its history that was the focus of attention and not its combat ability. There were, indeed, are, very few fighter pilots who would not want to fly a Spitfire for the sheer joy of the type; a desire that largely rests on the reputation of the Spitfire rather than, in most cases, any personal knowledge of the type – thus perpetuating the legend.

Thousands of Spitfires were disposed of in the immediate post-war years, many falling under the axe of the scrapman as being of no interest and no value. However, as the RAF looked back to its heritage the Spitfire became a popular gate guard at airfields, even those that had no association with the type. Spitfire gate guards began to vanish as airfields closed or more relevant types became available and where once there were dozens on show the numbers dwindled to a handful. The handful were also soon to go as aircraft preservation became an issue – leave an aircraft outside for years and it will soon deteriorate; corrosion was literally eating away at the aircraft. A second motive for taking them off the gates was an interest from museums and warbird collectors to restore and even fly Spitfires. Thus it was that real aircraft went indoors, were sold or swapped and plastic replicas popped up at those locations where it was deemed appropriate to display a 'Spitfire'.

Survivors

The warbird movement is a product of the last thirty years and has been particularly vibrant in the UK and America. The Spitfire has always been at the forefront of interest as far as British aircraft are concerned, not only because aircraft were available for restoration but also because the Spitfire 'legend' generated a ready market – and whilst warbird flying is about emotion it can never be separated from economics; people will pay for an airworthy Spitfire, therefore airworthy Spitfires are a marketable commodity. It is not the intention in this chapter to look at the restoration of Spitfires or the activities of warbird operators, but rather to look at the feelings that the Spitfire still generates – all part of the on-going legend.

There are approximately fifty airworthy Spitfires wordwide, the majority of which are in the UK, and in addition there are a significant number of museum examples. These cover most of the major Marks of Spitfire, from historic survivors from the Battle of Britain to aircraft that flew over the D-Day beaches. The largest single operator is the RAF's Battle of Britain Memorial Flight (BBMF), currently based at Coningsby, which is also home to the RAF's newest fighter – the Eurofighter Typhoon – one of the perks of being an instructor at Coningsby is that you might get the chance to be chosen as one of the BBMF fighter pilots. The flight operates Hurricanes and both Merlin and Griffon Spitfires; pilots invariably express a preference for the Spitfires but opinions are mixed as to which is the favourite Mark. Some pilots prefer the Merlin aircraft, for harmonisation of controls and for the sheer delight of the Merlin, whilst others prefer the raw power of the Griffon aircraft.

This book is about Spitfire tactics and whilst the warbird owners, and those who put on air displays, engage in mock combat or aerobatics, and by doing so show off the graceful lines and manoeuvrability of this great aircraft (not to mention that Merlin sound) to new generations of air enthusiasts, it is not the real world. There is no life-and-death struggle here; the Spitfire has become a showpiece and not the weapon of war it was when it dominated air combat for five years in the 1940s. I am a great supporter of keeping such aircraft in the air and watching the mass scramble and fly-by at Duxford a few years ago was an emotional experience, especially for the Spitfire veterans who watched from their special marquee.

Was there a Spitfire Legend? Indeed there was, and indeed there still is.

~ ANNEXE A ~

Variant Data and Squadrons

Despite the thousands of words and enormous amounts of research into the history of the Spitfire there are still many gaps and discrepancies in the information relating to the aircraft. This is particularly true when it comes to data such as that presented here. The following performance and operator data is based upon the best available research using primary documents in RAF and Company records plus a number of secondary (i.e. published) works, such as the author's *Source Book of the RAF*.

Performance Data

Facts and figures for performance data cause a great deal of debate and the numbers vary between published books, which is not surprising as they vary in official records, which in turn are often very different to the numbers provided by the manufacturer. This is particularly true of speeds, climb performance, service ceiling and range. The reader will note variation in the figures in this book between those given in the data tables below and those given in the trials reports and the main body of the text; it is quite likely that these figures are also at variance to those in other published works on the Spitfire. Sadly, there is no easy answer to the problem as it depends on the source of the data and that in turn depends on the date of that source and indeed the nature of that source. One of the commonest causes of confusion is knots versus miles per hour and it is always worth checking which unit of measurement is being used; most wartime records use mph whilst the post-war ones (from as early as 1946) use kts, although even this distinction is not always as clear as it might be. In the following tables mph/kts and Imperial gallons/US gallons are mixed – the tables reflect the original data and have not been converted. To put this into some perspective for the Spitfire speed range:

300mph is 250kts	250kts is 300mph
350mph is 292kts	300kts is 360mph
400mph is 334kts	350kts is 420mph

(The above calculations use 1kt = 1.2mph, the exact figure is between 1.15 and 1.2)

Squadron Lists

The list of RAF operators in each Mark entry includes Allied and Commonwealth units that were part of the RAF numbering sequence in the 300 series (Allies such as the Poles, French, Czechs, Dutch, Norwegians) and the 400 series (Commonwealth countries such as Canada, Australia and New Zealand). The lists do not include squadrons that were in the national sequence of a country, which means that, for example, the South African squadrons that flew Spitfires in the Desert War and Italy are not shown. Fleet Air Arm squadrons are included as a number of these operated Spitfires prior to or alongside Seafires; Seafire lists are at the end.

Summary Data Table: Spitfire and Seafire Variants

Mk	Engine	Max speed	First flight	IOC	Production
I	Merlin II, III	367mph	K5054, 5 Mar 1936	19 Sqn, Jun 1938	1567
II	Merlin XII, XX	370mph	K9788	611 Sqn, Aug 1940	920
IV	Merlin 45, 46, 50, 50A	365mph	DP845	140 Sqn, Sep 1941	229
V	Merlin 45, 46, 50, 50A	375mph	X4922, 20 Feb 1941	92 Sqn, Feb 1941	6487
VI	Merlin 47, 49	364mph	X4942, 4 Jul 1941	616 Sqn, Apr 1942	100
VII	Merlin 45, 46, 61, 64, 71	408mph	AB450, Apr 1942	HAF, Sep 1942	140
VIII	Merlin 61, 63, 63A, 66, 70	410mph	JF299, Apr 1942?	145 Sqn, Jun 1943	1658
IX	Merlin 61, 63, 63A, 66, 70	416mph	MH874	64 Sqn, Jul 1942	5665
X	Merlin 64, 71, 77	417mph	MD191	541 Sqn, May 1944	16
XI	Merlin 61, 63, 63A, 70	422mph	BR497?	541 Sqn, Dec 1942	471
XII	Griffon III, IV	393mph	DP845, 27 Nov 1941	41 Sqn, Feb 1943	100
XIII	Merlin 32	393mph	L1004		44
XIV	Griffon 65, 67, 85, 87, 88	448mph	JF316	610 Sqn, Jan 1944	957
XVI	P-Merlin 266	352kts	MJ556?	Nov 1944	1054

Mk	Engine	Max speed	First flight	IOC	Production
XVIII	Griffon 65, 67	437mph	NH872, Jun 1945	208 Sqn, Aug 1946	300
XIX	Griffon 65, 66	457mph	SW777	542 Sqn, May 1944	225
21	Griffon 61, 64, 85	454mph	DP139, 24 Jul 1943	91 Sqn, Jan 1945	120
22	Griffon 61, 64, 85	454mph	PK312	73 Sqn, Jul 1947	278
24	Griffon 61, 64, 85	454mph	VN302	80 Sqn, Jan 1948	81
Seafire					
1B	Merlin 45	355mph	AB205	807 Sqn, Sep 1942	166
IIC	Merlin 43, 45, 46, 50	345mph	AD371, 2 Feb 1942	807 Sqn, Jun 1942	372
III	Merlin 55, 55M	358mph	MA970, Nov 1942	887 Sqn, Dec 1943	355
XV	Griffon VI	383mph	NS847, Dec 1943?	802 Sqn, Aug 1945	390
XVII	Griffon	387mph	NS493	807 Sqn, Sep 1946	
45	Griffon 61	442mph	TM379	700 Sqn, 1945	
46	Griffon 85		TM383, 8 Sep 1944	777 Sqn, 1945	26
47	Griffon 87, 88	434mph	PS944, 25 Apr 1946	804 Sqn, Jan 1948	90

Notes: First flight = either prototype or first production aircraft.
Where question marks are shown, the author found conflicting sources.
P-Merlin = Packard Merlin.
IOC = Initial Operational Capability i.e. the first operational user, usually a squadron but in the case of the Spitfire VII, the High Altitude Flight (HAF).
Including sub-variants under each entry keeps the table simpler but does not always reflect max speed performance e.g. the Spitfire HF.VII is declared at 408mph but with its Merlin 71 is declared at 416mph, whereas the PR.VII with a Merlin 45 or 46 is down at 349mph. Additional detail for sub-variants is given in the appropriate entry for each Mark of Spitfire.

Fighter Spitfire Variants – Merlin Engine

	I	IIA	VB	VIII	HF.IX	XIII	XVI
Max power	1,030bhp at 16,250ft	1,150bhp at 14,500ft	1,210bhp at 18,250ft	1,710bhp at 8,500ft (c)	1,710bhp at 11,000ft (a)	1,760bhp at 1,000ft (e)	1,670hp at 15,700ft (g)
Range	G-85 M-575	G-85 M-530	G-85 M-480	G-120 M-660 G-165 M-935 G-210 M-1,180	G-85 M-434 G-130 M-721 G-175 M-980	G-85 M-329 G-130 M-574 G-175 M-791	G-102 M-378nm G-156 M-626nm G-210 M-851nm
MEC	190mph at 15,000ft	190mph at 15,000ft	208mph at 20,000ft	220mph at 20,000ft	220mph at 20,000ft	263mph at 20,000ft	191kts at 20,000ft
Max speed	355mph at 19,000ft	363mph at 17,000ft	375mph at 20,500ft	408mph at 25,000ft (d)	416mph at 27,500ft (b)	393mph at 18,000ft (f)	352kts at 22,500ft
Ceiling	34,500ft	36,500ft	38,000ft	42,000ft	44,000ft	39,000ft	42,500ft
Climb	6.2min to 15,000ft	4.9min to 15,000ft	7min to 20,000ft	7.1min to 20,000ft	6.4min to 20,000ft	8min to 20,000ft	6.4min to 20,000ft
AUW	6,256lbs	6,238lbs	6,460lbs	7,900lbs	7,450lbs	7,413lbs	7,500lbs
Armament	8 x 0.303-in	8 x 0.303-in	4 x 0.303-in + 2 x 20-mm	4 x 0.303-in + 2 x 20-mm	4 x 0.303-in + 2 x 20-mm	4 x 0.303-in + 2 x 20-mm	4 x 0.303-in + 2 x 20-mm

Notes: Max power = Maximum power at rated altitude.
Range = Fuel in gallons (G) and still-air range (M – miles) at MEC.
Ceiling = Service ceiling.
(a) Merlin 70; also 1,475bhp at 23,250ft.
(b) Also 396mph at 15,000ft.
(c) Also 1,520bhp at 21,000ft.
(g) War Emergency; 1,310hp at 19,000ft in military power.

MEC = Most economical cruise speed and height.
Max speed = maximum speed at given altitude.
Climb = Time to given height.
(d) Also 383mph at 12,500ft.
(e) Also 1,460bhp at 13,500ft.
(f) Also 372mph at 5,500ft.

Statistics from 'Confidential Register of British Aircraft Performance' (OR.4a tables)

Fighter Spitfire Variants – Griffon Engine

	XII (a)	XIV (a)	XVIII	F.21 (b)	F.22 (a)
Max power	1,495hp at 14,500ft (c)	2,100hp at 17,500ft (d)		2,050bhp at 8,000ft (e)	2,100hp at 22,000ft (f)
Range	G-102 M-286nm G-136 M-428nm	G-134 M-400nm G-170 M-530nm G-243 M-740nm		G-120 M-490 G-165 M-715 G-290 M-1,200	G-144 M-425nm G-182 M-670nm G-422 M-1,390nm
MEC	228kts at 20,000ft	213kts at 20,000ft	.	284mph at 20,000ft	246kts at 20,000ft
Max speed	341kts at 18,000ft	389kts at 26,000ft		454mph at 26,000ft	393kts at 26,000ft
Ceiling	40,000ft	43,500ft at max AUW		43,000ft	43,500ft
Climb	6.7min to 20,000ft	7min to 20,000ft		8min to 20,000ft	8min to 20,000ft
AUW	7,400lbs	8,488lbs		9,186lbs	9,186lbs
Armament	4 x 0.303-in + 2 x 20-mm	4 x 0.303-in + 2 x 20-mm		4 x 20-mm	4 x 20-mm

Notes: Max power = Maximum power at rated altitude.
Range = Fuel in gallons (G) and still-air range (M – miles) at MEC.
MEC = Most economical cruise speed and height.
Ceiling = Service ceiling.
Max speed = maximum speed at given altitude.
Climb = Time to given height.
(a) Fuel is US gallons, speeds are kts and distances nm.
(b) Statistics from 'Confidential Register of British Aircraft Performance' (OR.4a tables) dated May 1947.
(c) War Emergency rating; 1,365hp at 17,000ft in military power.
(d) War Emergency rating; 1,810hp at 22,000ft in military power.
(e) Also 1,780bhp at 21,000ft.
(f) War Emergency using 150 octane; 1,810hp at 22,000ft with 100 octane; 1,365hp at 27,000ft in military power.

PR Spitfire Variants

	PR.IV	PR.VII	PR.XI	PR.XIII	PR.XIX (f)
Max power	1,110bhp at 19,000ft	1,150bhp at 17,000ft	1,710bhp at 8,500ft (a)	1,620bhp at 1,500ft (b)	1,810bhp at 22,000ft
Range	G-217 M-1,460	G-113 M-710	G-217 M-1,200 G-262 M-1,450 G-307 M-1,650	G-84 M-500 G-114 M-700	G-260 M-930 G-314 M-1120 G-369 M-1270
MEC	228mph at 15,000ft	208mph at 20,000ft	260mph at 30,000ft	175mph at 5,000ft	252kts at 35,000ft
Max speed	365mph at 22,000ft	37mph at 20,500ft	422mph at 26,500ft (c)	349mph at 5,000ft (d)	397kts at 26,000ft
Ceiling	36,000ft	37,200ft	42,000ft (e)	37,000ft	44,500ft
Climb	8min to 20,000ft	7min to 20,000ft	12min to 30,000ft	4.5min to 15,000ft	14.5min to 35,000ft
AUW	7,105lbs	6,585lbs	7,872lbs	6,350lbs	8,575lbs
Cameras	2 x F8, F52 or F24 1 x F24 oblique	2 x F24 split vertical 1 x F24 oblique	2 x F8, F52 or F24 1 x F24 oblique	2 x F24 split vertical 1 x F24 oblique	

Notes: Max power = Maximum power at rated altitude.
Range = Fuel in gallons (G) and still-air range (M – miles) at MEC.
MEC = Most economical cruise speed and height.
Ceiling = Service ceiling.
Max speed = maximum speed at given altitude.
Climb = Time to given height.
(a) Merlin 63; also 1,505bhp at 21,000ft. For Merlin 70 figures of 1,655bhp at 10,000ft and 1,475bhp at 22,250ft.
(b) Using 18lb boost for 3,000rpm.
(c) Merlin 70; also 396mph at 14,000ft. For Merlin 63 figures of 388mph at 12,000ft and 414mph at 24,500ft.
(d) Also 323mph at sea level and 335mph at 20,000ft.
(e) Merlin 63; 43,000ft for Merlin 70.
(f) Statistics from different source; fuel is US galls, speed is kts, distance is nms.
Statistics from 'Confidential Register of British Aircraft Performance' (OR.4a tables)

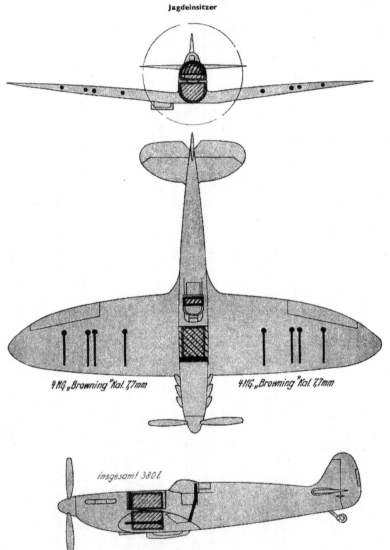

Großbritannien

Supermarine „Spitfire I"
Jagdeinsitzer

4 MG. „Browning" Kal. 7,7mm   4 MG. „Browning" Kal. 7,7mm

insgesamt 380 ℓ

8 starre ungesteuerte MG. Je MG. 320 Schuß. Munitionszuführung durch Zerfallgurte in den Flügeln. Auffallend die große Entfernung der MG. von der Längsachse. Abstand des äußersten rechten MG. vom äußersten linken MG. 7,8 m. Frontscheibe des Flugzeugführersitzes aus schußsicherem Glas.

A. Luftwaffe recognition three-view of Spitfire I; the drawing highlights the armament, protection and fuel elements of the aircraft – all things that a fighter pilot wants to know about his enemy.

Spitfire Variants – Data

Spitfire I

Role:	Fighter
Engine:	one Rolls-Royce Merlin II or III
Wing span:	36ft 10in
Length:	29ft 11in
Service ceiling:	31,500ft
Max speed:	I – 364mph
	IA – 367mph
	IB – 328mph
Range:	IA – 504miles (with 102 US gall)
	Other records show 575 miles with 85 gall
Armament:	I – 4 x 0.303-in (nil on PR versions)
	IA – 8 x 0.303-in (300rpg)
	IB – 4 x 0.303-in, 2 x 20-mm
First flight:	Prototype K5054 (5 Mar 1936)
	Production K9787
First sqn:	19 Sqn, Aug 1938
Last sqn:	140 Sqn, Apr 1943
Total production:	1,567
RAF squadrons:	

Spitfire C	140 Sqn	Sep 1941–Aug 1942
	212 Sqn	Feb 1940–Jun 1940
Spitfire D	541 Sqn	Oct 1942–Jan 1943
Spitfire I	19 Sqn	Aug 1938–Dec 1940
	41 Sqn	Jan 1939–Nov 1940
		Mar 1941–Apr 1941
	54 Sqn	Mar 1939–Feb 1941
	64 Sqn	Apr 1940–Jan 1941
	65 Sqn	Mar 1939–Apr 1941
	66 Sqn	Oct 1938–Nov 1940
		Feb 1941–Mar 1941
	72 Sqn	Apr 1939–Apr 1941
	74 Sqn	Feb 1939–Sep 1940
	92 Sqn	Mar 1940–Feb 1941
	111 Sqn	Apr 1941–May 1941
	118 Sqn	Feb 1941–Apr 1941
	122 Sqn	May 1941–Oct 1941
	123 Sqn	May 1941–Sep 1941
	124 Sqn	May 1941–Nov 1941
	129 Sqn	Jun 1941–Aug 1941
	131 Sqn	Jun 1941–Nov 1941
	132 Sqn	Jul 1941–Nov 1941
	140 Sqn	Sep 1941–Apr 1943
	145 Sqn	Jan 1941–Mar 1941
	152 Sqn	Dec 1939–Mar 1941
	222 Sqn	Mar 1940–Mar 1941

	234 Sqn	Mar 1940–Apr 1941
	238 Sqn	May 1940–Jun 1940
	249 Sqn	May 1940–Jun 1940
	257 Sqn	May 1940–Jun 1940
	266 Sqn	Jan 1940–Sep 1940
		Oct 1940–Apr 1941
	303 Sqn	Jan 1941–Mar 1941
		Aug 1941–Oct 1941
	308 Sqn	Mar 1941–May 1941
	313 Sqn	May 1941–Aug 1941
	403 Sqn	May 1941–Jul 1941
	411 Sqn	Jun 1941–Sep 1941
	452 Sqn	Apr 1941–May 1941
	457 Sqn	Jun 1941–Oct 1941
	485 Sqn	Mar 1941–Jun 1941
	501 Sqn	Apr 1941–Jun 1941
	510 Sqn	Oct 1942–Apr 1944
	602 Sqn	May 1939–Jun 1941
	603 Sqn	Sep 1939–Nov 1940
	609 Sqn	Aug 1939–May 1941
	610 Sqn	Sep 1939–Feb 1941
	611 Sqn	May 1939–Sep 1940
		Oct 1940–Mar 1941
	616 Sqn	Oct 1939–Feb 1941
FAA squadrons:		
Spitfire I	748 Sqn	Oct 1942–Apr 1943
	759 Sqn	?–Aug 1944
	761 Sqn	Sep 1942–Jul 1944
	762 Sqn	Feb 1943–Jun 1943
	775 Sqn	Jun 1943
	791 Sqn	Oct 1942–May 1943
	794 Sqn	Apr 1943–Nov 1943
	880 Sqn	Nov 1943–Jan 1944
	897 Sqn	Mar 1943–Jul 1943

Spitfire II

Role:	Fighter (F/ASR for IIC)
Engine:	one Merlin XII (Merlin XX for IIC)
Wing span:	36ft 10in
Length:	29ft 11in
Service ceiling:	31,500ft
Max speed:	370mph
Range:	530 miles (85 gall)
Armament:	IIA – 8 x 0.303-in
	IIB – 4 x 0.303-in, 2 x 20-mm
First flight:	Prototype K9788
	Production P7280

First sqn: IIA – 611 Sqn, Aug 1940

                IIB – 222 Sqn, Mar 1941

Last sqn: IIA – 278 Sqn, May 1944

                IIB – 277 Sqn, May 1944

Total production: IIA – 750, IIB – 170, IIC – 50 (total includes conversions)

RAF squadrons:

Spitfire IIA

19 Sqn	Sep 1940–Nov 1941
41 Sqn	Nov 1940–Aug 1941
54 Sqn	Feb 1941–May 1941
	Aug 1941
64 Sqn	Jan 1941–Nov 1941
65 Sqn	Jan 1941–Sep 1941
66 Sqn	Oct 1940–Apr 1942
71 Sqn	Aug 1941–Sep 1941
72 Sqn	Apr 1941–Jul 1941
74 Sqn	Jun 1940–Dec 1941
91 Sqn	Jan 1941–Jun 1941
111 Sqn	May 1941–Aug 1941
118 Sqn	Apr 1941–Jul 1941
121 Sqn	Oct 1941–Nov 1941
122 Sqn	Sep 1941–Oct 1941
123 Sqn	Sep 1941–Apr 1942
129 Sqn	Aug 1941
130 Sqn	Jun 1941–Dec 1941
131 Sqn	Sep 1941–Jan 1942
133 Sqn	Oct 1941–Jan 1942
134 Sqn	Dec 1941–Feb 1942
145 Sqn	Feb 1941–Feb 1942
152 Sqn	Mar 1941–Jun 1942
154 Sqn	Nov 1941–Apr 1942
222 Sqn	Mar 1941–Jun 1941
234 Sqn	Mar 1941–Sep 1941
266 Sqn	Sep 1940–Oct 1940
	Mar 1941–Sep 1941
276 Sqn	Mar 1942–Apr 1942
	Feb 1943–May 1944
278 Sqn	Apr 1944–May 1944
302 Sqn	Oct 1941–Nov 1941
303 Sqn	Mar 1941–Jun 1941
306 Sqn	Oct 1941–Dec 1941
308 Sqn	May 1941–Aug 1941
	Jan 1942–Feb 1942
310 Sqn	Oct 1941–Dec 1941
312 Sqn	Oct 1941–Dec 1941
313 Sqn	Aug 1941–Nov 1941
315 Sqn	Jul 1941–Aug 1941
316 Sqn	Oct 1941–Nov 1941
331 Sqn	Nov 1941–Apr 1942

	340 Sqn	Nov 1941–Mar 1942
	350 Sqn	Nov 1941–Apr 1942
	401 Sqn	Sep 1941–Oct 1941
	403 Sqn	Jul 1941–Sep 1941
	411 Sqn	Jun 1941–Oct 1941
	412 Sqn	Jul 1941–Oct 1941
	416 Sqn	Nov 1941–Mar 1942
	417 Sqn	Dec 1941–Feb 1942
	452 Sqn	May 1941–Aug 1941
	457 Sqn	Sep 1941–Mar 1942
	485 Sqn	Jun 1941–Aug 1941
	501 Sqn	Jun 1941–Oct 1941
	504 Sqn	Oct 1941–Feb 1942
	602 Sqn	May 1941–Aug 1941
	603 Sqn	Oct 1940–May 1941
	609 Sqn	Feb 1941–Jun 1941
	610 Sqn	Feb 1941–Nov 1941
	611 Sqn	Aug 1940–Oct 1940
		Feb 1941–May 1941
		Nov 1941–Feb 1942
	616 Sqn	Feb 1941–Jul 1941
Spitfire IIB	54 Sqn	Nov 1941–Mar 1942
	65 Sqn	Sep 1941–Oct 1941
	72 Sqn	Apr 1941–Jul 1941
	118 Sqn	Jul 1941–Sep 1941
	122 Sqn	Oct 1941–Jan 1942
	124 Sqn	Oct 1941–Nov 1941
	132 Sqn	Sep 1941–Apr 1942
	145 Sqn	May 1941–Jul 1941
		Sep 1941–Feb 1942
	154 Sqn	Jan 1942–Apr 1942
	222 Sqn	Mar 1941–Aug 1941
	266 Sqn	Sep 1941
	303 Sqn	May 1941–Aug 1941
	306 Sqn	Jun 1941–Sep 1941
	312 Sqn	Nov 1941–Jan 1942
	315 Sqn	Aug 1941–Sep 1941
	504 Sqn	Dec 1941–Feb 1942
	616 Sqn	Oct 1941–Nov 1941
Spitfire IIC	277 Sqn	Feb 1943–May 1944

FAA squadrons:
Spitfire II   759 Sqn   Aug 1943–Oct 1943

Spitfire IV

Role: PR
Engine: one Rolls-Royce Merlin 46, 50, 50A, 55 or 56
Wing span: 36ft 10in
Length: 29ft 11in

Service ceiling:	36,000ft
Max speed:	365mph
Range:	1,460 miles (217 gall)
Armament:	Nil; cameras: 2 x F8, F52 or F24 + 1 x F24 oblique
First flight:	DP845, Production BP888
First sqn:	140 Sqn, Sep 1941
Last sqn:	681 Sqn, Nov 1944
Total production:	229

RAF squadrons:

Spitfire IV	69 Sqn	Jan 1942–Feb 1943
	140 Sqn	Sep 1941–Nov 1943
	234 Sqn	Oct 1942–Apr 1943
	680 Sqn	Feb 1943 – Jun 1944
	681 Sqn	Jan 1943 – Dec 1944
	682 Sqn	Feb 1943 – Dec 1943
	683 Sqn	Feb 1943 – Jul 1943
	538 Sqn	Oct 1942–Oct 1943
	540 Sqn	Oct 1942–Dec 1942
	541 Sqn	Oct 1942–Sep 1944
	542 Sqn	Oct 1942–Jul 1943
	543 Sqn	Oct 1942–Oct 1943
	544 Sqn	Oct 1942–Oct 1943

Spitfire V

Role:	Fighter, fighter-bomber
Engine:	one Rolls-Royce Merlin 45, 46, 50 or 50A; VB Merlin 45 or 46
Wing span:	36ft 10in, 32ft 7in for clipped wing variant, 32ft 2in for LF.VB
Length:	29ft 11in
Service ceiling:	VA – 36,500ft
	VB – 38,000ft (35,500ft for LF.VB and 35,000 for VB Trop)
	VC – 36,500ft
Max speed:	VA – 369mph
	VB – 375mph
	VC – 357mph
Range:	VB – 417nm (with 102 US gall and no bombs)
	VB – 985nm (with 210 US gall and no bombs)
	Other records show 480 miles with 85 gallons
Armament:	VA – 8 x 0.303-in
	VB/VC – 4 x 0.303-in, 2 x 20-mm, 500-lb bombs
	VB Trop – 4 x 0.303-in
First flight:	VA prototype X4922 (20 Feb 1941)
	VB production W3134
First sqn:	VA – 92 Sqn, Feb 1941
Last sqn:	335 Sqn, Jul 1946
Total production:	6,487

RAF squadrons:

Spitfire V	16 Sqn	Feb 1943
	521 Sqn	Jul 1942–Mar 1943

Großbritannien

Supermarine „Spitfire V"
Jagdeinsitzer

Abdeckplatte Duralumin 3,2mm
Panzer 4,25mm   Panzerglas 38mm

Panzer 6,4mm
„   4,25 „
insges. 380 ℓ

Die Bewaffnung der Baureihe „**Spitfire V**" besteht aus 2 starren ungesteuerten Kanonen, Kal. 20 mm, „Hispano Mk I" und
4 starren ungesteuerten MG., Muster „Browning Mk II", Kal. 7,7 mm. Panzerung und Anordnung der Kraftstoffbehälter
wie bei Muster „**Spitfire I**".

B. Luftwaffe recognition three-view of Spitfire V; the drawing highlights the armament, protection and fuel elements of the aircraft – all things that a fighter pilot wants to know about his enemy.

Spitfire VA	26 Sqn	Mar 1944–Nov 1944
	54 Sqn	May 1941–Aug 1941
	66 Sqn	Feb 1942–Mar 1942
	81 Sqn	Dec 1941–Apr 1942
	124 Sqn	Nov 1941–Feb 1942
	130 Sqn	Oct 1941–Dec 1941
	133 Sqn	Jan 1942–Mar 1942
	134 Sqn	Dec 1941–Feb 1942
	154 Sqn	Feb 1942–Apr 1942
	164 Sqn	Apr 1942–Sep 1942
	165 Sqn	Apr 1942–Jun 1942
	332 Sqn	Jan 1942–Apr 1942
	349 Sqn	Jun 1943–Sep 1943
	421 Sqn	Apr 1942–May 1942
	602 Sqn	Sep 1942–Oct 1942
	603 Sqn	May 1941–Dec 1941
	611 Sqn	May 1941–Jul 1941
	695 Sqn	Sep 1944 – Jul 1945
	1435 Sqn	Aug 1942–Nov 1943
Spitfire VB	19 Sqn	Oct 1941–Aug 1943
	33 Sqn	Feb 1943–June 1943
		Nov 1943–Feb 1944
	41 Sqn	Aug 1941–Mar 1943
	54 Sqn	Mar 1942–Jun 1942
	63 Sqn	May 1944–Jan 1945
	64 Sqn	Nov 1941–Jul 1942
		Mar 1943–Sep 1943
	65 Sqn	Oct 1941–Aug 1941
	66 Sqn	Mar 1942–Nov 1943
	71 Sqn	Sep 1941–Sep 1942
	72 Sqn	Jul 1941–Jul 1942
		Aug 1942–Nov 1942
	74 Sqn	May 1941–Mar 1942
		Aug 1943–Apr 1944
	80 Sqn	Jan 1944–Apr 1944
	81 Sqn	Apr 1942–Oct 1942
	87 Sqn	Apr 1943–Aug 1944
	91 Sqn	Mar 1941–May 1943
	92 Sqn	Feb 1941–Feb 1942
		Aug 1942–Sep 1943
	93 Sqn	Jun 1942–Oct 1942
	94 Sqn	Aug 1943–Sep 1943
		Aug 1944–Feb 1945
	111 Sqn	Aug 1941–Oct 1942
	118 Sqn	Sep 1941–Jan 1944
		Mar 1944–Jul 1944
	121 Sqn	Nov 1941–Sep 1942
	122 Sqn	Nov 1941–Oct 1942
		Apr 1943–Aug 1943

123 Sqn	Jan 1942–Apr 1942
124 Sqn	Nov 1941–Jul 1942
	Mar 1943–Jun 1943
126 Sqn	Mar 1942–Mar 1944
127 Sqn	Mar 1944
129 Sqn	Aug 1941–Jun 1943
130 Sqn	Oct 1941–Nov 1942
	Mar 1943–Aug 1944
131 Sqn	Dec 1941–Sep 1943
132 Sqn	Mar 1942–Oct 1943
133 Sqn	Feb 1942–Sep 1942
134 Sqn	Jan 1942–Mar 1942
	Jun 1943–Aug 1943
145 Sqn	Nov 1941–Feb 1942
	Apr 1942–Sep 1943
152 Sqn	Apr 1942–Mar 1943
154 Sqn	Feb 1942–Aug 1943
164 Sqn	Sep 1942–Feb 1943
165 Sqn	May 1942–Oct 1943
167 Sqn	Apr 1942–Jun 1943
184 Sqn	Oct 1943
186 Sqn	Feb 1944–Apr 1944
222 Sqn	Aug 1941–Jun 1943
225 Sqn	Jan 1943–Dec 1943
232 Sqn	Apr 1942–Nov 1942
	Jan 1943–Feb 1944
234 Sqn	Sep 1941–Oct 1944
237 Sqn	Dec 1943–Feb 1944
238 Sqn	Feb 1943–Apr 1943
242 Sqn	Apr 1942–Dec 1943
243 Sqn	Jun 1942–Oct 1942
	Jan 1943–Feb 1944
249 Sqn	Mar 1942–Jan 1944
253 Sqn	Feb 1944–Apr 1944
257 Sqn	Apr 1942–May 1942
266 Sqn	Sep 1941–Jun 1942
269 Sqn	Feb 1944–Mar 1946
274 Sqn	Apr 1943–Aug 1943
	Nov 1943–Feb1944
276 Sqn	May 1944–Jun 1945
277 Sqn	Apr 1944–Feb 1945
278 Sqn	May 1944–Feb 1945
287 Sqn	Nov 1943–Mar 1944
288 Sqn	Dec 1942–?*
290 Sqn	Dec 1944–Oct 1945
302 Sqn	Oct 1941–Sep 1943

* ? indicates that the information is uncertain or conflicting; this applies throughout the Annexe.

303 Sqn	Oct 1941–Jul 1943
	Nov 1943–Feb 1945
306 Sqn	Sep 1941–Oct 1942
	Mar 1943–Apr 1944
308 Sqn	Aug 1941–Nov 1943
310 Sqn	Nov 1941–Feb 1944
	Jul 1944–Sep 1944
312 Sqn	Dec 1941–Feb 1944
313 Sqn	Oct 1941–Feb 1944
	Jul 1944–Oct 1944
315 Sqn	Aug 1941–Nov 1942
316 Sqn	Oct 1941–Jul 1943
	Sep 1943–Apr 1944
317 Sqn	Oct 1941–Sep 1943
318 Sqn	Mar 1944–Mar 1945
322 Sqn	Jun 1943–Apr 1944
329 Sqn	Feb 1944–Mar 1944
331 Sqn	Apr 1942–Oct 1942
332 Sqn	Apr 1942–Nov 1942
	May 1943–Jun 1943
335 Sqn	Jan 1944–Sep 1944
340 Sqn	Mar 1942–Oct 1942
	Mar 1943–Feb 1944
341 Sqn	Jan 1943–Mar 1943
	Oct 1943–Feb 194
345 Sqn	Mar 1944–Sep 1944
349 Sqn	Sep 1943–Feb 1944
350 Sqn	Mar 1942–Dec 1943
	Mar 1944–Jul 1944
352 Sqn	Jun 1944–Aug 1944
401 Sqn	Oct 1941–Aug 1942
	Jan 1943–Oct 1943
402 Sqn	Mar 1942–May 1942
	Mar 1943–Jun 1944
403 Sqn	Aug 1941–Jan 1943
411 Sqn	Oct 1941–Oct 1943
412 Sqn	Oct 1941–Nov 1943
416 Sqn	Mar 1942–Mar 1943
	Jun 1943–Feb 1944
417 Sqn	Feb 1942–Mar 1942
	Oct 1942–Sep 1943
421 Sqn	May 1942–May 1943
441 Sqn	Feb 1944–Mar 1944
442 Sqn	Feb 1944–Mar 1944
443 Sqn	Feb 1944–Mar 1944
452 Sqn	Aug 1941–May 1942
453 Sqn	Jun 1942–Apr 1943
	Jun 1943–Jan 1944
457 Sqn	Dec 1941–May 142

	485 Sqn	Aug 1941–Jul 1943
		Nov 1943–Feb 1944
	501 Sqn	Sep 1941–Jul 1944
	504 Sqn	Jan 1942–Jan 1944
		Mar 1944–Jul 1944
	527 Sqn	Jul 1944–Apr 1946
	567 Sqn	Jun 1945–Sep 1945
	577 Sqn	Jun 1945–Aug 1945
	595 Sqn	Dec 1944–1945
	601 Sqn	Mar 1942–Apr 1942
	602 Sqn	Jul 1941–Sep 1942
		Jan 1943–Oct 1943
	602 Sqn	Jan 1944–Mar 1944
	603 Sqn	Aug 1941–Mar 1942
	609 Sqn	Jun 1941–May 1942
	610 Sqn	Jul 1941–Aug 1941
	611 Sqn	Jan 1942–Jul 1942
		Jul 1943–Jul 1944
	616 Sqn	Jul 1941–Jun 1942
	1435 Sqn	Aug 1942–Nov 1943
Spitfire VC	19 Sqn	Sep 1942–Mar 1943
	32 Sqn	Apr 1943–Nov 1943
		May 1944–Sep 1945
	33 Sqn	Dec 1943–Apr 1944
	43 Sqn	Mar 1943–Jan 1944
	54 Sqn	Nov 1942–May 1944
	64 Sqn	Sep 1943–Jul 1944
	66 Sqn	Mar 1942–Nov 1943
	72 Sqn	Jul 1942–Feb 1943
		Jun 1943–Jan 1944
	73 Sqn	Jun 1943–Sep 1944
	74 Sqn	Aug 1943–Apr 1944
	80 Sqn	Apr 1943–Apr 1944
	81 Sqn	Oct 1942–Nov 1943
Spitfire VB/VC	87 Sqn	Apr 1943–Aug 1944
	92 Sqn	Aug 1942–Sep 1943
Spitfire VC	93 Sqn	Nov 1942–Feb 1944
	94 Sqn	Dec 1942–Jan 1943
		Mar 1944–Feb 1945
	111 Sqn	Oct 1942–Jan 1944
	123 Sqn	May 1943–Sep 1943
	126 Sqn	Mar 1942–Mar 1944
	127 Sqn	Jan 1943–Oct 1943
		Mar 1944
	129 Sqn	Dec 1942–Jan 1943
	130 Sqn	Apr 1942–Mar 1943
		Jan 1944–Feb 1944
	131 Sqn	Dec 1942–Jan 1943

	Jun 1943–Sep 1943
132 Sqn	May 1943–Jun 1943
	Jan 1944–Mar 1944
136 Sqn	Oct 1943–Feb 1944
152 Sqn	Mar 1943–Nov 1943
154 Sqn	Nov 1942–Feb 1944
165 Sqn	Jul 1943–Oct 1943
167 Sqn	Oct 1942–Jun 1943
185 Sqn	May 1942–Sep 1944
208 Sqn	Dec 1943–May 1947
213 Sqn	Feb 1944–May 1944
225 Sqn	Jul 1943–Jan 1945
229 Sqn	Aug 1942–Apr 1944
232 Sqn	Jul 1943–Feb 1944
237 Sqn	Dec 1943–Mar 1944
238 Sqn	Feb 1943–Apr 1943
	Aug 1943–Mar 1944
241 Sqn	Feb 1943–Mar 1943
242 Sqn	Jul 1943–Feb 1944
243 Sqn	Jan 1943–Feb 1944
249 Sqn	May 1942–Sep 1944
253 Sqn	Mar 1943
	Aug 1943–Nov 1944
274 Sqn	Apr 1943–Aug 1943
	Nov 1943–Apr 1944
275 Sqn	Apr 1944–Feb 1945
302 Sqn	Jul 1943–Sep 1943
310 Sqn	Jul 1942–Jun 1943
	Sep 1943–Feb 1944
312 Sqn	Aug 1942–Jun 1943
	Sep 1943–Feb 1944
313 Sqn	Jul 1942–Jul 1943
	Nov 1943–Feb 1944
318 Sqn	Mar 1944–Mar 1945
322 Sqn	Feb 1944–Apr 1944
326 Sqn	Dec 1943–Oct 1944
327 Sqn	Dec 1943–Nov 1945
328 Sqn	Dec 1943–Sep 1944
329 Sqn	Feb 1944–Mar 1944
335 Sqn	Jan 1944–Jul 1946
336 Sqn	Oct 1943–Jun 1946
349 Sqn	Oct 1943–Feb 1944
350 Sqn	Dec 1942–Mar 1943
	Dec 1943
352 Sqn	Jun 1944–Jun 1945
402 Sqn	Apr 1943–Jun 1944
416 Sqn	Jun 1943
417 Sqn	Oct 1942–Sep 1943

	451 Sqn	Mar 1943–Mar 1944
	452 Sqn	Sep 1942–Jan 1945
	453 Sqn	Jun 1943–Oct 1943
	457 Sqn	Sep 1942–Jul 1944
	501 Sqn	May 1942–Oct 1942
	504 Sqn	Oct 1942–Sep 1943
	520 Sqn	Feb 1944–Apr 1944
	601 Sqn	May 1942–Jan 1944
	602 Sqn	Oct 1942–Apr 1943
	603 Sqn	Apr 1942–Aug 1942
	607 Sqn	Sep 1943–Mar 1944
	610 Sqn	Aug 1942–Oct 1942
		May 1943–Feb 1944
	615 Sqn	Sep 1943–Jul 1944
	631 Sqn	Jun 1945 – Jul 1945
	1435 Sqn	Aug 1942–Nov 1943
		May 1944–Sep 1944

FAA squadrons:

Spitfire VA		
	715 Sqn	Aug 1944–Oct 1944
	748 Sqn	Feb 1943–Jul 1944
	759 Sqn	May 1943–Oct 1944
	761 Sqn	Apr 1943–Jan 1945
	768 Sqn	Jul 1943–Feb 1944
	794 Sqn	Sep 1942–Dec 1942
	801 Sqn	Sep 1942–Oct 1942
	809 Sqn	Mar 1943–Jun 1943
	879 Sqn	Mar 1943
	884 Sqn	Sep 1942–Oct 1942
	885 Sqn	Sep 1942–Oct 1942
	887 Sqn	Dec 1942–Apr 1943

Spitfire VB		
	719 Sqn	Jun 1944–Dec 1944
	748 Sqn	Mar 1945–Feb 1946
	759 Sqn	May 1943–Oct 1944
	761 Sqn	Apr 1943–Feb 1945
	768 Sqn	Oct 1942–Feb 1945
	778 Sqn	Nov 1941
	787 Sqn	Mar 1942
	790 Sqn	Feb 1945
	794 Sqn	Nov 1943–May 1945
	798 Sqn	Apr 1945–Jun 1945
	801 Sqn	Sep 1942–Oct 1942
	808 Sqn	Dec 1942–Apr 1943
		Feb 1944–Jul 1944
	879 Sqn	Mar 1943
	880 Sqn	Aug 1942–Feb 1943
	884 Sqn	Sep 1942–Oct 1942
	885 Sqn	Sep 1942–Oct 1942
	886 Sqn	Feb 1943–Mar 1943

		Feb 1944–Mar 1944
	897 Sqn	Mar 1943–Dec 1943
		Mar 1944–Jul 194
	899 Sqn	Dec 1943–Mar 1944
Spitfire VC	775 Sqn	Jun 1943

Spitfire VI

Role: Fighter
Engine: one Rolls-Royce Merlin 47 or 49
Wing span: 40ft 2in
Length: 29ft 11in
Service ceiling: 39,000ft
Max speed: 364mph
Range: 475 miles at 150mph
Armament: four .303-in + two 20-mm
First flight: Prototype X4942 (4 Jul 1941)
Production AB176
First sqn: 616 Sqn, Apr 1942
Last sqn: 519 Sqn, Nov 1944
Total production: 100
RAF squadrons:

Spitfire VI	66 Sqn	May 1943–Jun 1943
	118 Sqn	Sep 1943–Oct 1943
	124 Sqn	Jul 1942–Jul 1943
	129 Sqn	Dec 1942–Jan 1943
	132 Sqn	Jan 1944–May 1944
	234 Sqn	Jan 1943–May 1943
	310 Sqn	Jul 1943–Sep 1943
	313 Sqn	Jun 1943–Jul 1943
	504 Sqn	Sep 1943–Jan 1944
	519 Sqn	Aug 1943–Nov 1944
	602 Sqn	Sep 1942–Nov 1942
	616 Sqn	Apr 1942–Nov 1943
	680 Sqn	Mar 1943 – Jun 1943

Spitfire VII

Role: Fighter, PR
Engine: one Rolls-Royce Merlin 61, 64 or 71 (HF.VII – Merlin 71)
Wing span: 40ft 2in
Length: 31ft
Service ceiling: 43,000ft (44,000ft for HF.VII and 37, 200ft PR.VII)
Max speed: VII – 408mph
HF.VII – 416mph
PR.VII – 372mph
Range: PR.VII 710 miles with 113-gallon tanks
Armament: VII – 4 x 0.303-in
HF.VII – 4 x 0.303-in + 2 x 20-mm

PR.VII – 8 x 0.303-in OR nil with cameras: 2 x F24 split vertical + 1 x F24 oblique.

First flight:	AB450 (Apr 1942)	
First sqn:	High Altitude Flight, Sep 1942	
Last sqn:	518 Sqn, Oct 1946	
Total production:	140	
RAF squadrons:		
Spitfire VII	118 Sqn	Mar 1944–Jul 1944
	124 Sqn	Mar 1943–Jul 1944
	131 Sqn	Mar 1944–Oct 1944
	154 Sqn	Nov 1944–Feb 1945
	313 Sqn	Jul 1944–Aug 1944
	518 Sqn	Sep 1945–Oct 1946
	519 Sqn	Nov 1944–Dec 1945
	611 Sqn	Dec 1944
	616 Sqn	Sep 1943–Aug 1944

Spitfire VIII

Role:	Fighter, fighter-bomber	
Engine:	one Rolls-Royce Merlin 61, 63 or 63A	
	(HF.VIII – Merlin 70, LF.VIII – Merlin 66)	
Wing span:	36ft 10in	
Length:	30ft 4.25in	
Service ceiling:	VIII, HF.VIII – 43,000ft	
	LF.VIII – 41,500ft	
Max speed:	VIII – 410mph	
	HF.VIII – 408mph	
	LF.VIII – 404mph	
Range:	HF.VIII – 574nm (144 US gall and no bombs)	
	HF.VIII – 1,025nm (252 US gall and no bombs)	
Armament:	4 x 0.303-in + 2 x 20-mm or 4 x 20-mm, bombs	
First flight:	Production JF299 (Apr 1942)	
First sqn:	145 Sqn, Jun 1943	
Last sqn:	253 Sqn, May 1947	
Total production:	1,658 all variants	
RAF squadrons:		
Spitfire VIII	17 Sqn	Mar 1944–Jun 1945
	20 Sqn	Sep 1945–Apr 1946
	28 Sqn	Oct 1945–Nov 1945
	32 Sqn	Dec 1943–Jul 1944
	43 Sqn	Aug 1944–Nov 1944
	54 Sqn	Apr 1944–Sep 1945
	67 Sqn	Feb 1944–Jul 1945
	73 Sqn	Jul 1944–Sep 1944
	81 Sqn	Nov 1943–Jun 1945
	87 Sqn	Dec 1943–May 1944
	92 Sqn	Jul 1943–Dec 1946
	94 Sqn	Feb 1945–Apr 1945

131 Sqn	Feb 1945–Jun 1945
132 Sqn	Jan 1945–May 1945
136 Sqn	Jan 1944–May 1946
140 Sqn	Jun 1943–Jul 1943
145 Sqn	Jun 1943–Aug 1945
152 Sqn	Dec 1943–Mar 1946
	May 1946–Jul 1946
153 Sqn	Aug 1944–Sep 1944
154 Sqn	Aug 1944–Oct 1944
155 Sqn	Jan 1944–Dec 1945
185 Sqn	Aug 1944–Sep 1944
	Mar 1945–Apr 1945
208 Sqn	Jul 1944–Sep 1944
238 Sqn	Jun 1944–Oct 1944
241 Sqn	Jan 1944–Oct 1944
253 Sqn	Nov 1944–May 1947
256 Sqn	May 1944–Aug 1944
273 Sqn	Mar 1944–Dec 1945
326 Sqn	Apr 1944
327 Sqn	Jun 1944–Nov 1945
328 Sqn	Jul 1944–Nov 1945
417 Sqn	Aug 1943–Apr 1945
451 Sqn	Aug 1944–Oct 1944
452 Sqn	Jan 1944–Oct 1945
457 Sqn	Jul 1944–Oct 1945
548 Sqn	Apr 1944–Sep 1945
549 Sqn	Apr 1944–Sep 1945
601 Sqn	Jul 1943–Jun 1944
607 Sqn	Mar 1944–Aug 1945
615 Sqn	Jun 1944–Jun 1945

Spitfire IX

Role: Fighter, fighter-bomber, PR
Engine: one Rolls-Royce Merlin 61, 63 or 63A
(HF.IX – Merlin 70, LF.IX – Merlin 66)
Wing span: 36ft 10in
Length: 30ft 6in (IXE – 31ft 0.5in, HF.IX and LF.IX – 30ft)
Service ceiling: 44,000ft (HF.IX – 45,000ft, LF.IX – 42,500ft)
Max speed: 416mph (LF.IX – 404mph)
Range: LF.IX – 377nm (with 102 US gall); 850nm (with 210 US gall)
HF.IX – 378nm (with 102 US gall); 851nm (with 210 US gall)
Armament: 4 x 0.303-in + 2 x 20-mm
(IXE and HF.IX – 2 x 0.5-in + 2 x 20-mm); 1,000-lb bombs
First flight: Prototype IX – MH874 ; Prototype HF.IX – AB505
Production LF.IX – MJ823
First sqn: 64 Sqn, Jul 1942
Last sqn: 73 Sqn, Apr 1948

Total production: 5,665 (some sources give 5,710), includes 280 conversions of Spitfire V.

RAF squadrons:

   Spitfire IX

1 Sqn	Apr 1944–May 1945	
2 Sqn	Sep 1945–Mar 1946	
6 Sqn	Feb 1946–Jan 1947	
16 Sqn	Jul 1944–Nov 1944	
19 Sqn	Aug 1943–Jan 1944	
32 Sqn	Jun 1943–Jul 1944	
	Aug 1945–May 1947	
33 Sqn	Apr 1944–Dec 1944	
43 Sqn	Aug 1943–May 1947	
56 Sqn	Apr 1944–Jun 1944	
64 Sqn	Jun 1942–Mar 1943	
	Jun 1944–Nov 1944	
65 Sqn	Aug 1943–Jan 1944	
66 Sqn	Nov 1943–Sep 1944	
	Sep 1944–Nov 1944	
72 Sqn	Jul 1942–Aug 1942	
	Feb 1943–Dec 1946	
73 Sqn	Oct 1943–Apr 1948	
74 Sqn	Oct 1943–Apr 1944	
	Apr 1944–Mar 1945	
80 Sqn	Sep 1943–Jan 1944	
	May 1944–Aug 1944	
81 Sqn	Jan 1943–Nov 1943	
87 Sqn	Jun 1943–Jun 1944	
	Aug 1944–Dec 1946	
91 Sqn	Aug 1944–Apr 1945	
92 Sqn	Apr 1943–Aug 1943	
	Jun 1946–Dec 1946	
93 Sqn	Jul 1943–Sep 1945	
94 Sqn	Feb 1944–Aug 1944	
	Feb 1945–Apr 1945	
111 Sqn	Jun 1943–May 1947	
118 Sqn	Jan 1944–Mar 1944	
	Jul 1944–Jan 1945	
122 Sqn	Sep 1942–May 1943	
	Aug 1943–Feb 1944	
	Aug 1945–Feb 1946	
123 Sqn	Jul 1943–Aug 1943	
124 Sqn	Jan 1943–May 1943	
	Jul 1944–Aug 1945	
126 Sqn	Mar 1943–Nov 1943	
	Apr 1944–Dec 1944	
127 Sqn	Mar 1944	
	May 1944–Jul 1944	
	Jul 1944–Nov 1944	

129 Sqn	Jun 1943–Apr 1944
	May 1945–Sep 1946
130 Sqn	May 1945–Oct 1946
131 Sqn	Sep 1943–Mar 1944
132 Sqn	Sep 1943–Jan 1944
	Mar 1944–Nov 1944
133 Sqn	Sep 1942
145 Sqn	Mar 1943–Sep 1943
	May 1945–Aug 1945
152 Sqn	Aug 1943–Nov 1943
153 Sqn	Aug 1944–Sep 1944
154 Sqn	Jul 1943–Oct 1944
164 Sqn	Jun 1945–Jul 1946
165 Sqn	Sep 1943–Jan 1945
	May 1945–Sep 1946
185 Sqn	Jun 1943 -Aug 1945
208 Sqn	Mar 1944–May 1947
213 Sqn	Feb 1944–Jun 1944
222 Sqn	May 1943–Aug 1943
	Aug 1943–Dec 1944
225 Sqn	Jun 1944–Dec 1946
229 Sqn	Oct 1943–Apr 1944
	May 1944–Dec 1944
232 Sqn	Jun 1943–Oct 1944
234 Sqn	Aug 1945–Feb 1946
237 Sqn	Mar 1944–Sep 1945
238 Sqn	Aug 1943–Oct 1944
241 Sqn	Dec 1943–Aug 1945
242 Sqn	Jul 1943–Nov 1944
243 Sqn	Jun 1943–Sep 1944
249 Sqn	Jun 1943–Nov 1943
	Apr 1945–May 1945
253 Sqn	Nov 1944–May 1947
256 Sqn	May 1944–Aug 1944
274 Sqn	May 1944–Aug 1944
287 Sqn	Nov 1944–Sep 1945
302 Sqn	Sep 1943–May 1944
	May 1944–Feb 1945
303 Sqn	Jun 1943–Nov 1943
	Jul 1944–Apr 1945
303 Sqn	Jul 1944–Apr 1945
306 Sqn	Oct 1942–Mar 1943
308 Sqn	Nov 1943–Mar 1945
310 Sqn	Jan 1944–Jul 1944
	Aug 1944–Feb 1946
312 Sqn	Jan 1944–Jun 1944
	Jun 1944–Feb 1946

313 Sqn	Feb 1944–Jul 1944
	Oct 1944–Feb 1946
315 Sqn	Nov 1942–Apr 1944
316 Sqn	Mar 1943–Sep 1943
317 Sqn	Sep 1943–May 1945
318 Sqn	Sep 1944–Jul 1946
322 Sqn	Aug 1944–Nov 1944
326 Sqn	Apr 1944–Nov 1945
327 Sqn	Apr 1944–Nov 1945
328 Sqn	Apr 1944–Nov 1945
329 Sqn	Feb 1944–Mar 1945
	Apr 1945–Nov 1945
331 Sqn	Oct 1942–Apr 1945
	Apr 1945–Nov 1945
332 Sqn	Nov 1942–Apr 1945
	Apr 1945–Nov 1945
336 Sqn	May 1944–Jun 1944
340 Sqn	Oct 1942–Mar 1943
	Feb 1944–Feb 1945
341 Sqn	Mar 1943–Oct 1943
	Feb 1944–Feb 1945
345 Sqn	Sep 1944–Apr 1945
349 Sqn	Feb 1944–Feb 1945
	Apr 1945–May 1945
350 Sqn	Dec 1943–Mar 1944
	Jul 1944–Aug 1944
401 Sqn	Jul 1942–Dec 1942
	Oct 1943–Apr 1945
402 Sqn	Aug 1942–Mar 1943
	Jul 1944–Aug 1944
403 Sqn	Jan 1943–Dec 1944
411 Sqn	Oct 1943–Sep 1944
	Sep 1944–May 1945
412 Sqn	Nov 1943–Sep 1944
	Sep 1944–May 1945
414 Sqn	Aug 1944–Apr 1945
416 Sqn	Mar 1943–Jun 1943
	Jan 1944–Dec 1944
417 Sqn	Mar 1944–May 1944
	Apr 1945–Jul 1945
421 Sqn	May 1943–Feb 1944
	Feb 1944–Dec 1944
441 Sqn	Mar 1944–Jan 1945
	Jan 1945–May 1945
442 Sqn	Mar 1944–Sep 1944
	Sep 1944–Mar 1945
443 Sqn	Mar 1944–Feb 1945

451 Sqn	Dec 1943–Oct 1944
	Dec 1944–Jan 1945
453 Sqn	Mar 1943–Jun 1943
453 Sqn	Jan 1944–Jul 1944
	Sep 1944–Nov 1944
485 Sqn	Jul 1943–Nov 1943
	Feb 1944–Jul 1944
	Apr 1945–Aug 1945
501 Sqn	Jun 1943–Apr 1944
504 Sqn	Jan 1944–Mar 1944
	Jul 1944–Mar 1945
521 Sqn	Sep 1943–Nov 1945
541 Sqn	Nov 1942–Dec 1942
595 Sqn	Jul 1945–1948
601 Sqn	Jun 1943–Aug 1943
	Jun 1944–Aug 1945
602 Sqn	Oct 1943–Jan 1944
	Mar 1944–Nov 1944
611 Sqn	Jul 1942–Jul 1943
	Jul 1944–Mar 1945
680 Sqn	Feb 1943–Jun 1944
684 Sqn	Dec 1945–?
1435 Sqn	Mar 1943–Apr 1945

FAA squadrons:

Spitfire IX	778 Sqn	Apr 1944–May 1945
	798 Sqn	Dec 1944–Feb 1945

Spitfire X

Role:	PR
Engine:	one Rolls-Royce Merlin 64, 71 or 77
Wing span:	36ft 10in
Service ceiling:	42,000ft
Max speed:	417mph
Range:	2,301 miles with 170-gallon ferry tank; (5½ hours endurance)
Armament:	nil
First flight:	Prototype MD191
	Production MD192
First sqn:	541 Sqn, May 1944
Last sqn:	542 Sqn, Aug 1945
Total production:	16

RAF squadrons:

Spitfire X	541 Sqn	May 1944–Apr 1945
	542 Sqn	May 1944–Aug 1945

Spitfire XI

Role:	PR
Engine:	one Rolls-Royce Merlin 61, 63, 63A or 70
Wing span:	36ft 10in
Length:	31ft 4.5in
Service ceiling:	43,000ft
Max speed:	422mph
Range:	1,650 miles (with 307 gall)
Armament:	nil; cameras: 2 x F8, F52 or F24 + 1 x F24 oblique
First flight:	BR497 (converted PR.IX)?
First sqn:	541 Sqn, Dec 1942
Last sqn:	13 Sqn, Dec 1947
Total production:	471
RAF squadrons:	

Spitfire XI		
	4 Sqn	Jan 1944–Aug 1945
	13 Sqn	Apr 1947–Dec 1947
	16 Sqn	Aug 1943–Sep 1945
	26 Sqn	Sep 1945–Apr 1946
	28 Sqn	Jul 1945–Sep 1945
	140 Sqn	Sep 1943–Apr 1944
	253 Sqn	Mar 1947–May 1947
	400 Sqn	Dec 1943–Aug 1945
	538 Sqn	Apr 1943–Oct 1943
	541 Sqn	Dec 1942–Mar 1946
	542 Sqn	Mar 1943–Aug 1945
	543 Sqn	Apr 1943–Oct 1943
	544 Sqn	Aug 1943–Oct 1943
	680 Sqn	Aug 1943–Jul 1946
	681 Sqn	Sep 1943–Apr 1946
	682 Sqn	Feb 1943–Sep 1945
	683 Sqn	Apr 1943–Sep 1943

Spitfire XII

Role:	Fighter, fighter-bomber
Engine:	one Rolls-Royce Griffon III or IV
Wing span:	32ft 7in
Length:	31ft 10in
Service ceiling:	40,000ft
Max speed:	341kts at 18,000ft
Range:	286nm (with 102 US gall)
	428nm (with 138 US gall)
Armament:	4 x 0.303-in + 2 x 20-mm
First flight:	Prototype DP845 (27 Nov 1941)
	Production EN221
First sqn:	41 Sqn, Feb 1943
Last sqn:	595 Sqn, Jul 1945
Total production:	100

RAF squadrons:

Spitfire XII	41 Sqn	Feb 1943–Sep 1944
	91 Sqn	Apr 1943–Mar 1944
	595 Sqn	Dec 1944–Jul 1945

FAA squadrons:

Spitfire XII	778 Sqn	Feb 1943–Mar 1943

Spitfire XIII

Role:	PR
Engine:	one Rolls-Royce Merlin 32
Wing span:	36ft 10in
Length:	30ft
Service ceiling:	37,500ft
Max speed:	349mph
Range:	PR.XIII – 700 miles (with 114 gall)
Armament:	cameras: 2 x F24 split vertical + 1 x F24
First flight:	Prototype L1004
Total production:	XIII – 18, PR.XIII – 26

RAF squadrons:

Spitfire XIII	4 Sqn
	400 Sqn
	541 Sqn
	542 Sqn

FAA squadrons:

Spitfire PR.XIII	718 Sqn	Jun 1944–Oct 1945
	761 Sqn	Oct 1943–Jun 1944
	808 Sqn	Mar 1944
	886 Sqn	

Spitfire XIV

Role:	Fighter-bomber, FR, PR
Engine:	one Rolls-Royce Griffon 65, 67, 85 or 87; (FR.XIVE, Griffon 88)
Wing span:	FR.XIV – 36ft 10in; (PR.XIV – 40ft 2in)
Length:	FR.XIV – 32ft 8in; (PR.XIV – 30ft)
Service ceiling:	FR.XIV – 43,000ft at 8,488lb load
Max speed:	PR.XIV – 396kts at 26,000ft
	FR.XIV – 389kts at 26,000ft
Range:	PR.XIV – 1,095nms (with 309 US gall);
	1,435nm (with 417 US gall)
	FR.XIV – 400nm (with 134 US gall); 740nm (with 243 US gall)
Armament:	FR.XIV – 4 x 0.303-in + 2 x 20-mm
First flight:	JF316
First sqn:	610 Sqn, Jan 1944
Last sqn:	2 Sqn, Jan 1951
Total production:	957

RAF squadrons:

Spitfire XIV	2 Sqn	Nov 1944–Jan 1951
	11 Sqn	Jun 1945–Feb 1948
	16 Sqn	Sep 1945–Apr 1946
	17 Sqn	Jun 1945–Feb 1948
	20 Sqn	Nov 1945–Dec 1946
	26 Sqn	Jun 1945–Apr 1946
	28 Sqn	Oct 1945–May 1947
	41 Sqn	Sep 1944–Sep 1945
	91 Sqn	Mar 1944–Aug 1944
	130 Sqn	Aug 1944–May 1945
	132 Sqn	May 1945–Apr 1946
	136 Sqn	Feb 1946–May 1946
	152 Sqn	Jan 1946–Mar 1946
	155 Sqn	Dec 1945–Aug 1946
	268 Sqn	Apr 1945–Sep 1945
	273 Sqn	Nov 1945–Jan 1946
	322 Sqn	Mar 1944–Aug 1944
	350 Sqn	Aug 1944–Oct 1946
	401 Sqn	May 1945–Jun 1945
	402 Sqn	Aug 1944–Jun 1945
	411 Sqn	Jun 1945–Mar 1946
	412 Sqn	Jun 1945–Mar 1946
	414 Sqn	Apr 1945–Aug 1945
	416 Sqn	Sep 1945–Mar 1946
	430 Sqn	Nov 1944–Aug 1945
	443 Sqn	Jan 1946–Mar 1946
	451 Sqn	Aug 1945–Jan 1946
	453 Sqn	Aug 1945–Jan 1946
	600 Sqn	Oct 1946–Nov 1947
	602 Sqn	Oct 1946–Oct 1948
	607 Sqn	Nov 1946–Mar 1949
	610 Sqn	Jan 1944–Mar 1945
		Nov 1946–Apr 1949
	611 Sqn	Nov 1946–Aug 1949
	612 Sqn	Nov 1946–Oct 1949
	613 Sqn	Dec 1946–Dec 1948
	615 Sqn	Oct 1946–Jan 1949

Spitfire XVI

Role:	Fighter, fighter-bomber
Engine:	one Rolls-Royce Merlin 266
Wing span:	36ft 10in
Length:	31ft
Service ceiling:	42,500ft
Max speed:	352kts at 22,500ft
Range:	378nm (102 US galls and no bombs)
	851nm (with 210 US gall and no bombs)

Armament: 2 x 20-mm + 4 x 0.303-in, 1,000-lb bombs
First flight: MJ556
First sqn: Nov 1944
Last sqn: 288 Sqn, May 1953
Total production: 1,054
RAF squadrons:

Spitfire XVI	5 Sqn	Feb 1949–Aug 1951
	16 Sqn	Sep 1945–Apr 1946
	17 Sqn	Feb 1949–Mar 1951
	19 Sqn	Mar 1946–Nov 1946
	20 Sqn	Feb 1949–Sep 1951
	31 Sqn	Mar 1949–May 1954
	34 Sqn	Feb 1949–Mar 1951
	63 Sqn	Sep 1946–May 1948
	65 Sqn	Feb 1946–Oct 1946
	66 Sqn	Nov 1944–Apr 1945
		Sep 1946–Mar 1947
	74 Sqn	Mar 1945–May 1945
	126 Sqn	Feb 1946–Mar 1946
	127 Sqn	Nov 1944–Apr 1945
	164 Sqn	Jul 1946–Aug 1946
	229 Sqn	Dec 1944–Jan 1945
	287 Sqn	Aug 1945–Jun 1946
	288 Sqn	Mar 1953–May 1953
	302 Sqn	Jan 1945–Dec 1946
	303 Sqn	Feb 1945–Apr 1945
	308 Sqn	Mar 1945–Dec 1946
	317 Sqn	May 1945–Dec 1946
	322 Sqn	Nov 1944–Oct 1945
	329 Sqn	Feb 1945–Apr 1945
	340 Sqn	Feb 1945–Nov 1945
	341 Sqn	Feb 1945–Nov 1945
	345 Sqn	Apr 1945–Nov 1945
	349 Sqn	May 1945–Oct 1946
	350 Sqn	Aug 1946–Oct 1946
	401 Sqn	Jun 1945
	402 Sqn	Jun 1945–Jul 1945
	403 Sqn	Dec 1944–Jul 1945
	411 Sqn	May 1945
	412 Sqn	May 1945–Jun 1945
	416 Sqn	Dec 1944–Sep 1945
	421 Sqn	Dec 1944–Jul 1945
	443 Sqn	Jan 1945–Jan 1946
	451 Sqn	Jan 1945–Jun 1945
	453 Sqn	Nov 1944–Jun 1945
	501 Sqn	Oct 1946–May 1949
	567 Sqn	Jul 1945–Jun 1946
	577 Sqn	Jun 1945–Jun 1946

587 Sqn	Jul 1945–Jun 1946
595 Sqn	Sep 1945–Feb 1949
601 Sqn	Oct 1946–Jan 1950
602 Sqn	Nov 1944–May 1945
603 Sqn	Jan 1945–Aug 1945
	Oct 1946–Jun 1948
604 Sqn	Oct 1946–May 1950
609 Sqn	Apr 1948–Feb 1951
612 Sqn	Nov 1948–Jun 1951
614 Sqn	Jan 1947–Sep 1948
631 Sqn	Jun 1945–Feb 1949
667 Sqn	Jul 1945–Dec 1945
691 Sqn	Aug 1945–Feb 1949
695 Sqn	Jul 1945–Feb 1949

FAA squadrons:
    Spitfire XVI   761 Sqn   Jul 1945

Spitfire XVIII, 18

Role:	Fighter, FR
Engine:	one Rolls-Royce Griffon 65, 67
Wing span:	36ft 10in
Max speed:	437mph
Armament:	4 x 20-mm, up to 3 x 500-lb bombs, RPs
First flight:	NH872, Jun 1945
First sqn:	208 Sqn, Aug 1946
Last sqn:	208 Sqn, Apr 1951
Total production:	300
RAF squadrons:	

    Spitfire FR.18

28 Sqn	Apr 1947–Feb 1951
32 Sqn	Apr 1947–Mar 1949
60 Sqn	Jan 1947–Jan 1951
81 Sqn	Jul 1948–Mar 1950
	Nov 1950–Jan 1951
208 Sqn	Aug 1946–Apr 1951

Spitfire XIX, 19

Role:	PR (data below for PR.XIX)
Engine:	one Rolls-Royce Griffon 65
Wing span:	36ft 10in
Length:	30ft
Service ceiling:	44,500ft
Max speed:	397kts at 26,000ft
Range:	930nm (with 260 US gall); 1,270nm (with 369 US gall)
Armament:	nil
First flight:	SW777
First sqn:	542 Sqn, May 1944
Last sqn:	81 Sqn, Jun 1954

Total production: 225
RAF squadrons:

Spitfire PR.XIX	2 Sqn	Jan 1946–Jun 1951
	16 Sqn	Mar 1945–Apr 1946
	31 Sqn	Jul 1948–Apr 1949
	34 Sqn	Aug 1946–Jul 1947
	81 Sqn	Sep 1946–Jan 1950
		Jan 1951–Jun 1954
	82 Sqn	Oct 1946–Oct 1947
	268 Sqn	Sep 1945
	541 Sqn	Jun 1944–Oct 1946
		Nov 1947–May 1951
	542 Sqn	May 1944–Aug 1945
	681 Sqn	Jul 1945–Aug 1946
	682 Sqn	Jun 1944–Sep 1945
	683 Sqn	Sep 1944–Sep 1945

Spitfire XXI, F.21

Role: Fighter
Engine: one Griffon 61
Wing span: 37ft 1in
Length: 32ft 6in
Service ceiling: 44,000ft
Max speed: 395kts at 26,000ft
Range: 712nm (with 231 US gall and no bombs)
1,478nm (with 435 US gall and no bombs)
Armament: 4 x 20-mm, 500-lb bomb
First flight: DP851, Aug 1942 (as Spitfire 20 with Griffon II);
PP139, 24 Jul 1943; LA187 (first production), 15 Mar 1944
First sqn: 91 Sqn, Jan 1945
Last sqn: 602 Sqn, Jan 1951
Total production: 120
RAF squadrons:

Spitfire F.21	1 Sqn	May 1945–Oct 1946
	41 Sqn	Apr 1946–Aug 1947
	91 Sqn	Jan 1945–Oct 1946
	122 Sqn	Feb 1946–Apr 1946
	595 Sqn	Jun 1948–Feb 1949
	600 Sqn	Apr 1947–Nov 1950
	602 Sqn	Aug 1947–Jan 1951
	615 Sqn	Jan 1947–Jun 1950

Spitfire 22

Role:	Fighter
Engine:	one Rolls-Royce Griffon 61
Wing span:	37ft 1in
Length:	32ft 6in
Service ceiling:	43,500ft
Max speed:	393kts at 26,000ft
Range:	425nm (with 144 US gall and no bombs)
	1,390nm (with 422 US gall and no bombs)
Armament:	4 x 20-mm, 1,000-lb bombs
First flight:	SX549, TM383
First production:	PK312 (delivered Mar 1945)
First sqn:	73 Sqn, Jul 1947
Last sqn:	611 Sqn, Nov 1951
Total production:	278
RAF squadrons:	

Spitfire F.22	73 Sqn	Jul 1947–Oct 1948
	500 Sqn	May 1948–Oct 1948
	502 Sqn	Sep 1948–Mar 1951
	504 Sqn	May 1948–Mar 1950
	600 Sqn	Sep 1948–Mar 1950
	602 Sqn	Oct 1948–May 1951
	603 Sqn	Feb 1948–Jul 1951
	607 Sqn	Jan 1949–Jun 1951
	608 Sqn	May 1948–Jan 1951
	610 Sqn	Mar 1949–Aug 1951
	611 Sqn	Feb 1949–Nov 1951
	613 Sqn	Oct 1948–Mar 1951
	614 Sqn	Jul 1948–Jul 1950
	615 Sqn	Jul 1948–Oct 1950

Spitfire 24

Role:	Fighter, fighter-bomber
Engine:	one Rolls-Royce Griffon 61 or 64
Wing span:	36ft 10in (some sources say same as Spitfire 22)
Length:	32ft 6in
Service ceiling:	43,000ft
Max speed:	454mph at 26,000ft
Armament:	4 x 20-mm, RPs or 3 x 500-lb bombs
First flight:	VN302
First sqn:	80 Sqn, Jan 1948
Last sqn:	80 Sqn, Dec 1951
Total production:	81 (including 27 conversions of F.22)
RAF squadrons:	

Spitfire F.24	80 Sqn	Jan 1948–Dec 1951

Seafire Variants – Data

Seafire IB

Role:	Fighter
Engine:	one Rolls-Royce Merlin 45
Wing span:	36ft 10in
Length:	30ft 2½in
Useful ceiling:	28,000ft
Max speed:	355mph at 13,000ft
Range:	radius of action – 125 miles (with 250-gallon drop tank)
Armament:	2 x 20-mm, 4 x 0.303-in
First flight:	AB205
First sqn:	807 Sqn, Sep1942
Last sqn:	708 Sqn, Feb 1946
Total production:	166; conversions of Spitfire VB

FAA squadrons:

Seafire IB		
	700 Sqn	Feb 1945–Sep 1945
	708 Sqn	May 1945–Feb 1946
	715 Sqn	Aug 1944–?1945
	719 Sqn	?1944–Dec 1944
	731 Sqn	May 1944–Feb 1945
	748 Sqn	Jun 1943–Feb 1946
	759 Sqn	Aug 1943–Jan 1945
	761 Sqn	Apr 1943–Mar 1945
	768 Sqn	Jul 1943–Feb 1945
	775 Sqn	Jul 1943–Mar 1944
	778 Sqn	Jan 1942–Feb 1945
	779 Sqn	May 1943–Oct 1944
	781 Sqn	Jul 1943
	787 Sqn	Jul 1942–Aug 1944
	790 Sqn	Mar 1945
	798 Sqn	May 1945–Jul 1945
	801 Sqn	Sep 1942–Jun 1944
	807 Sqn	Jun 1942–Sep 1942
	809 Sqn	Apr 1943–Aug 1943
	816 Sqn	Aug 1943–Dec 1943
	842 Sqn	Jul 1943–Mar 1944
	879 Sqn	Mar 1943–Jun 1943
	885 Sqn	Oct 1942–Aug 1943
	894 Sqn	Feb 1943–Apr 1943
	897 Sqn	Mar 1943–Jul 1943

Seafire IIC

Role:	Fighter
Engine:	one Rolls-Royce Merlin 32, 45, 46, 50A
Wing span:	36ft 10in (32ft 7in clipped-wing)
Length:	30ft 2½in
Useful ceiling:	29,500ft

Max speed:	398mph at 21,000ft with Merlin 46	
	335mph at 6,000ft with Merlin 32	
Range:	radius of action – 125 miles (with 45-gall drop tank)	
Armament:	2 x 20-mm, 4 x 0.303-in	
First flight:	AD371 (Feb 1942); MA970 (first production)	
First sqn:	807 Sqn, Jun 1942	
Last sqn:	768 Sqn, Apr 1946	
Total production:	372	
FAA squadrons:		
Seafire IIc	700 Sqn	Nov 1945–Dec 1945
	708 Sqn	May 1945–?
	718 Sqn	Jul 1945–Oct 1945
	719 Sqn	?1944–Dec 1944
	728 Sqn	Jan 1945–Jan 1946
	731 Sqn	?1945–Nov 1945
	748 Sqn	Mar 1943–Feb 1946
	757 Sqn	Jun 1944
	759 Sqn	Feb 1944–Feb 1945
	761 Sqn	Jul 1944–Aug 1945
	768 Sqn	Jan 1944–Apr 1946
	770 Sqn	Jul 1945–Oct 1945
	775 Sqn	Aug 1944–Nov 1945
	776 Sqn	May 1945–Oct 1945
	778 Sqn	Jul 1942–Apr 1944
	787 Sqn	Nov 1942–Mar 1945
	790 Sqn	Mar 1945
	794 Sqn	Jan 1945–Feb 1945
	798 Sqn	Jun 1945
	799 Sqn	Aug 1945–?
	801 Sqn	Oct 1942–May 1943
		Apr 1944–Jun 1944
	807 Sqn	Jun 1942–Oct 1944
	808 Sqn	Dec 1942–May 1944
	809 Sqn	Mar 1943–Feb 1945
	816 Sqn	Jun 1943–Aug 1943
	833 Sqn	Jun 1943–Sep 1943
	834 Sqn	Jun 1943–Aug 1944
	842 Sqn	Jul 1943
	879 Sqn	Jun 1943–Nov 1945
	880 Sqn	Sep 1942–Mar 1944
	884 Sqn	Sep 1942–Jul 1943
	885 Sqn	Sep 1942–Nov 1943
		Aug 1944–Nov 1944
	886 Sqn	Mar 1943–Feb 1944
	887 Sqn	Jan 1943–Dec 1943
	889 Sqn	Apr 1944–Jul 1944
	894 Sqn	Mar 1943–Nov 1943
	895 Sqn	Mar 1943–Jun 1943

897 Sqn	Aug 1942–Sep 1942
	Aug 1943–May 1944
899 Sqn	Dec 1942–Jan 1944
1700 Sqn	Dec 1945–Jan 1946

Seafire III

Role: Fighter
Engine: one Rolls-Royce Merlin 55 series
Wing span: 36ft 10in (32ft 7in clipped wing)
Length: 30ft 2½in
Useful ceiling: 31,300ft
Max speed: 358mph at 6,000ft (LIII)
Range: radius of action 200 miles (with 90-gallon drop tank)
Armament: 2 x 20-mm, 4 x 0.303-in
First flight: MA970 (Nov 1942)
First sqn: 778 Sqn, Jun 1943
Last sqn: 1832 Sqn, Jan 1950
Total production: 355
FAA squadrons:

Seafire III	700 Sqn	Feb 1945–Feb 1946
	706 Sqn	Mar 1945–Nov 1945
	708 Sqn	May 1945–Aug 1945
	709 Sqn	Aug 1944–Dec 1944
	718 Sqn	Jun 1944–Oct 1945
		Aug 1946–Mar 1947
	721 Sqn	?1946–?1947
	728 Sqn	Jul 1945–Jul 1946
	733 Sqn	Oct 1946–Dec 1946
	736 Sqn	Mar 1945–May 1945
	740 Sqn	Jul 1945–Aug 1945
	741 Sqn	Feb 1947–Nov 1947
	744 Sqn	May 1946
	748 Sqn	Nov 1945–Feb 1946
	757 Sqn	May 1945–Jan 1946
	759 Sqn	Dec 1945–Feb 1946
	760 Sqn	Oct 1945–Jan 1946
	761 Sqn	Apr 1944–Jan 1946
	766 Sqn	Aug 1946–Sep 1947
	767 Sqn	Mar 1946–Jun 1947
	768 Sqn	Jun 1944–Apr 1946
	771 Sqn	Mar 1946–Jan 1947
	772 Sqn	Mar 1946–Aug 1946
	777 Sqn	Oct 1945–Dec 1945
	778 Sqn	Jun 1943–Mar 1947
	781 Sqn	Aug 1944
	782 Sqn	May 1947–Jan 1948
	787 Sqn	Dec 1943–Jun 1946
	790 Sqn	Nov 1946–Feb 1947

794 Sqn	Jun 1946–Feb 1947
799 Sqn	Aug 1945–Jul 1947
801 Sqn	May 1944–Nov 1945
802 Sqn	May 1945–Aug 1945
803 Sqn	Jun 1945–Dec 1945
805 Sqn	Jul 1945–Aug 1945
806 Sqn	Aug 1945–Sep 1945
807 Sqn	Jun 1944–Dec 1945
	Sep 1946–Oct 1946
808 Sqn	Jun 1944–Oct 1944
809 Sqn	Jul 1944–Dec 1945
879 Sqn	Mar 1944–Nov 1945
880 Sqn	Mar 1944–Sep 1945
883 Sqn	Sep 1945–Dec 1945
885 Sqn	Feb 1944–Nov 1944
886 Sqn	Mar 1944–Jul 1944
887 Sqn	Dec 1943–Mar 1946
889 Sqn	Apr 1944–Jul 1944
894 Sqn	Nov 1944–Mar 1946
899 Sqn	Feb 1944–Sep 1945
1832 Sqn	Jul 1947–Jan 1950

Seafire XV/F.15

Role:	Fighter
Engine:	one Rolls-Royce Griffon VI
Wing span:	36ft 10in
Length:	31ft 10in
Useful ceiling:	32,000ft
Max speed:	383mph at 13,500ft
Range:	radius of action 150 miles
Armament:	2 x 20-mm + 4 x 0.303-in, 500-lb bombs, RPs
First flight:	NS847 (Dec 1943?)
First sqn:	802 Sqn, Aug 1954
Last sqn:	766 Sqn, Nov 1951
Total production:	390
FAA squadrons:	

Seafire XV		
	700 Sqn	Feb 1945–Mar 1948
	701 Sqn	Mar 1946–Jul 1946
	706 Sqn	1946
	709 Sqn	Nov 1945–Jan 1946
	721 Sqn	Nov 1946–Nov 1947
	728 Sqn	Sep 1946–Sep 1948
	733 Sqn	Jan 1947–Dec 1947
	736 Sqn	Jul 1945–Sep 1945
	737 Sqn	Apr 1949–Jan 1950
	751 Sqn	Jul 1947–Sep 1947
	759 Sqn	Jan 1946–Feb 1946
	761 Sqn	Jul 1945–Jan 1946

766 Sqn   Jun 1947–Nov 1951
767 Sqn   May 1946–Feb 1952
768 Sqn   Dec 1948–Mar 1949
771 Sqn   Nov 1946–Jan 1951
773 Sqn   Jan 1950–Mar 1950
777 Sqn   May 1945–Jul 1945
778 Sqn   Mar 1944–Aug 1946
780 Sqn   Apr 1946–Nov 1946
781 Sqn   Dec 1949–Feb 1950
787 Sqn   Sep 1944–Jun 1946
790 Sqn   May 1947–Jan 1949
791 Sqn   Dec 1946–Jun 1947
799 Sqn   Oct 1945–Nov 1951
800 Sqn   Aug 1946–Feb 1947
801 Sqn   Sep 1945–Feb 1946
802 Sqn   Aug 1945–Apr 1948
803 Sqn   Aug 1945–Jul 1947
804 Sqn   Oct 1946–Mar 1948
805 Sqn   Aug 1945–Aug 1946
806 Sqn   Oct 1945–Oct 1947
809 Sqn   Nov 1945–Dec 1945
883 Sqn   Nov 1945–Feb 1946
               May 1947–Sep 1948
1831 Sqn   Jun 1947–Aug 1951
1832 Sqn   Apr 1949–Aug 1951
1833 Sqn   Jul 1949–Aug 1951

Seafire XVII/F.17

Role: Fighter
Engine: one Rolls-Royce Griffon VI
Wing span: 36ft 10in
Length: 32ft 10in
Useful ceiling: 31,000ft
Max speed: 387mph at 13,500ft
Range: radius of action 220 miles
Armament: 2 x 20-mm + 4 x 0.303-in, 1,000-lb bombs, RPs
First flight: NS493
First sqn: 807 Sqn, Sep 1946
Last sqn: 764 Sqn, Nov 1954
FAA squadrons:

Seafire XVII/F.17 701 Sqn   Sep 1945–Nov 1945
                   703 Sqn   1947–Aug 1949
                   709 Sqn   Dec 1945–Jan 1946
                   715 Sqn   Aug 1944–Dec 1945
                   727 Sqn   Dec 1946–Feb 1947
                   728 Sqn   May 1948–Mar 1952
                   736 Sqn   Jul 1945–Sep 1945
                   737 Sqn   Apr 1949–May 1950

738 Sqn	May 1950–Sep 1951
746 Sqn	Dec 1945
759 Sqn	Aug 1951–Jul 1954
761 Sqn	Nov 1945–Jan 1946
764 Sqn	?1945–Aug 1945
	May 1953–Nov 1954
766 Sqn	Jul 1947–Nov 1952
777 Sqn	Dec 1945–Mar 1946
778 Sqn	Jul 1945–Jul 1948
781 Sqn	May 1949–Oct 1949
782 Sqn	Dec 1947–Oct 1948
787 Sqn	Apr 1945–Jan 1948
799 Sqn	Dec 1947–Jun 1952
800 Sqn	Jan 1947–Apr 1949
805 Sqn	Apr 1947–Jun 1948
807 Sqn	Sep 1946–Oct 1946
809 Sqn	Nov 1945–Jan 1946
879 Sqn	Nov 1945–Jan 1946
1830 Sqn	Aug 1947–May 1948
1831 Sqn	Jun 1947–Aug 1951
1832 Sqn	Jun 1948–May 1953
1833 Sqn	Aug 1947–Jul 1952

Seafire 45

Role:	Fighter, FR
Engine:	one Rolls-Royce Griffon 61
Wing span:	36ft 11in
Length:	32ft 8in
Service ceiling:	39,000ft
Max speed:	442mph at 20,000ft
Range:	
Armament:	4 x 20-mm
First flight:	TM379
First sqn:	778 Sqn, Jun 1945
Last sqn:	771 Sqn, Sep 1950
Total production:	
FAA squadrons:	

Seafire F.45	700 Sqn	mid-1945?
	703 Sqn	Dec 1945–?1946
	709 Sqn	Dec 1945–Jan 1946
	771 Sqn	Dec 1947–Sep 1950
	777 Sqn	May 1945–Dec 1945
	778 Sqn	Jun 1945–Oct 1947
	780 Sqn	Nov 1946–Dec 1946
	787 Sqn	Mar 1946–Feb 1948

Seafire 46

Role:	Fighter
Engine:	one Rolls-Royce Griffon 85
Wing span:	36ft 11in
Length:	34ft 4in
First flight:	TM383 (Sep 1944)
First sqn:	777 Sqn, May 1945
Last sqn:	738 Sqn, Aug 1950
Total production:	26

FAA squadrons:

Seafire F.46	736 Sqn	Jan 1946–Dec 1946
	738 Sqn	May 1950–Aug 1950
	767 Sqn	Mar 1950–Jul 1950
	771 Sqn	May 1947–Dec 1947
	777 Sqn	May 1945–Jun 1945
	778 Sqn	Jul 1946–Jan 1948
	781 Sqn	Mar 1947–Sep 1947
	1832 Sqn	Aug 1947–Jan 1950

Seafire 47

Role:	Fighter, FR
Engine:	one Rolls-Royce 87 or 88
Wing span:	36ft 11in
Length:	34ft 4in
Useful ceiling:	39,500ft
Max speed:	434mph at 24,500ft
Range:	radius of action 250 miles
Armament:	4 x 30-mm, 1,500-lb bombs, RPs
First flight:	PS944 (Apr 1946)
First sqn:	804 Sqn, Jan 1948
Last sqn:	1833 Sqn, May 1954
Total production:	90

FAA squadrons:

Seafire F.47	759 Sqn	Sep 1952–Nov 1953
	777 Sqn	May 1945–Jun 1945
	778 Sqn	Dec 1946–Mar 1947
	787 Sqn	May 1947–Sep 1949
	800 Sqn	Apr 1949–Nov 1950
	804 Sqn	Jan 1948–Aug 1949
	1833 Sqn	Jun 1952–May 1954

~ ANNEXE B ~

RAF Orders of Battle
– Spitfire Squadrons

The following Orders of Battle (ORBATS) show the growth of the Spitfire in terms of numbers of operational squadrons from August 1940 to July 1945; this last date was the high point of Spitfire strength and, whilst some units had already converted to new types, including the first jets (Meteors), it was the Spitfire that remained the most significant single-seat tactical aircraft in the RAF, although other types, such as the Typhoon with its specific ground-attack role cannot be discounted in the RAF's overall air strength.

With the exception of the Battle of Britain table showing August and September 1940, where the entire Fighter Command ORBAT is shown, *all other listings are purely Spitfire units*. There were a number of support units, and even some squadrons, that had Spitfires in strength but if the aircraft was not one of the primary types being used then the unit has been omitted.

Fighter Command – ORBAT– Battle of Britain

	1 Aug 1940		1 Sep 1940	
Airfield	*Squadron*	*Aircraft*	*Squadron*	*Aircraft*
No 10 Group				
Boscombe Down			56	Hurricane
Exeter	87, 213	Hurricane	87, 213	Hurricane
Middle Wallop	238	Hurricane		
Middle Wallop	604	Blenheim	604	Blenheim
Middle Wallop	609	Spitfire	234, 609	Spitfire
Pembrey	92	Spitfire	92	Spitfire
St Eval	234	Spitfire	236	Blenheim
St Eval			238	Hurricane
Warmwell	152	Spitfire	152	Spitfire

Airfield	1 Aug 1940		1 Sep 1940	
	Squadron	Aircraft	Squadron	Aircraft
No 11 Group				
Biggin Hill	32	Hurricane	79	Hurricane
Biggin Hill	610	Spitfire		
Gravesend	501	Hurricane	501	Hurricane
Croydon	111	Hurricane	72	Spitfire
Debden	17	Hurricane	111, 257, 601	Hurricane
Hornchurch	41, 65, 74	Spitfire	54, 222, 603	Spitfire
Hornchurch			600	Blenheim
Kenley	615	Hurricane	253	Hurricane
Kenley	64	Spitfire	616	Spitfire
Manston	600	Blenheim		
Martlesham Heath	25	Blenheim		
Martlesham Heath	85	Hurricane		
Northolt			1, 1 (Can)	Hurricane
North Weald	56, 151	Hurricane	249	Hurricane
North Weald			25	Blenheim
Stapleford			46	Hurricane
Tangmere	1, 601	Hurricane	17, 43, 607	Hurricane
Tangmere	266	Spitfire		
Westhampnett	145	Hurricane		
No 12 Group				
Bircham Newton			229	Hurricane
Collyweston	23	Blenheim		
Coltishall	66	Spitfire	66	Spitfire
Coltishall	242	Hurricane	242	Hurricane
Digby	29	Blenheim		
Digby	46	Hurricane	151	Hurricane
Digby	611	Spitfire	611	Spitfire
Duxford			310	Hurricane
Fowlmere	19	Spitfire	19	Spitfire
Kirton-in-Lindsey		Spitfire		
Kirton-in-Lindsey	264	Defiant	264	Defiant
Wellingore			29	Blenheim
Wittering	229	Hurricane	74, 266	Spitfire

Airfield	1 Aug 1940		1 Sep 1940	
	Squadron	Aircraft	Squadron	Aircraft
No 13 Group				
Acklington	72	Spitfire	32	Hurricane
Acklington	79	Hurricane	610	Spitfire
Aldergrove	245	Hurricane		
Castletown	504	Hurricane	504	Hurricane
Castletown	808	Fulmar		
Catterick	54	Spitfire	41	Spitfire
Church Fenton	73, 249	Hurricane	73	Hurricane
Drem	602	Spitfire		
Drem	605	Hurricane	605	Hurricane
Grangemouth	263	Hurricane	263	Hurricane
Leconfield	616	Spitfire	64	Spitfire
Leconfield			302	Hurricane
Leeming	219	Blenheim	219	Blenheim
Montrose			145	Hurricane
Prestwick	141	Defiant		
Sumburgh	232	Hurricane		
Turnhouse	603	Spitfire		
Usworth	607	Hurricane		
Wick	3	Hurricane	3	Hurricane
Wick	804	Gladiator		

RAF ORBAT May 1941

Fighter Command

No 10 Group:

Exeter	66 Sqn
Portreath	152 Sqn
Warmwell	118 Sqn, 234 Sqn

No 11 Group:

Biggin Hill	74 Sqn, 92 Sqn
Hawkinge	91 Sqn
Hornchurch	64 Sqn, 611 Sqn
Northolt	303 Sqn
Southend	4 Sqn
Tangmere	145 Sqn

No 12 Group:

Coltishall	222 Sqn
Driffield	485 Sqn
Duxford	19 Sqn
Kirton-in-Lindsey	65 Sqn, 452 Sqn
Wittering	266 Sqn

No 13 Group:

Acklington	72 Sqn
Catterick	41 Sqn
Prestwick	602 Sqn
Turnhouse	603 Sqn

No 81 Group:

Grangemouth	58 OTU
Hawarden	57 OTU
Heston	53 OTU

Coastal Command

Wick, St Eval	PRU

RAF ORBAT April 1942

Fighter Command

No 9 Group:

Andreas	452 Sqn
Woodvale	315 Sqn

No 10 Group:

Angle	312 Sqn
Church Stanton	306 Sqn
Exeter	308 Sqn
Fairwood Common	402 Sqn
Harrowbeer	302 Sqn
Ibsley	118 Sqn, 234 Sqn, 501 Sqn
Perranporth	310 Sqn, 130 Sqn
Portreath	66 Sqn

No 11 Group:

Biggin Hill	72 Sqn, 124 Sqn
Debden	65 Sqn, 111 Sqn, 350 Sqn
Gravesend	401 Sqn
Hawkinge	91 Sqn
Hornchurch	122 Sqn, 313 Sqn
Kenley	485 Sqn, 602 Sqn
Martlesham	71 Sqn
Merston	340 Sqn
Northolt	303 Sqn, 316 Sqn, 317 Sqn
North Weald	121 Sqn, 222 Sqn, 403 Sqn
Redhill	457 Sqn
Southend	64 Sqn
Westhampnett	41 Sqn, 129 Sqn

No 12 Group:

Coltishall	154 Sqn (one Flight)
Fowlmere	154 Sqn (one Flight)
Digby	411 Sqn, 412 Sqn, 609 Sqn
Hutton Cranswick	19 Sqn
Kingscliffe	616 Sqn
Kirton-in-Lindsey	133 Sqn
Ludham	610 Sqn

No 13 Group:

Ayr	134 Sqn
Catterick	332 Sqn

Drem	611 Sqn	Hawarden	57 OTU
Turnhouse	81 Sqn	Llandow	53 OTU
Castletown	54 Sqn, 123 Sqn	Rednal	61 OTU
Dyce, Montrose	416 Sqn		
Peterhead	603 Sqn	*No 82 Group:*	
Skeabrae	132 Sqn, 331 Sqn	Eglinton	152 Sqn
Tain	417 Sqn	Kirkistown	504 Sqn
		Long Kesh	74 Sqn
No 81 Group:			
Grangemouth	59 OTU		

RAF ORBAT April 1943

Fighter Command		Redhill	416 Sqn
		Southend	453 Sqn
No 9 Group:		Tangmere	129 Sqn
High Ercall	41 Sqn	Merston	485 Sqn
		Westhampnett	165 Sqn, 610 Sqn
No 10 Group:			
Church Stanton	312 Sqn, 313 Sqn	*No 12 Group:*	
Bolt Head	310 Sqn	Coltishall	118 Sqn
Fairwood Common	412 Sqn	Digby	411 Sqn
Harrowbeer	276 Sqn (plus other types such as Walrus)	Hutton Cranswick	306 Sqn
		Kirton-in-Lindsey	302 Sqn, 317 Sqn
Ibsley	129 Sqn, 504 Sqn, 616 Sqn	Ludham	167 Sqn
		Ayr	222 Sqn
Perranporth	19 Sqn, 130 Sqn, 602 Sqn	Catterick	401 Sqn
		Drem	65 Sqn
		Turnhouse	341 Sqn
No 11 Group:			
Biggin Hill	340 Sqn, 611 Sqn	*No 14 Group:*	
Gravesend	277 Sqn	Castletown	131 Sqn
Hawkinge	91 Sqn	Skeabrae	66 Sqn, 234 Sqn
Heston	303 Sqn		
Hornchurch	64 Sqn, 122 Sqn	*No 81 Group:*	
Fairlop	350 Sqn	Aston Down	52 OTU
Kenley	402 Sqn, 403 Sqn, 421 Sqn	Eshott	57 OTU
		Grangemouth	58 OTU
Martlesham	132 Sqn	Llandow	53 OTU
Northolt	308 Sqn, 315 Sqn, 316 Sqn	Millfield	59 OTU (plus other types)
North Weald	124 Sqn, 331 Sqn, 332 Sqn	*N. Ireland:*	
		Kirkistown	501 Sqn

Coastal Command

No 16 Group:

Benson	541 Sqn, 542 Sqn, 543 Sqn
Benson	544 Sqn (plus other types)
Bircham Newton	521 Sqn (plus other types)

Army Co-operation Command

No 35 Wing:

Odiham	140 Sqn (plus other types)

Mediterranean Air Command

North Africa:

Constantine	72 Sqn
Maison Blanche	682 Sqn

Souk El Khemis	92 Sqn, 111 Sqn, 152 Sqn, 243 Sqn
Tingley	81 Sqn, 154 Sqn, 232 Sqn, 242 Sqn
Hazbub	92 Sqn, 145 Sqn, 601 Sqn

AHQ Malta:

Hal Far	185 Sqn
Krendi	229 Sqn, 249 Sqn
Luqa	126 Sqn, 683 Sqn, 1435 Sqn

Middle East Command

Matariya	680 Sqn

India Command

Dum Dum	681 Sqn (plus other types)

RAF ORBAT July 1944

Allied Expeditionary Air Force (AEAF)

No 83 Group:

B11/Longues	132 Sqn, 441 Sqn, 453 Sqn, 602 Sqn
B8/Sommervieu	400 Sqn
B2/Bazenville	403 Sqn, 416 Sqn, 421 Sqn, 245 Sqn
B4/Beny-sur-Mer	401 Sqn, 411 Sqn, 412 Sqn, 442 Sqn
Odiham	414 Sqn

No 84 Group:

Odiham	4 Sqn
Tangmere	66 Sqn, 331 Sqn, 332 Sqn
Funtington	222 Sqn, 349 Sqn, 485 Sqn
Ford	302 Sqn, 308 Sqn, 317 Sqn
Lympne	310 Sqn, 312 Sqn, 313 Sqn
Selsey	329 Sqn, 340 Sqn, 341 Sqn

No 85 Group:

Deanland	91 Sqn
Bradwell Bay	124 Sqn
West Malling	322 Sqn

No 34 Wing:

Northolt	16 Sqn

Air Defence of Great Britain

No 9 Group:

Eshott	57 OTU
Grangemouth	2 TEU
Kirton-in-Lindsey	53 OTU
Millfield	FLS (plus other types)
Rednal	61 OTU

No 10 Group:

Culmhead	126 Sqn, 131 Sqn, 616 Sqn
Friston	41 Sqn, 610 Sqn
Lympne	1 Sqn, 165 Sqn

No 11 Group:

Bradwell Bay	278 Sqn (plus other types)
Coltishall	229 Sqn
Friston	350 Sqn, 501 Sqn
Harrowbeer	64 Sqn, 611 Sqn
Lee-on-Solent	26 Sqn, 63 Sqn
Lympne	33 Sqn, 74 Sqn, 127 Sqn
Manston	1401 Flt
Merston	130 Sqn, 303 Sqn, 402 Sqn
Predannack	234 Sqn
Shoreham	345 Sqn
Shoreham	277 Sqn (plus other types)
Warmwell	275 Sqn (plus other types)
West Malling	80 Sqn, 274 Sqn

No 12 Group:

Digby	504 Sqn

No 13 Group:

Skeabrae	118 Sqn

Coastal Command

St Eval, Benson	541 Sqn, 542 Sqn
Benson	544 Sqn

Mediterranean Allied Air Force (MAAF)

Piombino	43 Sqn, 72 Sqn, 93 Sqn, 111 Sqn
Follonica	225 Sqn
Perugia	145 Sqn
Calenzana	154 Sqn, 232 Sqn, 242 Sqn, 243 Sqn
Calvi	237 Sqn, 238 Sqn, 451 Sqn
Fermo	241 Sqn, 318 Sqn
Venafro	92 Sqn, 208 Sqn, 417 Sqn, 601 Sqn

Mediterranean Allied Coastal Air Force (MACAF)

Foggia	32 Sqn

AHQ Malta

Catania	87 Sqn
Hal Far, Palermo	185 Sqn

No 214 Group:

Alghero, San Severo	682 Sqn

No 242 Group:

Brindisi	1435 Sqn
Foggia	72 Sqn, 253 Sqn

AHQ Eastern Mediterranean

Bersis	335 Sqn
Bu Amud	94 Sqn
Mersa Matruh	336 Sqn

Air Command South-East Asia (ACSEA)

No 222 Group:

Minneriya	17 Sqn
Ratmalana	273 Sqn

No 231 Group:

Alipore	681 Sqn

3rd Tactical Air Force:

Baigachi	67 Sqn, 155 Sqn

No 221 Group:

Imphal	607 Sqn
Kumbhirgram	81 Sqn
Palel	615 Sqn

No 224 Group:

Chittangong	136 Sqn
Palel	152 Sqn

RAF ORBAT July 1945

2nd Tactical Air Force

No 34 Wing:
B78/Eindhoven	16 Sqn

No 83 Group:
B16/Luneburg	400 Sqn, 414 Sqn, 430 Sqn
B172/Husum	41 Sqn, 350 Sqn
B152/Fassberg	411 Sqn, 412 Sqn, 416 Sqn

No 84 Group:
Warmwell	2 Sqn
Turnhouse	164 Sqn
B116/Wunstorf	322 Sqn, 349 Sqn
B155/Dedelsdorf	274 Sqn, 302 Sqn, 308 Sqn
B150/Hustedt	268 Sqn
B113/Varrelsbusch	317 Sqn
B105/Drope	340 Sqn, 341 Sqn, 345 Sqn, 485 Sqn
Lasham	451 Sqn, 453 Sqn

No 85 Group:
B83/Knocke le Zout	290 Sqn
Grossachenheim	326 Sqn, 328 Sqn
Sersheim	327 Sqn

Fighter Command

No 11 Group:
Manston	310 Sqn, 312 Sqn, 313 Sqn
Chilbolton	183 Sqn
Harrowbeer	329 Sqn, 275 Sqn (plus other types)
Bentwaters	65 Sqn, 126 Sqn

No 12 Group:
Hutton Cranswick	124 Sqn
Ludham	1 Sqn, 91 Sqn
Keevil	61 OTU (plus other types)
Acklington	19 Sqn
Chilbolton	26 Sqn
Morpeth	80 OTU (plus other types)

No 13 Group:
Skeabrae	603 Sqn
Drem	164 Sqn
Dyce	129 Sqn, 165 Sqn

No 88 Group:
Dyce	130 Sqn
Gardemoen	331 Sqn, 332 Sqn

Coastal Command

No 106 Group:
Benson	541 Sqn, 542 Sqn, 544 Sqn

Mediterranean Allied Air Force (MAAF)

Bellaria	92 Sqn, 145 Sqn, 241 Sqn, 417 Sqn, 601 Sqn
Florence	208 Sqn
Forli	318 Sqn
Pontedera	87 Sqn, 185 Sqn
Rimini	43 Sqn, 72 Sqn, 93 Sqn, 111 Sqn

Balkan Air Force:
Biferno	249 Sqn
Canne	73 Sqn, 253 Sqn, 351 Sqn

Mediterranean Allied Coastal Air Force (MACAF)

Falconara, Rosignano	237 Sqn
Florence, Nancy	682 Sqn
San Severo	680 Sqn

Australia

Darwin	54 Sqn, 548 Sqn, 549 Sqn

Air Command South-East Asia (ACSEA)

Brown	136 Sqn

AHQ Burma:		*No 224 Group:*	
Alipore	681 Sqn	Dabaing	67 Sqn
No 221 Group:		Kyaukpyu	273 Sqn
Kwetnge	155 Sqn, 607 Sqn	Nidania	615 Sqn
Sinthe	152 Sqn		
		No 228 Group:	
No 222 Group:		Amarda Road	131 Sqn
Ratmalana	81 Sqn		
Vavuniya	132 Sqn		

~ ANNEXE C ~

Spitfire Prototype Trial

AEROPLANE AND ARMAMENT EXPERIMENTAL ESTABLISHMENT
MARTLESHAM HEATH
Handling trials of the Spitfire K-5054

Controls

Ailerons

In the air the ailerons are light to handle when climbing and on the glide they become heavier with increase in speed, but by no more than is required to impart good 'feel'.

The aeroplane was dived to 380mph A.S.I. and up to that speed the ailerons were not unduly heavy, and gave adequate response.

The ailerons are effective down to the stall and give adequate control when landing and taking off. The response is quick under all conditions of flight, and during all manoeuvres required from a fighting aeroplane.

There was no snatch or aileron vibration at any speed, and in general the aileron control is excellent for a high speed fighting aeroplane.

Rudder

In the air it is moderately light and extremely effective. The rudder becomes heavier with increase of speed, but by no more than is necessary in a high speed aeroplane, and at the highest speeds it is still effective.

The aeroplane responds easily and quickly to the rudder under all conditions of flight.

Although the rudder is heavier than the ailerons, it should not be made lighter as with a very light rudder the pilot might overload the aeroplane at high speeds.

Rudder Bias Gear
[Omitted]*

Elevators
In the air the elevator control is light and very effective down to the stall.

* Omitted from Annexe for reasons of space; this applies in all subsequent uses of [Omitted]

Heaviness increases with speed, but by no more than is necessary. In the dive the aeroplane is steady. The elevators give rapid response with a small movement of the control column.

Tail Trimming Gear [Omitted]

Engine Controls [Omitted]

Flaps [Omitted]

Brakes [Omitted]

Flying Controls

Stability

Laterally the aeroplane is stable. If one wing is depressed and the control column released the aeroplane will return to a level keel in a reasonable time. Directionally the aeroplane is stable under all conditions of flight, engine on or off. Longitudinally the aeroplane is neutrally stable with engine on and stable in the glide. The aeroplane is unstable in the glide with flaps and undercarriage down.

In general the stability characteristics are satisfactory for a fighting aeroplane and give a reasonable compromise between controllability and steadiness as a gun platform.

Characteristics at the Stall

As the elevator control is very powerful the aeroplane will stall long before the control column is moved right back. The stall is normal. There is no vice nor snatch on the controls. In tight turns, giving approximately 3g as registered on the accelerometer, at speeds from 140mph A.S.I. downwards there was a distinct juddering on the whole aeroplane. Under these conditions the aeroplane is probably in a semi-stalled condition and this juddering effect may be due to slight buffeting on the tail. This can be stopped at once if the control column is eased forward.

Tests according to A.D.M. *[Omitted]*

Aerobatics [Omitted]

Landing and Take-off [Omitted]

Sideslipping [Omitted]

Ground Handling [Omitted]

Undercarriage *[Omitted]*

Flying View

View forwards is fair and upwards is good. View to the rear is fair for a covered cockpit. The present windscreen gives great distortion. If a curved windscreen of this shape cannot be made in either moulded glass or in suitable material to give no distortion, it is considered that it should be replaced by a flat-sided type, even though this might involve a slight reduction in performance.

Cockpit Comfort

The cockpit is comfortable and there is plenty of room, even for a big pilot. The head room is somewhat cramped for a tall pilot. It is not unduly noisy and the instruments and controls are well arranged. The cockpit is easy to enter and leave when the aeroplane is on the ground and foot steps on the wing are not considered necessary.

Although no heating is provided the cockpit was kept warm by heat from the engine and exhaust at 25,000ft. Gloves were not necessary.

Instruments [*Omitted*]

Summary of Flying Qualities

The aeroplane is simple and easy to fly and has no vices. All controls are entirely satisfactory for this type and no modification to them is required, except that the elevator control might be improved by reducing the gear ratio between the control column and elevator. The controls are well harmonised and appear to give an excellent compromise between manoeuvrability and steadiness for shooting. Take-off and landing are straightforward and easy.

The aeroplane has rather a flat glide, even when the under-carriage and flaps are down and has a considerable float if the approach is made a little too fast. This defect could be remedied by fitting higher drag flaps.

In general the handling of this aeroplane is such that it can be flown without risk by the average fully trained service fighter pilot, but there can be no doubt that it would be improved by having flaps giving a higher drag.

~ ANNEXE D ~

AFDU Tactical Trials:
Spitfire VB versus Fw 190

The Fw 190 was compared with a Spitfire VB from an operational squadron for speed and all-round manoeuvrability at heights up to 25,000 feet. The Fw 190 is superior in speed at all heights, and the approximate differences are as follows:

a At 1,000ft the Fw 190 is 25–30mph faster than the Spitfire VB.
b At 3,000ft the Fw 190 is 30–35mph faster than the Spitfire VB.
c At 5,000ft the Fw 190 is 25mph faster than the Spitfire VB.
d At 9,000ft the Fw 190 is 25–30mph faster than the Spitfire VB.
e At 15,000ft the Fw 190 is 20mph faster than the Spitfire VB.
f At 18,000ft the Fw 190 is 20mph faster than the Spitfire VB.
g At 21,000ft the Fw 190 is 20–25mph faster than the Spitfire VB.

Climb
The climb of the Fw 190 is superior to that of the Spitfire VB at all heights. The best speeds for climbing are approximately the same, but the angle of the Fw 190 is considerably steeper. Under maximum continuous climbing conditions the climb of the Fw 190 is about 450ft/min better up to 25,000 feet.

With both aircraft flying at high cruising speed and then pulling up into a climb, the superior climb of the Fw 190 is even more marked. When both aircraft are pulled up into a climb from a dive, the Fw 190 draws away very rapidly and the pilot of the Spitfire has no hope of catching it.

Dive
Comparative dives between the two aircraft have shown that the Fw 190 can leave the Spitfire with ease, particularly during the initial stages

Manoeuvrability
The manoeuvrability of the Fw 190 is better than that of the Spitfire VB except in turning circles, when the Spitfire can quite easily out-turn it. The Fw 190 has better acceleration under all conditions of flight and this must obviously be most useful during combat.

When the Fw 190 was in a turn and was attacked by the Spitfire, the superior rate of roll enabled it to flick into a diving turn in the opposite direction. The pilot of the Spitfire found great difficulty in following this manoeuvre and even when prepared for it, was seldom able to allow the correct deflection. A dive from this manoeuvre enabled the Fw 190 to draw away from the Spitfire which was then forced to break off the attack.

Several flights were carried out to ascertain the best evasive manoeuvres to adopt if 'bounced'. It was found that if the Spitfire was cruising at low speed and was 'bounced' by the Fw 190, it was easily caught even if the Fw 190 was sighted when well out of range, and the Spitfire was then forced to take avoiding action by using its superiority in turning circles. If on the other hand the Spitfire was flying at maximum continuous cruising and was 'bounced' under the same conditions, it had a reasonable chance of avoiding being caught by opening the throttle and going into a shallow dive, providing the Fw 190 was seen in time. This forced the Fw 190 into a stern chase and although it eventually caught the Spitfire, it took some time and as a result was drawn a considerable distance away from its base. This is a particularly useful method of evasion for the Spitfire if it is 'bounced' when returning from a sweep. This manoeuvre has been carried out during recent operations and has been successful on several occasions.

If the Spitfire VB is 'bounced' it is thought unwise to evade by diving steeply, as the Fw 190 will have little difficulty in catching up owing to its superiority in the dive.

The above trials have shown that the Spitfire VB must cruise at high speed when in an area where enemy fighters can be expected. It will then, in addition to lessening the chances of being successfully 'bounced', have a better chance of catching the Fw 190, particularly if it has the advantage of surprise.

~ ANNEXE E ~

AFDU Trial: Spitfire VB
Clipped-wing versus Standard Version

Method of Test

Two Spitfire VB aircraft were selected with a performance which was almost identical, the loading and equipment carried were standard in each, and the propeller, engine and finish of each aircraft were similar. A test flight was made under maximum cruising conditions and no differences could be determined. The wing tips were then removed from one aircraft and trials were carried out, each trial being performed twice to enable the pilots to be changed. The wing tips were then replaced on one aircraft and removed on the other and similar tests carried out. Differences in speed were taken as relative increases or decreases owing to possible instrument inaccuracies, and position error differences with and without tips. Readings for level speeds were taken at 10,000, 15,000, 20,000 and 25,000 feet; zoom climbs were made 10,000–15,000ft and 20,000–25,000ft; dives were made with similar engine settings.

Results of Comparative Tests

Level Speed

- a 10,000 feet. In each case the clipped wing Spitfire proved the faster by a small margin estimated in the nature of 5mph.
- b 15,000 and 20,000 feet. The average results at these two heights showed that the difference in speed is not measurable.
- c 25,000 feet. The standard Spitfire is very slightly faster than the clipped wing Spitfire.

In all level speed runs the clipped wing Spitfire accelerated rather better than the standard Spitfire.

Climb

The average difference in time during zoom climbs from 20,000 to 25,000 feet was 15 seconds in favour of the standard Spitfire. From 10,000 to 15,000 feet no differences were indicated.

Dive
In all diving tests the clipped wing Spitfire drew away from the standard Spitfire.

Manoeuvrability
At all heights to 25,000 feet the rate of roll is considerably improved by removal of the wing tips. The response to aileron movements is very quick and very crisp. Four dog-fights were carried out, starting with the standard Spitfire on the tail of the clipped wing Spitfire. On two occasions the clipped wing Spitfire evaded so rapidly in the rolling plane that it was able to lose the standard Spitfire and reverse the positions in about 20 seconds. On the third occasion the clipped wing Spitfire was also able to lose the standard Spitfire. The fourth occasion was at 25,000 feet and the standard Spitfire was able to keep the clipped wing Spitfire in sight.

The minimum turning circle of the clipped wing Spitfire at 20,000ft has been increased by 55 feet at 1,025 feet compared with the Fw 190 turning circle of 1,450 feet. This slight increase does not therefore detract from the fighting qualities of the aeroplane in any way, since the clipped wing version is unlikely to be in combat with the standard Spitfire.

Take-off [Omitted]

Landing [Omitted]

General
The view downwards over the wing tips, for what it is worth, is improved by a not inconsiderable amount. The strengthening of the wing by removal of the wing tips may permit higher maximum IAS to be used.

AFDU
1942

AFDU Tactical Trials: Spitfire Mark VI

Introduction

In accordance with arrangements with Headquarters, Fighter Command, a Spitfire VI aircraft, No BR 289, was delivered to this Unit on 23rd May 1942 for tactical trials.

The all-up weight of the aircraft with full war load is approximately 6,738lbs, which is 180lbs more than the Spitfire VB, and it was flown throughout the trials in this condition. The aircraft had fittings for a jettisonable fuel tank holding 30 gallons but this was not available during the trials.

Brief Description of the Aircraft [*Omitted*]

Pressure Cabin [*Omitted*]

Cockpit Heating [*Omitted*]

Tactical Trials

Flying Characteristics
The Spitfire VI is similar to the Spitfire VB for take-off, but for landing a slightly faster approach is necessary due to the higher stalling speed.

The aileron controls are considerably heavier than the Spitfire VB. This appears to be partly due to the air-tight seals attached to the control cables passing through the cockpit. As a result the manoeuvrability is much slower in the rolling plane and the 'going in' and 'coming out' of steep turns is slowed down.

The longer wing tips on the Spitfire VI add to the lateral stability especially above 25,000 feet, but the elevator control is unstable at altitudes over 30,000 feet.

The balloon hood distorts the pilot's vision near the forward frame, and sometimes gives a double image. This has a slight adverse effect on landing and formation flying, but the hood is excellent for search and general flying.

Taxying [*Omitted*]

Performance
Comparative performances were carried out with a Spitfire VC as a VB was not available. Both aircraft took off with a full war load. Below 20,000 feet the Spitfire VI was slightly slower but by 22,000 feet (its rated altitude) it was about 6mph faster.

Climb
Comparative climbs were carried out with a Spitfire VB and up to 20,000 feet there is little to choose between the two aircraft. The Spitfire VB is faster up to 10,000 feet and climbs at a steeper angle, but from 10,000 feet to 20,000 feet the Spitfire VI is slightly faster. From 20,000 to 30,000 feet the Spitfire VI is about 1 minute faster than the Spitfire VB. Above 30,000 feet the superiority of the Spitfire VI is even more marked and it climbs from 30,000 to 35,000 feet in half the time of the Spitfire VB.

The highest altitude reached was 37,500 feet indicated. At this height excessive hunting and intermittent cutting out of the engine was experienced due to the petrol vapourising in the feed line due to insufficient fuel pressure. On a very hot day (28°C [82°F] on the ground) it was impossible to climb above 28,500 feet due to this trouble.

The rate of climb falls off to 1,000 feet per minute at about 34,000 feet and this is considered to be the operational ceiling for a squadron, but sections of two could operate up to 37,000 feet.

Manoeuvrability
Although the aileron controls are heavier than the Spitfire VB, the rate of turn is as good up to 25,000 feet and above this height is appreciably better. At 32,000 feet the Spitfire VI got on the tail of the Spitfire VB after 1½ turns. At these heights and above the increased wing area and higher rated altitude of the engine gave the Spitfire VI a great advantage over the Spitfire VB.

The Spitfire VI was fitted with a 6½lb inertia device and below 25,000 feet there was no tendency to tighten-up in the turn if the elevators were trimmed correctly. If incorrectly trimmed the aircraft tended to tighten the rate of turn. During dog-fights, above 30,000 feet there was a definite tightening of the turn.

Evasive action of half rolling the aircraft and doing aileron turns was slowed down considerably by the heavy aileron control. A better method of evasion is considered to be diving steeply, as the engine only cuts out momentarily when negative 'G' is applied due to the restrictor fitted in the fuel supply pipe.

High Flying
Numerous flights have been carried out between 30,000 and 37,500 feet and the pilot has greatly benefited by the pressure cabin. There have been no complaints of ill-effects from being at altitude, even for long periods, and pilots have nothing but praise for the comfort of the cockpit. At 37,500 feet the pressure inside the cockpit was equal to 28,500 feet. The cockpit was warmed by the air so that at -42°C [-49°F] outside the cockpit it was +8°C [+46°F] inside. For comfort above 30,000 feet, only flying boots and light overalls are needed by the pilot

No serious icing-up of the cockpit was experienced and during rapid descents from high altitude the cockpit was almost free from internal misting-up, while the Spitfire VB misted up badly.

The elevator control above 30,000 feet is most sensitive and at 36,000 feet the aircraft often loses as much as 1,000 feet while the pilot is searching or looking at his instruments.

Freezing-up of the elevator and rudder trimmers was experienced during the first two flights above 30,000 feet, but after treatment with anti-freeze oil it was possible to trim the aircraft correctly at all heights.

Vapour trails, non persistent, were generally experienced around 30,000 feet (-36°C [-33°F]), but disappeared above 36,000 feet. On one occasion vapour trails were made at 25,000 feet (-42°C [-43°F]) and disappeared at 30,000 feet (-54°C [-65°F]).

Endurance

The Spitfire VI consumes approximately the same amount of petrol as the Spitfire VB. During the climb to 30,000 feet starting at +2 boost, 2,600 rpm, and 45 minutes spent at this height, the Spitfire VI used 48 gallons of petrol and the Spitfire VB, formatting at a distance, used 50 gallons.

Armament

No firing trials were carried out as the gun installations are identical with those of the Spitfire VB.

Conclusions

The pressure cabin adds greatly to the pilot's comfort at high altitude. He is kept warmer and needs less oxygen, but on a hot day below 15,000 feet the cabin is unbearably hot. The cabin showed no signs of misting up.

The rated altitude of the Spitfire VI is 22,000 feet and above this height the performance is better than the Spitfire VB. This difference becomes more marked above 30,000 feet, its climb from there to 35,000 feet being twice as fast as that of the Spitfire VB. The operational ceiling for a squadron is considered to be about 34,000 feet, although sections of two could operate up to 37,000 feet.

The Spitfire VI is more manoeuvrable than the Spitfire VB above 30,000 feet and below this height has an equally good rate of turn, although it is slow in the rolling plane. Owing to the slow rate of roll the best method of evasion is to dive steeply.

The cockpit is uncomfortably hot at low altitudes flying in summer conditions.

Wing Commander
Commanding, AFDU
May 1942

~ ANNEXE G ~

AFDU Short Tactical Trials: Spitfire VIII (Report No 85)

Introduction

On instructions from Headquarters, Fighter Command, a Spitfire VIII, No JF664 (Merlin 63) was delivered to this Unit on 7.7.43 for short tactical trials. The trials took the form of a direct comparison with a Spitfire IX (Merlin 63) made available by No 332 (Norwegian) Squadron at R.A.F. Station, North Weald.

Brief Description

The Spitfire VIII has a strengthened airframe primarily designed to take the 61 series of Merlin; as a result it is slightly heavier than the Spitfire IX. The fuel capacity has been increased to 96 gallons in the main tank, with 27 gallons carried in two wing tanks, making a total of 123 gallons. The wing tanks were filled for the trial but the fuel could not be used as the system had not received A.I.D.'s approval at the time. The wings are of a greater span, having extended wing tips similar to those on the Spitfire VI. The ailerons are smaller, having about 8½ inches less span than on the standard universal Mark VC wing. The aircraft used on the trial was a tropical version but the tropical air filter was never used, so that its performance was directly comparable with the Spitfire IX. The weight of the Spitfire VIII was 7,760lbs.

Tactical

General

The trials took the form of comparing the two aircraft at all heights up to 40,000 feet. Two experienced pilots took part, taking turns in flying the two aircraft so as to rule out any differences in piloting. Other pilots of the Unit and two pilots from Norwegian Squadrons at North Weald have also flown the aircraft and their opinions are incorporated in this report.

Performance

There was very little to choose between the performance of the two aircraft which were similarly loaded as regards armament, ammunition and radio, except that at altitude the Mark VIII gave slightly better results than the Mark IX available for the trial. This may be due to the individual engines or airframes of these two aircraft. In particular the following was noticed:-

(i) SPEEDS
   (a) Up to 20,000 feet   Nothing to choose between the aircraft.
   (b) 30,000 feet   Spitfire VIII slightly faster.
   (c) 36,000 feet   Spitfire VIII again faster, this time by a greater margin than before.

(ii) CLIMBS (a) Zero to 10,000ft   Spitfire IX very slightly ahead.
             (b) 10,000 to 20,000ft   Both aircraft the same.
             (c) 20,000 to 30,000ft   Spitfire VIII very slightly better.
             (d) 30,000 to 40,000ft   Spitfire VIII very slightly better.

Manoeuvrability

There was nothing to choose between either aircraft as regards turning circles at any height; whether on offensive or defensive manoeuvres neither could make any impression on the other. In rate of roll, however, the Spitfire IX was considerably better especially at low altitude. A number of full rolls through 360 degrees were timed by the same pilot flying each aircraft in turn and although quantitative tests are difficult to produce, it appeared that there was often more than 1.5 seconds superiority for the Mark IX over the Mark VIII. The Mark VIII feels fairly light on the ailerons but at high speeds it becomes very heavy, and so this new combination of extended wing and small aileron cannot be considered satisfactory.

Other Points

(i)   The fuel transfer cock when in operation works in the opposite direction from the main fuel cock, i.e. it is up when 'OFF' and it is considered that it should be down for 'OFF' and more progressively through 'port' and 'starboard' as it reaches the up position.
(ii) A.K.D.G. fuel contents gauge is fitted to this aircraft which does not appear at all accurate and it certainly no use to a fighter pilot when manoeuvring.
(iii) The enlarged horn balanced elevator fitted to this aircraft, suits it far better than the Spitfire V on which previous flying with it had been done at this Unit. In particular at altitude the longitudinal stability is considered an improvement.

Conclusions

There is no difference in performance between the Spitfire VIII and Spitfire IX with Merlin 63 engines, except that with the extended wing tips the Spitfire VIII is performing a little bit better at high altitude.

The smaller span ailerons combined with extended wing tips give the Spitfire VIII an inferior rate of roll.

Wing Commander
Commanding AFDU
29th July 1943

AFDU Trial: Spitfire VIII JF299 with Tear-drop Canopy

Description

Windscreen

This is made up of a sheet of bullet-proof glass set behind a curved windscreen of perspex. The side panels which are smaller than standard are of bullet-proof glass and the aft frames of these panels are raked further forward than on the standard Spitfire.

Sliding Hood

This is an entirely new design and consists of a long moulded perspex hood giving direct vision to the rear. It is a trifle wider than the old type flat hood but not so wide as a balloon hood. The hood is manipulated in a similar fashion to the standard hoods. Armour protection is provided as before.

Flying Trials

General

The aircraft was flown by pilots of this Unit and the Naval Air Fighting Development Unit, also by four pilots from other Fighter Command Units, whose comments and criticisms are summarised below.

Rearward View

This is an enormous improvement over the standard Spitfire rear view. The pilot can see quite easily round to his fin and past it, almost to the further edge of the tailplane, ie if he looks over his left shoulder he can practically see to the starboard tip of the tail. By banking the aircraft slightly during weaving action, the downward view to the rear is opened up well. The whole field of search is increased very appreciably.

Forward View

In general, this is now better than on the standard Spitfire, since the original small panel at the top to which the rearview mirror was mounted has been removed and a longer piece of bullet proof glass runs right up to the top of the hood. There are, however, the following criticisms:

    a Slight reflections are picked up by the curved windscreen in a similar fashion to those described in Report No 78 [on the curved windscreen fitted to a Spitfire

V], but now that the cowlings have been treated with a matt black dope forward of the windscreen and between the curved screen and the bullet proof screen, these have been cut down to a minimum and are considered acceptable. Slight distortion is found when looking through this screen.

b The bullet proof side panels are now smaller than those on previous Spitfires with the result that the pilot has to be leaning well forward to make full use of them and the landing view is not as good as normal.

c The frames supporting the rear part of the bullet proof side panels are thought to be unnecessarily wide; together with frames of the sliding hood when closed they form quite a large obstruction. The pilot can see round them by moving his head, but he is always conscious of them since they are more in his line of vision than previously.

Reflections

Besides those mentioned in the previous paragraph, reflections off the top of the front bullet proof glass and off the hood catches and handle appear in the top of the sliding hood at its front end. Matt black paint on the frame of the bullet proof glass causes this almost to disappear.

Misting and Icing-up [Omitted]

Reflector Sight

The sight has been raised almost 3 inches to improve the view for deflection shooting. This is considered a great benefit and full use of it can be made with the new hood and screen. The view over the nose cowling is almost equal to that from the Spitfire XII's cockpit. The reflector glass was removed from the GM 2 sight by this Unit and an excellent image was thrown direct on to the bullet proof glass.

Operation of the Hood [Omitted]

Draught [Omitted]

Rear View Mirror

Owing to the very great improvement in all-round search view, particularly to the rear, the omission of the rear view mirror is not considered to be of any disadvantage to pilots flying with this new hood.

Armour Plate

This is at present the same as fitted to the standard Spitfire, and there is room for improvement. The armour is a little too far behind the pilot's head when he is in the normal sitting position, but it has been found that if it is moved forward and is retained the same size, some of the newly acquired view is lost. It is considered that the armour plating could profitably be made higher because pilots look round the armour plating not over it, and also the possibility of fitting full width armour glass behind the pilot's head could be investigated.

Comparison with the Tempest [*Omitted*]

Maintenance [*Omitted*]

Conclusions

Sliding Hood
The all-round rearward view has been enormously improved. This type of hood should be made standard, but the following suggested modifications will effect still greater improvement:

 (i) The hood needs to be ballooned – the cockpit is now too cramped, and the hood is easily scratched by the pilot's head gear.
 (ii) A handle is needed for easy manipulation.
 (iii) The armour plate should be increased in height or possibly replaced by bullet proof glass.

Windscreen
The general forward view is also improved over the standard Spitfire, but attention to the following points is thought necessary:

 (i) The side panels are too small to be really useful. They might also be set at a wider angle – at the expense of narrowing the centre panel – with good effect. The curved screen in front of the centre bullet proof glass should be removed. It is viewed with suspicion as it may easily mist up in winter conditions and certainly makes cleaning the front of the bullet proof glass difficult. In spite of a matt black finish to the top cowlings, slight reflections are still found.
 (ii) [*Omitted*]
 (iii) The frames between the centre panel and the side panels need to be inclined inwards to present the pilot with the least possible obstruction.
 (iv) The frames on the aft sides of the side panels must be made smaller and preferably set more upright so as to increase the size of the side panels and cause less of an obstruction to the view.
 (v) The side panels freeze up seriously.

Reflector Sight
This has been raised 3 inches and can be reflected direct on to the screen. The shooting view is comparable to that of the Spitfire XII.

Wing Commander
Commanding, AFDU
August 1943

~ ANNEXE I ~

AFDU Tactical Trials: Spitfire Mark IX (Report No 46)

Introduction

In accordance with the instructions from Headquarters, Fighter Command, one Spitfire IX aircraft, AB505, was delivered from Messrs. Rolls-Royce Ltd., to this unit on 26th April 1942, for a period of one week, for tactical trials.

In order to bring the weight of the aircraft up to its full was load it was necessary to fit 2 x 20-mm cannons, full ammunition for all guns, V.H.F., and I.F.F. The aircraft has fittings for a jettisonable fuel tank but this was not available. Without this tank the all-up weight is about 7,400lbs.

During the trials minor adjustments had to be made to the undercarriage and sliding hood, and after 5 days flying engine failure occurred. It was found that the butterflies in the carburettor were pitted, one spray nozzle on the enrichment side was missing, and several pieces of metal had reached the oil filters. A new engine is being sent from Messrs. Rolls-Royce, Hucknall.

Brief Description of the Aircraft

General
The Spitfire IX is a Spitfire VC modified to incorporate a Merlin 61 engine fitted with the latest negative 'G' carburettor. The main differences between the two aircraft are the slightly longer nose due to the larger engine, a 4-bladed Rotol constant speed propeller, two thermostatically controlled radiators and two-speed super chargers which are automatically controlled. The fuel capacity is increased 10 gallons, and the tanks are pressurised.

Pilot's Cockpit [Omitted]

Sighting View
The Spitfire IX is fitted with the G.M.2 pilot's reflector sight and although the aircraft is longer in the nose than the Spitfire VC, the 100mph ring of the sight is still just clear of the nose.

The oxygen supply is obtained from two bottles provided with an economiser and is the same as that used in the standard spitfire.

Tactical Trials

The Spitfire IX was compared with a Spitfire VC with similar armament and a Typhoon I for performance and manoeuvrability; all aircraft were carrying full war load.

Flying Characteristics

The Spitfire IX is similar to the Spitfire VC for take-off and length although the landing speed is slightly higher. The extra weight and length of the aircraft has made the elevators a little heavier and as a result . . . are better harmonised. It was noticed that during dives there was less tendency for the aircraft to yaw and this was thought to be due to the extra radiator fitted on the port wing. Tight turns were made up to 5G and there was a sign of 'tightening up', the aircraft recovering normally when the control column was released.

Performance

The speed of the Spitfire IX was compared with a Spitfire VC and a Typhoon I at various heights. Its maximum true speed in M.S. gear is developed at a height of 16,300 feet and is approximately 386mph and in F.S. gear 28,000 feet and is approximately 409mph. Those figures are slightly less than those obtained by Messrs. Rolls Royce, but it is understood that the aircraft they used was not fitted with cannons and did not carry full war load. The speed of the Spitfire IX at all heights was vastly superior to that of the Spitfire VC.

Two speed runs were made against a Typhoon I from an operational Squadron. At 15,000 feet the Spitfire IX was approximately 10mph faster and at 18,000 feet approximately 2mph faster.

Comparative climbs were carried out and it was found that the Spitfire IX was superior to the Spitfire VC and Typhoon I at all heights. This superiority becomes even more marked as height increases. The Spitfire IX was climbed under maximum continuous climbing conditions, to an indicated height of 39,500 feet where the rate of climb was about 700 feet per minute. It was particularly noticed that the oil and glycol temperatures were normal throughout. The operational ceiling is considered to be about 38,000 feet where the rate of climb is 1,000 feet per minute. This height can be reached by a single aircraft in 18½ minutes.

Manoeuvrability

The Spitfire IX was compared with a Spitfire VC for turning circles and dog-fighting at heights between 15,000 and 30,000 feet. At 15,000 feet there was little to choose between the two aircraft although the superior speed and climb of the Spitfire IX enabled it to break off its attack by climbing away and then attacking again in a dive. The manoeuvre was assisted by the negative 'G' carburettor, as it was possible to change rapidly from climb to dive without the engine cutting. At 30,000 feet there is still little to choose between the two aircraft in manoeuvrability, but the superiority in speed and climb of the Spitfire IX becomes outstanding. The pilot of the Spitfire VC found it difficult to maintain a steep turn without losing height, whereas the pilot of the Spitfire IX found that he had a large reserve of power which enabled him to maintain height without trouble. The all-round performance of the Spitfire IX at 30,000 feet is most impressive.

Short trials were carried out against a Typhoon I and the Spitfire IX was found to be more manoeuvrable and superior in climb but inferior in dive. During a dog-fight at 18,000 feet the Spitfire out-turned the Typhoon and got on its tail after 1½ turns.

High Flying
Several climbs were made to heights between 39,000 and 40,000 feet and the pilot felt that the aircraft was capable of going even higher. Although the operational ceiling is considered to be 38,000 feet, it is thought that Sections of two could operate up to 39,000 feet and probably higher. The aircraft is easy to fly at high altitudes, but freezing up of the trimming tabs occurred. It was therefore difficult to keep the aircraft level as it was still trimmed for climb. During manoeuvres there is otherwise little tendency to lose height even at 38,000 feet. At this height the aircraft was dived for 1,500 feet and zoomed up to 39,000 feet. Steep turns were carried out at 38,000 feet where it was necessary to maintain an indicated airspeed of at least 110mph to prevent stalling. The cockpit heating kept the pilot warm at all heights and flying clothing was unnecessary.

Slight icing up of the cockpit was experienced during turns but this dispersed as soon as the aircraft was flown straight. The cold air spray to the windscreen was turned on during descents and no misting up was experienced.

During the high flying trials vapour trails were formed between 30,000 and 36,000 feet, but above this height trails were not visible. All flights took place under conditions of no cloud and extremely low temperatures, -64 degrees centigrade, being reported on one occasion.

Endurance
The fuel capacity of the Spitfire IX is 92 gallons, 57 in the top tank and 35 in the bottom tank. This is 10 gallons more than the Spitfire VC. There are fittings under the fuselage for a jettisonable tank holding 39 gallons. Petrol consumption during the trials was high and during a comparative flight of 75 minutes the Spitfire used 76 gallons and the Spitfire VC 54 gallons. In a flight of one hour, three speed runs of 4 minutes each and a maximum continuous climb to 39,000 feet were carried out and the Spitfire IX used 76 gallons. On investigation of engine trouble experienced at the latter stage of the trials it was found that the aircraft had been delivered with the mixture trial locked in the 'RICH' position instead of the 'WEAK'.

Armament Characteristics
The Spitfire IX, like the Spitfire VC is fitted with the universal wing and for the trials 2 x 20-mm cannons and 4 x 0.303 Brownings were carried. When fitting the 20-mm cannons it was found that the inboard rib on the gun panel housing fouled the feed mechanism and the gun panel had to be eased by filing. Time did not permit firing trials to be carried out but this installation has already been reported on by this unit.

Cine Camera Gun [Omitted]

Conclusions

The performance of the Spitfire IX is outstandingly better than the Spitfire V especially at heights above 20,000 feet. On the level the Spitfire is considerably faster and its climb is exceptionally good. It will climb easily to 38,000 feet and when levelled off there can be made to climb in stages to above 40,000 feet by building up speed on the level and a slight zoom. Its manoeuvrability is as good as a Spitfire V up to 30,000 feet and above that is very much better. At 38,000 feet it is capable of a true speed of 368mph and is still able to manoeuvre well for fighting.'

Wing Commander
Commanding, AFDU
4th May 1942

~ ANNEXE J ~

AFDU Tactical Trials:
Spitfire Mark IX versus Fw 190

The Fw 190 was compared with a fully operational Spitfire IX for speed and manoeuvrability at heights up to 25,000 feet. The Spitfire IX at most heights is slightly superior in speed to the Fw 190 and the approximate differences in speeds at various heights are as follows:

a   At 2,000ft the Fw 190 is 7–8mph faster than the Spitfire IX.
b   At 5,000ft the Fw 190 and Spitfire IX are approximately the same.
c   At 8,000ft the Spitfire IX is 8mph faster than the Fw 190.
d   At 15,000ft the Spitfire IX is 5mph faster than the Fw 190.
e   At 18,000ft the Fw 190 is 3mph faster than the Spitfire IX.
f   At 21,000ft the Fw 190 and Spitfire IX are approximately the same.
g   At 25,000ft the Spitfire IX is 5–7mph faster than the Fw 190.

Climb

During comparative climbs at various heights up to 23,000 feet, with both aircraft flying under maximum continuous climbing conditions, little difference was found between the two aircraft although on the whole the Spitfire IX was slightly better. Above 22,000 feet the climb of the Fw 190 is falling off rapidly, whereas the climb of the Spitfire IX is increasing. When both aircraft were flying at high cruising speed and were pulled up into a climb from level flight, the Fw 190 had a slight advantage in the initial stages of the climb due to its better acceleration. This superiority was slightly increased when both aircraft were pulled up into the climb from a dive.

It must be appreciated that the differences between the two aircraft are only slight and that in actual combat the advantage in climb will be with the aircraft that has the initiative.

Dive

The Fw 190 is faster than the Spitfire IX in a dive, particularly during the initial stage. This superiority is not as marked as with a Spitfire VB

Manoeuvrability

The Fw 190 is more manoeuvrable than the Spitfire IX except in turning circles, when it is out-turned without difficulty.

The superior rate of roll of the Fw 190 enabled it to avoid the Spitfire IX if attacked when in a turn, by flicking over into a diving turn in the opposite direction and, as with the Spitfire VB, the Spitfire IX had great difficulty in following this manoeuvre. It would have been easier for the Spitfire IX to follow the Fw 190 in the diving turn if its engine had been fitted with a negative G carburettor, as this type of engine with ordinary carburettor cuts out very easily

The Spitfire IX's worst heights for fighting the Fw 190 were between 18,000 and 22,000 feet and below 3,000 feet. At these heights the Fw 190 is a little faster.

Both aircraft 'bounced' one another in order to ascertain the best evasive tactics to adopt. The Spitfire IX could not be caught when 'bounced' if it was cruising at high speed and saw the Fw 190 when well out of range. When the Spitfire IX was cruising at low speed its inferiority in acceleration gave the Fw 190 a reasonable chance of catching it up and the same applied if the position is reversed and the Fw 190 was 'bounced' by the Spitfire IX, except that overtaking took a little longer.

The initial acceleration of the Fw 190 is better than the Spitfire IX under all conditions of flight, except in level flight at such altitudes where the Spitfire has a speed advantage and then, provided the Spitfire is cruising at high speed, there is little to choose between the acceleration of the two aircraft.

The general impression gained by the pilots taking part in the trials is that the Spitfire IX compares favourably with the Fw 190 and that provided the Spitfire has the initiative, it has undoubtedly a good chance of shooting it down.

AFDU
July 1942

~ ANNEXE K ~

AFDU Comparative Trials: Spitfire IX versus Mustang X

Comparative trials of new low altitude fighters Spitfire IX (Merlin 66) and Mustang X (Merlin 65) (Interim Report No 64)

Introduction

In accordance with instruction from Air Ministry (DAT), CS 1800 dated 30th September 1942, tactical trials have now been carried out with the Mustang X. Aircraft No AM203 was delivered to this unit on 23.12.42 and this aircraft has been compared with Spitfire IX No BS552 fitted with a similar engine which was available throughout the trial. A second Spitfire IX with this type of engine, No BS543, had also been flown at this unit. Further flying is to be done by pilots from the USAAF on the Mustang X, when it will be compared with modern American fighters, but the arrangements of the USAAF made it impossible for these pilots to be made available during the early part of the trials and a report will therefore be rendered at the completion of their flying.

Description

General [Omitted]

Spitfire IX
The alterations made to this aircraft affect the engine and its installation only and it is otherwise a standard Spitfire IX. The fitting of the Bendix carburettor has been incorporated with an immersed fuel pump which this Unit was instructed to use for starting up, take-off and aerobatics. It was found, however, that the pump was unnecessary for starting, take-off of any flying manoeuvres, except possibly to restart the engine after a dead cut due to inverted flying with almost empty tanks. The pump was not used after the first week's flying and has never been needed, although unsuccessful attempts were made to make the engine cut with only a little fuel in the tanks. The pressurised fuel system is adequate for the needs of the engine at altitude. No fuel inter-coolers are fitted and they do not appear necessary. There is no mixture control in the cockpit and no gate on the throttle. Otherwise, no alterations have been made to the aircraft and its appearance is identical with other Spitfire IXs, which is a strong point tactically as the enemy will

never know which type of Spitfire he is fighting. Full throttle heights are 11,000ft and 22,000ft. The superchargers are changed automatically at 12,500ft on the climb.

Mustang X [Omitted]

Tactical

Flying Characteristics
   (i) Spitfire IX. There is very little difference in the general characteristics of this Spitfire from the other Spitfire IXs. It was, however, found that the aileron control was considerably worse than is usual on the IX and a considerable amount of flying had to be carried out with alterations of rigging and various pairs of ailerons in order to get lateral control that was acceptable, but even with the best pair of ailerons at the Unit's disposal the control was not as good as a standard Spitfire VB. The earlier part of the trials was carried out with wing tips in position and a few flights were made at the end with the wing tips clipped. This improved the all-round fighting capabilities of the IX without detracting noticeably from the excellent rate of climb.
  (ii) Mustang X [*Omitted*]

Performance

The Spitfire IX being the lighter aircraft has a slightly better acceleration from cruising flight to its maximum speeds. The Mustang varies between 12 and 22mph faster than the Spitfire up to about 34,000 feet, at which height the Spitfire becomes the faster. Maxima for the Spitfire and Mustang as given by the A&AEE are as follows:

	Spitfire	Mustang
11,000 feet in MS gear	384mph	404mph
22,000 feet in FS gear	407mph	430mph

Climb
The Spitfire climbs about 800ft/min faster than the Mustang up to 20,000 feet, after which its superiority drops off slightly. The rates of climb as obtained by the A&AEE were for a Spitfire with a dural propeller and other fittings likely to be removed in operations, which made it about 200lb heavier than the aircraft will probably be in service, so that better results still can be expected. In the case of the Mustang the figures given are for an aircraft with the smaller propeller, so that a better climb can be anticipated with the larger one as flown by this Unit. The operational ceiling of 1,000ft/min is reached at 37,500 feet in 13 minutes in the Spitfire and at 34,000 feet in 13¾ minutes in the Mustang. The angle of climb for both aircraft is very steep; in the Spitfire it is particularly difficult for the pilot to see the horizon in the initial parts of the climb owing to the high angle of the nose. The Mustang climbs at a higher speed (195mph IAS to 19,000 feet) and is much more stable than the Spitfire, it being possible to trim with hands and feet off. Zoom climbs were carried out to compare the two aircraft in which it was found that from fast cruising conditions the Spitfire was faster from ground level to 10,000 feet by 15 seconds, from 10,000 to 20,000 feet by 17 seconds; and from 20,000 to 30,000 feet by 40 seconds.

Dive

The Mustang out-dives the Spitfire very easily, being especially quick to accelerate away at full throttle. In the dive the rudder requires a considerable amount of left trim, but the elevator control is good, there being no tendency to recover fiercely and the amount of trim required from cruising flight is only very little. At the end of a dive the Mustang retains its speed very much longer than the Spitfire.

Manoeuvrability

The aircraft were compared at varying heights for their powers of manoeuvrability and it was found throughout that the Mustang, as was expected, did not have so good a turning circle as the Spitfire. By the time they were at 30,000 feet the Mustang's controls were found to be rather mushy, while the Spitfire's were still very crisp and even in turns during which 15 degrees of flap were used on the Mustang, the Spitfire had no difficulty in out-turning it. In rate of roll, however, it found that while the Spitfire is superior in rolling quickly from one turn to another at speeds up to 300mph, there is very little to chose between the two at 350mph IAS and at 400mph the Mustang is definitely superior, its controls remaining far lighter at high speeds than those of the Spitfire. When the Spitfire was flown with wings clipped, the rate of roll improved at 400mph so as to be almost identical with the Mustang. The manoeuvrability of the Mustang, however, is severely limited by the lack of directional stability which necessitates very heavy forces on the rudder to keep the aircraft steady. The trim requires re-setting for almost every alteration of engine setting of increase or decrease of speed. If trimmed for the climb and then suddenly rolled over into a dive, it is difficult to hold the Mustang in the required line of flight and shooting at or even following the curve of another aircraft in a dive is not easy unless the aircraft is re-trimmed as it gathers speed.

Sighting View

The replacing of the air intake below the engine on the Merlin 65 installation of the Mustang has improved the pilot's sighting view to 120mph.

Low Flying

Although the view forwards and downwards from the Mustang is better than from the Spitfire, low flying is extremely uncomfortable with the present difficulty of executing accurate turns. As a result, any flying except straight and level makes the pilot feel that he lacks sufficient control to fly with sufficient precision to evade ground defences or natural obstacles.

Night Flying

No night flying was carried out as both aircraft were fitted with open exhaust stubs.

Other Points

[First four paragraphs omitted – refer to Mustang only]

The Mustang has a more robust undercarriage and much wider track which can be used on rough ground with far greater safety than the Spitfire's.

Conclusions

The Development of the Merlin 61 and Merlin 65 and 66 and fitted in the Spitfire IX and Mustang X has made available two high performance low-altitude fighters than can be compared as follows:

(i)   In level speed the Mustang is 12–22mph faster than the Spitfire up to 30,000ft.

(ii)   In rate of climb the Spitfire is better than the Mustang by about 800ft/min up to 20,000ft, the operational ceiling of 1,000ft/min being 37,000ft for the Spitfire and 34,000 for the Mustang.

(iii)   In the dive the Mustang is able to out-pace the Spitfire without difficulty.

(iv)   In turning and rolling manoeuvres the Spitfire is better, save that at 400mph IAS, with standard wing it was a little inferior to the Mustang in rate of roll. With the Spitfire wing tips clipped their roll is identical at this speed. At altitude the Mustang's aileron control does not appear sufficient.

(v)   The Mustang suffers badly from lack of directional stability and adequate rudder control, both of which detract seriously from its fighting capabilities. Modifications are in hand to improve these qualities.

(vi)   The view for fighting and search generally from the Mustang is inferior to that from the Spitfire.

(vii)   The Mustang carries 150 gallons as compared with the Spitfire's 85 gallons. The latter can be increased by 30 gallons in a jettison tank.

D O Finlay
Wing Commander
Commanding AFDU
9th February 1943

~ ANNEXE L ~

AFDU Tactical Trials: Spitfire XII (Report No 61)

Introduction

On instructions from Headquarters, Fighter Command, a production Spitfire XII (EN223), was collected from A&AEE on 21st December 1942 for tactical trials.

Description

This aircraft is a standard Spitfire VC airframe modified to take a Griffon III engine in order to produce a high performance low altitude fighter. It differs otherwise from the VC in that the wing tips have been removed to improve manoeuvrability, the bulge over the cannon feed on the mainplane is much smaller, the rudder and trimming tabs are larger, and the engine cowlings and spinner differ considerably. It is fitted with facilities for beam approach and about the first seven, including the aircraft on trial, have the oil tank behind the pilot. This is not acceptable operationally and subsequent aircraft will have the oil tank mounted immediately aft of the fireproof bulkhead. The fuel capacity is retained at 85 gallons, and jettison tanks can be used if required. The first six aircraft, including EN223, have dural propellers, the remainder will have wooden ones. The external finish of EN223 was far better than has been seen on standard production Spitfire Vs and IXs.

   [*Next paragraph omitted*]

Tactical

General

The aircraft was flown throughout the trials with wings clipped and full armament, i.e. 2 x 20-mm cannon and 4 x .303 Browning guns. All guns were loaded with full ammunition. IFF was carried and one oxygen bottle. The all-up weight for the trials was about 7,400lbs. With wooden propeller and certain equipment such as IFF removed, the rate of climb and handling can be further improved.

Flying Characteristics
This aircraft has the normal Spitfire feel about it, but the take-off needs care, as the large amount of torque causes it to swing away to the right, not to the left as usual, and if the pilot is slow in reacting the swing is so strong that he will not be able to correct even with full left rudder. This is being considerably improved by fining off the fine pitch stop on the propeller and so enabling a full rpm to be obtained at lower boost values. In the air the handling of both EN223 and another production Spitfire XII, which was made available by Supermarine for one day, were felt to be far superior to the normal Spitfire IX or VB, being exceptionally good in the lateral control, which is crisper and lighter due to the clipped wings. The longitudinal stability is much better than that of the Spitfire V, and in the dive it was particularly noticed that when trimmed for cruising flight, it stays in easily at 400mph IAS, and does not recover fiercely. In turns the stick load is always positive and the control very comfortable. The rudder, however, is most sensitive to changes in engine settings and needs re-trimming for most alterations of flight, as it is too heavy to be held by the feet for long periods. The Spitfire XII has the usual Spitfire stall characteristics. The engine runs noticeably more roughly than a Merlin.

Performance
The Spitfire XII is capable of high speed at low altitude and is considerably faster than the Spitfire V. It is faster than the Spitfire IX by about 10mph at sea level, and slower by 9mph at 10,000ft. It is slower up to 15,000ft and it becomes slightly the faster until 19,000ft. The maximum speeds are 372mph at 5,700ft, and 397mph at 18,000ft. Checks were made with EN223 and the speeds were found to be almost identical with those quoted, the absence of wing tips probably making up for the special finish of the prototype.

Climb
The climb at full combat rating is not as good as that of the Spitfire IX with the dropped blower peak. Comparative zoom climbs were carried out with a Spitfire IX of this type which had the standard wing tips, with the following results:

Zero to 10,000ft:	Spitfire XII slower by about 30 seconds
10,000 to 20,000ft:	Spitfire XII slower by about 45 seconds

When compared in the climb below 10,000ft with the Spitfire V using 16lb boost, it was found there was little to choose between them during a full throttle climb away from take-off.

For the production aircraft with clipped wings the operational ceiling of 1,000ft/min is reached at 28,500ft, and the rate of climb for the earlier aircraft is slightly slower, but when modified as described in paras 3 and 4, the climb may well equal that of the prototype. The time taken for a section climbing easily to reach 28,500ft is about 25 minutes.

Dive
In comparative dives with the Spitfire IX when both aircraft maintained the engine settings they had had in formation, the XII pulled away slightly as being the cleaner design, but at full throttle there was nothing to choose between the two aircraft.

Manoeuvrability
The manoeuvrability of the Spitfire XII is considered to be excellent. It was compared with the Spitfire IX (RM.10SM engine), also designed as a high performance low-altitude fighter, over which it has an advantage in speed but not in climb, and found to be much better in rate of roll. Above 20,000ft however, the Spitfire IX with standard wing tips has a better all-round performance and was able to out-manoeuvre the XII. It was unfortunate that in the trials the Spitfire IX was only an average aircraft on controls and was inferior to both Mk XIIs flown. It is considered than when used below 20,000ft it will be able to out-pace, out-turn and roll as well as the Fw 190. The general manoeuvrability for dog-fighting is slightly limited by the fact that the engine cuts under negative acceleration forces.

Endurance
Accurate consumption figures are not yet available. One practice operation carried out in company with a VB gave a consumption 5 galls higher for 1hr 30mins.

Sighting View
Owing to the engine having been set lower than the Merlin in the V or IX, the sighting view over the centre of the cowlings is increased from 100mph standard to 120mph, which gives a total of four degrees downward view.

Low Flying
Owing to the slightly improved forward view and to the benefit obtained when looking sideways over the clipped wing tips, pilots have felt very confident in low flying in the Spitfire XII. The aircraft handles very well in all turns but when throttle alterations are made during turns close to the ground, pilots must be careful to guard against the alterations in trim, particularly in a right-hand turn when the nose is pulled down.

Night Flying [Omitted]

Cine Camera Gun [Omitted]

Maintenance [Omitted]

Conclusions

The Spitfire XII handles in general better than the previous marks of Spitfire. Its longitudinal stability has been improved, but the rudder control is not at present completely satisfactory, as it needs constant re-trimming and is rather heavy.

The aircraft fills the category of a low-altitude fighter extremely well, being capable of speeds of 372mph at 5,700ft and 397mph at 18,000ft.

The climb is not as good as the rest of the performance in general, being inferior to the Spitfire IX and similar to the Spitfire V at 16lb boost up to 10,000ft. The operational ceiling (with clipped wings) is about 28,500ft. Modifications already in hand should improve the rate of climb, especially at low altitudes.

The aircraft dives well and benefits from having its wing tips clipped.

Manoeuvrability is excellent particularly in its rate of roll.

The sighting view over the nose has been slightly increased to give a totals deflection allowance of 120mph.

The similarity of design to Spitfires V and IX will make its identification by the enemy difficult.

DO Finlay
Wing Commander
Commanding AFDU
6th February 1943

~ ANNEXE M ~

AFDU Tactical Trials:
Spitfire Mark XIV (Report No 117)

Introduction

In accordance with instructions from Headquarters, A.D.G.B. (letter reference ADGB/S.29156/Air Tactics dated 29.2.44 refers), tactical trials have been completed on the Spitfire XIV. Aircraft RB141 was delivered to this Unit on 28.1.44 for comparative trials with a Tempest V. It was discovered that this aircraft was not representative of production aircraft for Squadrons, and Spitfire XIV No RB179 was therefore made available and delivered on 25.2.44. the operational weight with full fuel and ammunition is 8,400lbs. To give a clear picture to the greatest number, the Spitfire IX (maximum engine settings +18lbs. Boost, 3000revs) has been chosen for full comparison, and not the Spitfire XII which is a low-altitude aircraft only built in small numbers. Tactical comparisons have been made with the Tempest V and Mustang III, and combat trials have been carried out against the Fw 190 (BMW.801D) and Me 109G.

Brief Description

The Spitfire XIV is a short-range medium-high altitude fighter, armed with 2 x 20-mm cannon and 4 x 0.303 Browning machine guns in the wings. It is fitted with a Griffin 65 engine of approximately 2000hp. Pick-up points are provided for the carrying of 30-gallon, 45-gallon, or 90-gallon long-range tanks. At present there are no bomb racks. In appearance it is very similar to the Spitfire XII with normal wings, except that it has a five-bladed propeller. The fin and rudder have been further modified.

The Cockpit [Omitted]

Flying Characteristics

In the most respects this aircraft is similar to Spitfire IX, except for some very marked changes of trim with alteration of throttle setting below q boost. This applies principally to the rudder, despite the incorporation of the servo-operated trimming tab. This is the one bad characteristic of the aircraft. The elevators also require more frequent trimming than in a Spitfire IX.

Taxying
The aircraft is nose-heavy and considerable care must be exercised in taxying, particularly in a strong wind.

Take-off
During take-off, the aircraft tends to swing to the right and to drag the right wing, full power should therefore not be used immediately on opening the throttle, but only when the aircraft is almost airborne, i.e. +6lbs. Boost is quite sufficient. The nose must not be allowed to fall lower than the horizon as the prop clearance is very slight.

Turning Stall
The Spitfire XIV gives less warning of a stall in a tight turn than a Spitfire IX, though the same pre-stall characteristic ('shuddering') occurs. This is a good point as it allows sighting to be maintained nearer the stall. The aircraft tends to come out of a dive in a similar manner to all other Spitfires.

Landing
The landing run is slightly longer and the aircraft sinks rather more rapidly than a Spitfire IX on landing. In all other respects the landing is quite normal and very easy. There is no tendency to swing.

Formation Flying
Quite straightforward, similar to the Spitfire IX.

Low Flying
The view from the cockpit is as good as from a Spitfire IX, the longer nose making no appreciable difference. Engine handling is a little more inconvenient because of the recurring trimming changes to elevators and rudder. The aircraft does not therefore handle quite as well as the Spitfire IX near the ground.

Night Flying [Omitted]

Tactical Comparison with Spitfire IX

The tactical differences are caused chiefly by the fact that the Spitfire XIV has an engine of greater capacity and is the heavier aircraft (weighing 8,400lbs against 7,480lbs of Spitfire IX).

Range and Endurance
The Spitfire XIV, without a long-range tank, carries 110 gallons of fuel and 9 gallons of oil. When handled similarly, the Spitfire XIV uses fuel at about 1¼ times the rate of the Spitfire IX. Its endurance is therefore slightly less. Owing to its higher speed for corresponding engine settings, its range is about equal. For the same reasons, extra fuel carried in a long-range tank keeps its range about equal to the Spitfire IX; its endurance being slightly less.

Speeds
At all heights the Spitfire XIV is approximately 30–35mph faster in level flight. The best performance heights are similar, being just below 15,00 feet and between 25,000 and 32,000 feet.

Climb
The Spitfire XIV has a slightly better maximum climb than the Spitfire IX having the best maximum rate of climb yet seen at this unit. In the zoom climb the Spitfire XIV gains slightly all the way, especially if full throttle is used in the climb.

Dive
The Spitfire XIV will pull away from the Spitfire IX in a dive.

Turning Circle
The turning circles of both aircraft are identical. The Spitfire XIV appears to turn slightly better to port than it does to starboard. The warning of an approaching high speed stall is less pronounced in the case of the Spitfire XIV.

Rate of Roll
The rate of roll of both aircraft is also very much the same.

Search View and Rear View
The all-round view from the pilot's cockpit is good; the longer nose of the aircraft interferes with the all round visibility, which remains the same as that of the Spitfire IX. Rear view is similar.

Sighting View and Fire Power
The sighting view is slightly better, being 4 degrees (140mph) as against 3$^1/_3$ degrees. The two bulges at the side cause little restriction. The fire power is identical with the Spitfire IX.

Armour
As for the Spitfire IX.

Conclusions
The all round performance of the Spitfire XIV is better than the Spitfire IX at all heights. In level flight it is 25–35mph faster and has correspondingly greater rate of climb. Its manoeuvrability is as good as a Spitfire IX. It is easy to fly but should be handled with care when taxying and taking off.

Combat Trial Against Fw 190 (BMW.801D)

Maximum Speeds
From 0–5,000 feet and 15,000–20,000 feet, the Spitfire XIV is only 20mph faster; at all other heights it is up to 60mph faster than the Fw 190 (BMW.801.D). It is estimated to have about the same maximum speed as the new Fw 190 (DB.603) at all heights.

Maximum Climb
The Spitfire XIV has a considerably greater rate of climb than the Fw 190 (BMW.801D) or (estimated) the new Fw 190 (DB.603) at all heights.

Dive
After the initial part of the dive, during which the Fw 190 gains slightly, the Spitfire XIV has a slight advantage.

Turning Circle
The Spitfire XIV can easily turn inside the Fw 190, though in the case of a right-hand turn this difference is not quite so pronounced.

Rate of Roll
The Fw 190 is very much better.

Conclusions
In defence, the Spitfire XIV should use its remarkable maximum climb and turning circle against any enemy aircraft. In the attack it can afford to 'mix it' but should beware the quick roll and dive. If this manoeuvre is used by an Fw 190 and the Spitfire XIV follows, it will probably not be able to close the range until the Fw 190 has pulled out of its dive.

Combat Trial Against Me 109G

Maximum Speed
The Spitfire XIV is 40mph faster at all heights except near 16,000 feet where it is only 10mph faster.

Maximum Climb
Same results. At 16,000 feet identical, otherwise the Spitfire XIV out-climbs the Me 109G. The zoom climb is practically identical when the climb is made without opening throttle. Climbing at full throttle, the Spitfire XIV draws away from the Me 109G quite easily.

Dive
During the initial part of the dive, the Me 109G pulls away slightly, but when a speed of 380mph is reached, the Spitfire XIV begins to gain on the Me 109G.

Turning Circle
The Spitfire XIV easily out turns the Me 109G in either direction.

Rate of Roll
The Spitfire XIV rolls much more quickly.

Conclusion
The Spitfire XIV is superior to the Me 109G in every respect.

Combat Performance with 90-Gallon Long-Range Tanks

As the Spitfire XIV has a very short range it has been assumed that when a long-range tank is to be carried, it is most likely to be the 90-gallon tank rather than the 30-gallon or 45-gallon. Pending further instructions, no drops or trials have been carried out with the 30- or 45-gallon tanks. The aircraft's performance with either can be estimated from the results given below of trials with the 90-gallon long-range tank.

Drops
The aircraft was fitted with Assistor Springs as for the Spitfire IX. Two drops were made with the empty tanks at 50 feet, and 25,000 feet, A.S.T. 250mph with no trouble. Cine photographs were taken and show the tank dropping quite clear of the aircraft. Further trials would be necessary to check these results thoroughly.

Speeds
About 80mph is knocked off the maximum speed and correspondingly off the speed at intermediate throttle settings. The aircraft is then still faster than the Fw 190 (BMW.801D) and Me 109G above 20,000 feet.

Climb
Climb is most affected. With a half-full tank its maximum climb becomes identical with the Spitfire IX without the tank. Even with a full tank it can therefore climb as fast as the Fw 190 or Me 109G. Its zoom climb is hardly affected.

Dibe
So long as the tank is more than 1/3 full, the dive acceleration is similar.

Turning Circle
The Spitfire XIV now has a definitely wider turning circle than before, but is still within the Fw 190 (BMW.801D) and Me 109G.

Rate of Roll
Similar.

Conclusions
Even with the 90-gallon long-range tank, the Spitfire XIV can equal or outclass the Fw 190 (BMW.801D) and Me 109G in every respect. Its main advantages remain the tight turn and maximum speed.

Technical

Gun Harmonisation [Omitted]

Gun Firing [Omitted]

Re-arming [Omitted]

Cine-gun Installation and Harmonisation [Omitted]

Radio [Omitted]

Oxygen [Omitted]

Engine Temperature [Omitted]

Starting Hints [*Omitted*]

Servicing Hints [*Omitted*]

General Conclusions

The Spitfire XIV is superior to the Spitfire IX in all respects.

It has the best all-round performance of any present-day fighter, apart from the range.

Modification to the compass bracket shown at Appendix 'B', to enable the pilot to obtain an unrestricted view of the compass, should be incorporated.

Wing Commander A. R. Wright
Commanding A.F.D.U.
19th March, 1944.

~ ANNEXE N ~

AFDU Tactical Trials:
Spitfire Mark F.21 LA201

Aircraft LA201 was allotted for these trials and was fully representative of the aircraft now being delivered to squadrons. It was flown throughout completely equipped and fully armed. Eight pilots from this Establishment and two outside pilots have flown the aircraft.

Description

Role

The Spitfire 21 is a short-range, medium-high altitude single seat fighter, designed to replace the Spitfire XIV.

Airframe [Omitted]

Engine [Omitted]

Fuel Capacity

Compared with the Spitfire XIV, the Spitfire 21 has two additional fuel tanks each of 5½ gallons inboard of the main-plane tanks, giving a total fuel capacity of 120 gallons as against 109 gallons

Armament

The armament consists of four Mk II 20-mm Hispano guns, mounted two in each mainplane outboard of the airscrew. Two ammunition boxes, one for each gun, are housed out-board of the guns and aft of the main spar. The forward box is for the inboard gun and the aft box for the outboard gun and hold 175 rounds and 150 rounds respectively. The cannon are fired pneumatically by means of a selective push button on the control column spade grip. Pressing the top of the button fires the inboard cannon, pressing the bottom fires the out-board cannon, and all four cannon are fired simultaneously if the centre of the button is pressed. The aircraft on trial was fitted with the standard Mark II sight. A bomb carrier for either a 250-pound or 500-pound bomb can be fixed underneath the fuselage on the drop tank fittings

Armour
The armour protection is designed to give protection against 20-mm AP Mauser ammunition within a 20° cone to the rear and against 13-mm AP ammunition within a 20° cone from ahead

Cockpit Layout [Omitted]

Flying Limitations [Omitted]

Handling in the Air

Take-Off [Omitted]

Landing [Omitted]

Flying Controls [Omitted]

General Handling
Whilst this aircraft is not unstable in pitch, above 25,000 feet the instability in yaw makes it behave as if it were unstable about all three axes. Because of its higher wing loading the high speed stall comes in earlier than with other marks of Spitfire and in a steep turn the general feeling of instability, combined with its critical trimming qualities, is unpleasant. The control characteristics are such that this aircraft is most difficult to fly accurately and compares most unfavourably with other modern fighters.

Search and Sighting View
The all-round search view from the pilot's cockpit is good although, as with the Spitfire XIV, the view straight ahead is poor due to the longer nose of the aircraft. No trouble was experienced with misting-up of the front panel. The sighting view is similar to the Spitfire XIV and gives 4° view over the nose as against 3½° on the Spitfire IX.

Low Flying
At low altitude in conditions of bad visibility, the comparatively poor view from the cockpit and the feeling of instability makes this aircraft almost dangerous to fly. It is far too sensitive on the elevator and the slightest twitch by the pilot is sufficient to cause a loss or gain in height. In conditions of good visibility the accurate flying which is at all times necessary still limits the pilot's ability to search.

Aerobatics
The aerobatic qualities of this aircraft may seem good on the first impression because of the excellent aileron control, but in fact the instability and constant trimming required more than outweigh this advantage and make the aircraft less easy for aerobatics than previous Spitfires.

Formation Flying [Omitted]

Operational Ceiling [Omitted]

Night Flying [Omitted]

Instrument Flying [Omitted]

Sighting Platform

The good aileron control of the Spitfire 21 enables the pilot to anticipate the manoeuvres of any other fighter, but due to lack of stability it is difficult to hold the sight on the target especially when changes of direction are rapid. The effects of instability on the aircraft as a sighting platform will be more pronounced when it is fitted with a gyro gun sight.

It can be flown accurately enough for ground attack purposes in the hands of an experienced pilot and under trial conditions but the elimination of skid is more difficult with this aircraft than with any other modern fighter and makes it unsuitable for the ground attack role.

Pilot's Comfort

The sliding hood is the normal Spitfire balloon hood, which has never been comfortable for a large pilot to operate; in particular the forward spring catch remains a latent danger to the pilot, as it strikes his head whenever the hood is pulled back with the seat in the up position. The hood on aircraft LA201 was not a good fit and allowed a stream of air to flow onto the right cheek of the pilot.

The position of the cine-gun switch at the bottom right hand side of the spade grip is unsatisfactory and requires adjustment so that the button can be operated without altering the position of the hand.

Tactical Comparison with Spitfire XIV using +18lbs Boost

Range and Endurance

As the consumption of the Griffon 61 is similar to that of the Griffon 65 the Spitfire 21 has greater range and endurance than the Spitfire XIV, measured by the extra 11 gallons of fuel. This has been calculated to represent a difference of 15 miles in radius of action and 10 minutes in endurance.

Speeds

As a result of checks carried out by this Establishment on figures from Supermarine, it appears that the Spitfire 21 is approximately 10–12mph faster than the Spitfire XIV at all altitudes.

Acceleration in Straight and Level Flight

The Spitfire 21 and the Spitfire XIV have approximately the same acceleration in straight and level flight. After opening to full power from maximum cruise settings (2,400revs +7 pounds boost on both aircraft) each aircraft takes about 2½ minutes to reach maximum speed.

Climbs

In the climb at maximum power (2,750revs +18 pounds boost on both aircraft) there was very little to choose between the two at all altitudes. Up to 15,000 feet the Spitfire XIV had a slight advantage, above 15,000 feet the Spitfire 21 was slightly the better.

Zoom Climbs

The Spitfire 21 has a slightly better zoom climb than the Spitfire XIV.

Dive

Initially the Spitfire 21 out-dives the Spitfire XIV, but after reaching a speed of 350mph Indicated there is little difference between the two aircraft.

Turning Circles

The Spitfire 21 is definitely out-turned by the Spitfire XIV at all speeds. As previously stated, the Spitfire 21 is not pleasant in the turn and the high speed stall comes on early.

Rate of Roll

At speeds below 300mph Indicated there is little to choose between the two aircraft, but above this speed the Spitfire 21 becomes increasingly superior due to its lighter ailerons

Conclusions

The Spitfire 21 possesses the following advantages over the Spitfire XIV:

   (i)   It has a slightly greater range
  (ii)   It is faster at all heights by some 10 to 12mph
 (iii)   It has slightly better acceleration in the dive
 (iv)   It has better aileron control at speeds above 300mph
  (v)   It has the greater fire power

The instability in the yawing plane and the critical trimming characteristics of this aircraft make it difficult to fly accurately under the easiest conditions and as a sighting platform it is unsatisfactory both for air-to-air gunnery and ground attack.

Its handling qualities compare unfavourably with all earlier marks of Spitfire and with other modern fighters and more than nullify its advantages in performance and fire power.

The Spitfire XIV is a better all round fighter than the Spitfire 21. The handling qualities of successive marks of the basic Spitfire design have gradually deteriorated until, as exemplified in the Spitfire 21, they prejudice the pilot's ability to exploit the increased performance.

Recommendations

It is recommended that the Spitfire 21 be withdrawn from operations until the instability in the yawing plane has been removed and that it be replaced by the Spitfire XIV or Tempest V until this can be done.

If it is not possible then it must be emphasised that, although the Spitfire 21 is not a dangerous aircraft to fly, pilots must be warned of its handling qualities and in its present state it is not likely to prove a satisfactory fighter.

No further attempts should be made to perpetuate the Spitfire family.

AFDU
December 1944

~ ANNEXE O ~

Tactics Used by Spitfire Day Fighter/ Bomber Squadrons of 2nd TAF (Tactical Paper No 4)

Introduction

The Tactical Airforce, which was created for the invasion of the Continent was mainly based on the fighter force which was then existing in Great Briain

The aircraft deployed by the new force were the same fighter aircraft modified so as to carry bombs and rocket-projectiles. In their role in 2nd T.A.F. the aircraft of the Spitfire XVI Squadrons normally carried the following armament:

  (a) Two 20-mm cannons with 260 rounds of ammunition.
  (b) Two 0.5-in machine-guns with 500 rounds of ammunition.
  (c) One 500-lb bomb plus two 250-lb (fully loaded).
  (d) Two 250-lb plus drop tank (45 gallons).

The bombs were of two types, high explosive and incendiary. The high explosive bombs were either instantaneous or had delayed action fuses from 0.025 second to 72 hours, depending on the kind of target. The bombing was carried out from low-level or from a dive. In the case of low level bombing the normal fuse was of at least 11 seconds delay in order that it should not endanger the bombing aircraft.

The first trials of using fighter aircraft for new purposes were the 'Rhubarb' operations. From the experience gained in these operations and in mass exercises of the fighter squadrons in Great Britain in the years 1943–1944, the basis of the formation of a Tactical Air Force was formed. The employment of fighter aircraft in the Tactical Air Force necessitated new tactics being evolved because of:

  (a) Flying at lower altitude in the reach of enemy flak defences.
  (b) The employment of fighter aircraft in attacks on ground targets.
  (c) The arming of fighter aircraft so that they could carry bombs and rocket projectiles.

The creation of a Tactical Air Force did not change the main tasks of the Fighter Force. It only added new tasks and the personnel and material had to carry out a more varied programme.

The general tactics of the Fighter Force were only changed in as much as the technical improvements of the material allowed it. We will limit ourselves in the review of the Tactical Air Force to the experience of certain Units who had Spitfires Mk XVI at their disposal. These Squadrons had the following tasks to carry out:

(a) Direct co-operation with our own first-line troops.
(b) Attacks on the enemy's front line and rear.
(c) Normal fighter force tasks.

Outline of Operations

Direct Co-operation with First-Line Troops
This co-operation had three main aims:

(a) The attacking of targets which were supplied in advance by the Army to the Air Force through regular channels. It used to take some time before the attack on the supplied target could be carried out. Thus, this method of co-operation could only be effective when the front was more or less stabilised or in the case of immobilised points of resistance such as dug-in artillery or tanks.
(b) [. . .] passed to the pilot from the Contact Car. The pilot who was linked by R / T to the Contact Car could attack any target upon receipt of instructions. The target could be a small one and even mobile.
(c) Patrols of defined regions with attacks on enemy artillery and personnel whose location was normally observed by the pilot patrolling or was betrayed through their own fire. Such patrols and eventual attacks forced the enemy personnel to seek cover and enabled our own troops to have more freedom of movement. These patrols were being carried out as a supplement or instead of the normal co-operation with Contact Car, and only in very special circumstances as, for example, during the crossing of Siegfried Line when the Sappers of the Polish 1st Armoured Division were completing a bridge on the river Mark, during the liquidation of the enemy bridgehead at Breskens opposite Waicheren Island etc.

This activity was not a result of direct requests by the Ground Forces, but was carried out by the Air Force on general lines supplied by higher authority, and had two main tasks:

(a) Attacks on targets supplied and strictly defined as for example, Enemy HQ's, launching points of V.1 and V.2, factories, groups of enemy units, motorised enemy formations, enemy airfields, etc. This kind of task required very minute preparations and especially exact data about the target. Preparation for this type of operation was, therefore, somewhat lengthy.
(b) In reconnaissance and attacks on targets in defined regions, the fighter force had to reconnoitre a defined region and find its own targets for attack. This kind of operation was called 'Armed Recce' and was mainly directed against enemy's lines of communication (road and rail transport). It was also directed against the enemy units and had as a general aim the disorganisation of the enemy in the line and in the rear of the front-line. Once the Air Force gained a definite superiority, and the enemy units

were disorganised, this kind of attack was also carried out to an extended depth.

Normal Fighter Force Tasks
The activity of the Tactical Air Force on the Continent was exercised in rather specific conditions, seeing that the enemy air force hardly ever appeared in order to resist any ventures by the Tactical Air Force. But the 'New Year's' attack of the German Air force, on the 1st January, 1945, was a proof that the general task of the fighter air force should not be left out of the programme of the Tactical Air Force. It was a proof that the Tactical Air Force should be ready at any time to carry out tasks normally carried out by a Fighter Force.

The three main tasks are:

(a) To gain and maintain air superiority. For that purpose, sections or whole squadrons of the Tactical Air Force ware prepared for combating the enemy Air Force, for maintaining readiness and for offensive patrols.
(b) To act as escort for other aircraft; this task being carried out on the lines of the strict fighter force system.
(c) Reconnaissance, which was the duty of every aircraft of Tactical Air Force. As the front line was very mobile, ordinary tactical reconnaissance could not be effective. The time for carrying out an attack on a reconnoitred target was limited owing to the very mobile nature of most targets. As a result of the above all Tactical Air Force aircraft were carrying out a continuous reconnaissance during their operations. Any target which was suitable for attack and destruction but could not be effectively tackled by the pilot who located it, for any reason at all, was passed by the pilot – immediately by R/T to any other section or formation who were operating in the same region and could be directed to the target. If the target was a large one, for example, concentrations of enemy motorised units or steamed-up trains at railway junctions, the pilot passed his information to G.C.C. All other information as for instance enemy movements etc. the pilot used to pass to the Intelligence Officer upon landing.

Factors Influencing the Carrying-out of a Task

Nature of Target
The nature of the target was the deciding factor of the number of aircraft which were to take part in the operation. On large targets or on targets whose destruction was essential two or even three squadrons were sent out. On small or mobile targets one or two sections (of two aircraft) were employed.

[*Seven paragraphs missing from original text*]

Each pilot had to know:

(a) The course back.

(b) The position of the bomb line and forward troops so that he could be certain at every moment on which side of, and how far from, the forward troops he was.

(c) The position of the nearest airfield in case of emergency landing.

Flight to Target
The flight to the target was divided into three parts:

(a) Over own territory. If there were no special restrictions from our own A.A. or troops, the flight to the targets was left to the discretion of the leader of the formation. The general rule was that the formation should fly as close as possible but not as close a formation as would tire the pilots. The height of the flight was decided by the visibility, base of clouds and ease of navigation.

(b) Crossing of the front line. Before reaching the front line the aircraft would take up battle formation and would climb so as to cross the front line at a minimum height of 5,000ft. It was usual to climb to a greater height (10,000ft) and cross the front line at high speed in a slight dive. At this stage the pilots would switch on their cameras and their sights and get the bombs ready for release so that in the event of meeting enemy aircraft they could release the bombs and be ready for dog-fighting.

(c) Over enemy territory. As a rule the height of 5,000ft was kept and the aircraft flew at high speed (+2 boost). They never flew on a straight line so as not to reveal to the enemy to which target they were flying, and as a safe-guard against enemy flak.

Bombing

Bombing by T.A.F. was divided into two main categories; dive-bombing and low-level bombing. Most of the bombing missions were dive-bombing as the accuracy of the bombing did not suffer and the aircraft were less vulnerable to flak. Sometimes it was essential to bomb from low-level, although in most cases the use of aircraft with rocket projectiles was more effective in this type of attack. Bombing could be carried out with a whole formation bombing at once or with one aircraft following the other. In the first case the aircraft were less endangered by flak, and in the second case, greater accuracy was achieved. Polish Squadrons normally bombed one aircraft after another. This ensured both liberty of action for each pilot and more accurate bombing, as the pilot who followed could correct his own bombing by the result achieved by the pilot who preceded him. In addition, the leader could give advice on aiming to the pilots by R/T, the main point being the effect of wind on bombs.

Approach
The approach to the attack was made in level flight at speed 220 to 230mph. At the moment when the target hid itself under the wing on a line of about 1/3 from the end of the wing-tip, the pilot made a gentle turn under the 'horizon in the direction of the target. He regulated the speed of the turn so that the target should be visible all the time. This turn had to be a very steady one and made without the excessive use of the rudder, so that the pilot could very quickly catch the target in his sight. There was another method of flying straight at the target and attacking it from a half roll, but in

this case the aircraft gathered high speed and the pilot had great difficulty steadying it and bringing it on the target.

Attack

The attack was usually carried out from a dive and at angle of 60 to 45 degrees. The leader dived at a steep angle, while the aircraft that were behind him and at his side were forced to dive at a shallower angle. When diving the pilots had to remember:

(a) The danger of a traverse as in this case the bombing was inaccurate.
(b) Not to get the aircraft into high speed as the aiming time would pass too quickly and the pulling out from the dive would be much more difficult and unpleasant. The bombs were released at 3,000ft. The angle of release for the bombs depended on the direction and strength of the wind.

Departure

The departure from the target after bombing was carried out in level flight at full boost in order to get out as quickly as possible from the orbit of enemy flak.

Low Level

Bombing at low level. This was carried out on the same lines as strafing.

Co-operation

The squadron was divided into three sections of four aircraft. The sections usually had different colours (Red, Blue, Yellow, White) while the aircraft in the sections were Red 1, Red 2, etc. Red 1 was the leader of the formation. Once the formation reached the region of their target, the leader would issue last minute instructions before attack, such as the location of the target, the direction of attack, direction of departure, etc. Upon receipt of these instructions, the pilots would get into the correct order ready for bombing and keep a distance of about four hundred yards between themselves. They kept this distance so that the formation should not be too long and in order that every aircraft should start diving at more or less the same point and at the same angle as the leader. Every pilot, upon the release of his bombs, informed the others that he had done so by R/T, for example 'Red 4, dropped'. Each pilot observed the hits of the bombs of the pilot who preceded him. Thus, after the attack, it was possible to decide how accurate the bombing was. If a pilot for any reason did not drop his bombs in his turn, he reported this by R/T and dropped his bombs as the last of the formation.

Strafing

Strafing with cannon and machine-guns was limited to special targets and was not usually carried out together with bombing. A typical case for strafing was during Armed Recce on mobile targets. The attack followed these general lines:

(a) General remarks. After locating the target the leader of the formation decided on the time, place and way of approach, passing the information by R/T to the rest of the pilots. The enemy had look-outs on all his transport vehicles. On MT they normally had two, one on the mudguard and one on the roof or at the back of the vehicle in question. As soon as our aircraft were sighted the vehicle usually hid under trees or in the vicinity of buildings. Thus the pilots were forced to leave the moving vehicles and not attack until they were on a part of the road where it could not easily find cover.

The attack had to be carried out rapidly so as to deny the vehicle time to find cover.

(b) The approach to attack was usually carried out from a wide turn with a loss of height so that when levelling out for the attack, the aircraft should not be higher than 1,500ft and as far as possible at normal speed.

(c) After steadying the aircraft and getting the target in the sights, the pilot would open fire at a height of about 700ft from a distance of about 500 yards and at an angle of 25 to 30 degrees. The angle of attack in relation to the direction of the moving target used to vary from 0 to 90 degrees and dependent mainly on the nature of the target, its position and the outlines of the terrain. The attacks on motor transport and locomotives were normally carried out as far as possible at an angle of 30 degrees from the front.

(d) The departure from the target after attack was carried out at full throttle low-level flying for about 30 seconds with a turn in order to get out of the line of fire of the next aircraft. Thus, in the case of a convoy, the leader would attack the first car on the side to which he intended to turn after carrying out his attack.

(e) Co-operation between aircraft. The usual practice was to send out two aircraft on such missions. In the case of more aircraft, the aircraft would take up a formation to be on the straight line for attack when the first aircraft started its attack. The following aircraft only started firing at the moment when the one who preceded him passed the target with a slight turn. On small targets or single targets, if there were not more targets than the number of aircraft, one attack should be sufficient. Only in the case of a greater number of vehicles, and after making sure that the flak was not dangerous, did the leader decide to repeat the attack. Normally, when the front line was more or less stabilised, the enemy had a great amount of flak concentrated and the repetition of an attack after the flak positions were manned was very risky. The enemy sometimes used dummy motor transport and locomotives, concentrating round those dummies a great amount of light flak, and pilots had to be very careful to avoid being caught.

(f) Effectiveness of the cannon and machine-guns in the Spitfire Mk XVI was very great, especially in attacks on road and rail transport or moving columns of enemy troops. Attacks on trains usually exploded the locomotive. The shooting up and destruction of the rail trucks, however, depended on the freight they were carrying. The attacks on road transport usually set fire to vehicles and completely destroyed them.

Special Tasks

The special tasks that were normally carried out consisted of patrols over the front line, which attacked targets of opportunity, and co-operation with the Contact Car which directed fighters to particular targets.

Patrols

Patrols over our own first line troops were normally carried out by two aircraft at a time. They patrolled a certain region at a certain time and attacked any targets, such as artillery and enemy troops, that were proving obstacles to the advance of our own troops.

Contact Car

The co-operation with a Contact Car was carried out by 2 or 4 aircraft at a time, sometimes carrying bombs. The aircraft would proceed to a rendezvous at about 5,000ft and then report by R/T to the Contact Car. The Contact Car would then pass to them the tasks and give them the information about the target with the aid of special grids which were previously drawn on the maps or with the aid of landmarks. (Hills or valleys could not be taken as landmarks for the pilot.) After carrying out the attack the pilot would return to the rendezvous point. The co-operation between the aircraft and Contact Car would go on until all ammunition was spent or the defined time elapsed. Other sections, if required, would then take the place of the one which had just finished its task.

Return

The return to base was normally carried out on the same lines as the flight to the target, our own front line being crossed at a minimum height of 5,000ft in order to give our own A.A. a chance to recognise the aircraft.

Emergencies

Airfield conditions and flying in the orbit of enemy flak often resulted in technical defects as well as damage caused by the enemy. Thus it was essential that each pilot should be mentally and technically prepared for all eventualities. Over enemy territory the closest co-operation between aircraft was essential. Pilots were instructed to watch whether their fellow pilots managed to get rid of their drop-tanks or drop their bombs. Pilots were told to escort their fellow-pilots who were hit by flak at least to the moment when they crossed our own lines, but usually until the aircraft in distress managed to land. The purpose of such an escort was to defend the damaged aircraft, to help the pilot find the nearest airfield or landing ground and then inform the base of the exact spot and how the landing was carried out. If the pilot did not manage to release his bombs or his drop tank, he used to land as the last in the formation. This was so that if he did damage the runway it would not stop the other aircraft landing.

Landing [Omitted]

Interrogation

[First paragraph omitted]

Apart from the change of armament (i.e. the carrying of bombs) and the novel circumstances of activity, the main characteristics of the T.A.F. as compared with Fighter Command was the fact that there was not a single sortie which did not result in some kind of action. On the whole the pilot could not return from a flight without having found a target for his bombs or cannons and machine-guns unless there were special instructions to the contrary. Most of the sorties were carried out by sections of two aircraft and each pilot was personally responsible for carrying out his task.

Thus we can assert that pilots who took part in sorties in T.A.F. had to possess all the characteristics required of a fighter pilot and had to display great courage, speed of decision and speed of action. Taking into consideration that it is very difficult to repeat an attack on the same target and that most of the targets are mobile, the main characteristic which should be sought in the future T.A.F. pilot should be accuracy of bombing and firing. This, apart from the technical side of it, depends mostly on the speedy orientation and quick action on the part of the pilot. Pilots should be good navigators, as the targets will be small ones, mobile and difficult to observe in the terrain, and the whole flight will have to be carried out at comparatively low altitude.

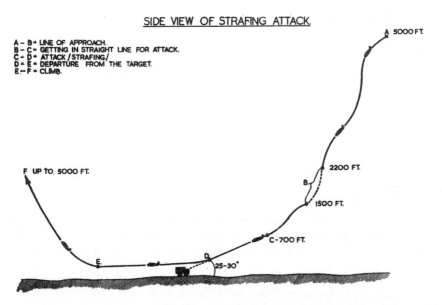

SIDE VIEW OF STRAFING ATTACK.

A – B = LINE OF APPROACH.
B – C = GETTING IN STRAIGHT LINE FOR ATTACK.
C – D = ATTACK /STRAFING./
D – E = DEPARTURE FROM THE TARGET.
E – F = CLIMB.

C. 2nd TAF employment of Spitfires in the ground-attack role: this graphic shows the ideal strafing attack profile.

D. The Spitfire proved to be a reasonable fighter-bomber; this 2nd TAF diagram shows the dive-bomb profile.

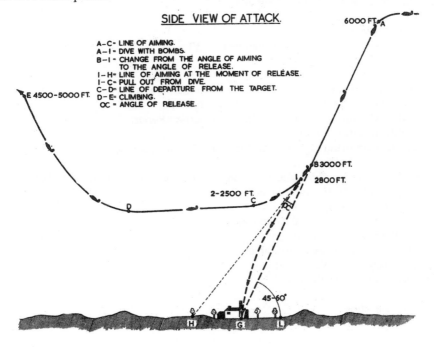

SIDE VIEW OF ATTACK.

A–C = LINE OF AIMING.
A–I = DIVE WITH BOMBS.
B–I = CHANGE FROM THE ANGLE OF AIMING
        TO THE ANGLE OF RELEASE.
I–H = LINE OF AIMING AT THE MOMENT OF RELEASE.
I–C = PULL OUT FROM DIVE.
C–D = LINE OF DEPARTURE FROM THE TARGET.
D–E = CLIMBING.
OC = ANGLE OF RELEASE.

Bibliography

Official Sources

The core of this book is based on official records, including those for trials and operational units, plus the post-war narratives produced by the Air Historical Branch. Many of the individual papers used have no reference other than their title and are listed here under 'miscellaneous papers'.

AIR 27 series of RAF Squadron Operational Record Books
AIR 28 series of RAF Station Operational Record Books
AIR 29 series of RAF Training and Support Unit Operational Record Books
Aircrew Training: Report on Conference held in the United Kingdom January/February 1942. Air Ministry, 1942
Air Fighting Committee Papers and Reports
Air Fighting Development Unit Reports

Air Historical Branch Narratives
    Air Defence of Great Britain, volumes I to VI
    Aircrew Training

Air Publication AP3232. Air Sea Rescue. Air Historical Branch, 195
    Fighter Command Order of Battle Tables 1938–1947
    Fighter Command Operational Research Section Reports
    Fighter Command Form Y
    Fighter Command Operational Record Book (Air 24 series)

Luftwaffe Documents (all translated from captured German documents, translated and held in the files of the Air Historical Branch)
    Air Operations against Britain
    Battle of Britain, General Adolf Galland
    Fighter Staff Conferences
    Strength and Serviceability Tables
    Summary of the War Situation
    War Diary of 1 Jagdkorps

Miscellaneous Papers
    Allied Expeditionary Air Force Strengths and Losses Tables

Fighter Command Research Branch Papers
History of Fighter Command; Fighter Command Summary Notes
Manoeuvrability in Air Fighting: Spitfire versus Hurricane
Note on Operational Strength and Wastage amongst Day Fighter Squadrons in the
Battle of Britain
Tactical Air Operations in the European Theatre
Tactics used by Spitfire Day Fighter/Bomber Squadrons of 2nd TAF

Pilots' Notes
Spitfire IIA, IIB
Spitfire FVII, FVIII, PRX
Spitfire IX, XI, XVI
Spitfire XIV, XIX
Supermarine Spitfire VI
Supermarine Spitfire XII
Supermarine Spitfire 18
Supermarine Spitfire 21
Supermarine Seafire XV, XVII
Supermarine Seafire 45, 46
Supermarine Seafire 47

Reports on Air Operations 1939–1945
SD161 Location of Units Tables, 1939–1946
SD737 Armament Volume 2, Air Historical Branch, 1954
Secret Organisational Memoranda 1939 to 1946
Tactical Bulletins, Papers and Memoranda issued by Air Ministry
Tactical Bulletins, Papers and Memoranda issued by HQ SW Pacific Area
Tactical Bulletins, Papers and Memoranda issued by HQ Mediterranean Allied Air
Force

Biographies and Secondary Sources

The volume of published material on the Spitfire in book and article form is almost as legendary as the aircraft itself. Over the years the author has acquired or read countless books and articles dealing with the aircraft itself, its squadrons or simply the general campaigns in which it was involved. The following bibliography includes only a fraction of this material to cover those books that were of direct and particular use during the research for this book. The author has also collected, and used, a large amount of personal anecdotal material obtained either through interview or letter, which are not listed here.

Avery, Max, with Shores, Christopher, *Spitfire Leader*, London: Grub Street, 1997.
Bashow, David, *All the Fine Young Eagles*, Toronto: Stoddart, 1996.
Bracken, Robert, *Spitfire: The Canadians*, Toronto: Stoddart, 1995.
Brown, David, *Seafire: The Spitfire that Went to Sea*, London: Greenhill Books, 1989.
Burns, Michael, *Bader, the Man and his Men*, London: Arms & Armour Press, 1994.
Closterman, Pierre, *The Big Show*, London: Chatto and Windus, 1951.

Crook, David, *Spitfire Pilot, A Personal Account of the Battle of Britain*, London: Faber & Faber, 1942 (reprinted London: Greenhill Books, 2006).

Crosley, Mike, 'Seafire Diary', *FlyPast*, Stanford: Key Publishing.

Cull, Brian, with Aloni, Shlomo and Nicolle, David, *Spitfires over Israel*, London: Grub Street, 1995.

Delve, Ken, with Pitchfork, Graham, *South Yorkshire's Own: History of 616 Squadron*, Doncaster: Doncaster Books, 1990.

Delve, Ken, *Source Book of the RAF*, Shrewsbury: Airlife, 1994.

Delve, Ken, *D-Day the Air Battle*, Ramsbury: Crowood Press, 2004.

Dundas, Hugh, *Flying Start: A Fighter Pilot's War Years*, London: Stanley Paul, 1989.

Dunn, Bill Newton, *Big Wing*, Shrewsbury: Airlife, 1992.

Franks, Norman, *Spitfires over the Arakan*, London: William Kimber, 1988.

Goss, Chris, *The Luftwaffe Bombers' Battle of Britain: The Inside Story – July–October 1944*, Manchester: Crecy, 2000.

Henshaw, Alex, *Sigh for a Merlin*, Manchester: Crecy, 1999.

Holmes, Tony, 'Jungle Fighter', *Spitfire Special*, Stanford: Key Publishing.

Jacobs, V., *Woodpecker Story: 136 (Fighter) Squadron RAF*, Edinburgh: Pentland Press, 1994.

Jarrold, Jerry, with Delve, Ken, *Did You Survive the War – An Ordinary Fighter Pilot's Story*. Kings Lynn: Aviation History Centre, 2006.

Jefford, Jeff, *RAF Squadrons* (2nd edition), Airlife: Shrewsbury, 2001.

Johnson, Johnnie, *Wing Leader*, Newton Abbot: David & Charles, 1974.

Jonsson, Tony, *Dancing in the Skies*, London: Grub Street, 1994.

Liskutin, Miroslav, *Challenge in the Air*, London: William Kimber, 1988.

Morgan, Eric, and Shacklady, Edward, *Spitfire: The History*, Stamford: Key Publishing, 1987.

Price, Alfred, *The Spitfire Story*, London: BCA, 1982.

Quill, Jeffrey, *Spitfire, a Test Pilot's Story*, Manchester: Air Data Publications, 1996.

Sampson, Ralph 'Sammy', with Franks, Norman, *Spitfire Offensive*, London: Grub Street, 1994.

Smith, Duncan, *Spitfire into Battle*, London: John Murray, 1981.

Spurdle, Bob, *The Blue Arena*, London: William Kimber, 1986.

Sturtivant, Ray, and Balance, Theo, *The Squadrons of the Fleet Air Arm*, Tunbridge Wells: Air-Britain, 1994.

Sturtivant, Ray, with Hamlin, John and Halley, James, *Royal Air Force Flying Training and Support Units*, Tunbridge Wells: Air-Britain, 1997.

Watkins, David, *Fear Nothing: History of 501 Squadron*, Cowden: Newton, 1990.

Wheeler, Neil, 'Unarmed and Unafraid', *Spitfire Special*, Stanford: Key Publishing.

Index

Note: Individual Spitfire Marks and engine variants are not referenced in the index.

Admiralty 102, 124
Aerodrome Dummy Deck
  Landing 124, 151
Aeroplane and Armament
  Experimental
  Establishment (AAEE) 13,
  27, 219–21, 244
AHQ Burma 217
AHQ Eastern Mediterranean
  216
AHQ Malta 215, 216
Air Command South East Asia
  (ACSEA) 216, 217
Airborne Division:
  82nd American 91
  101st American 91
Air Council 100–1
Aircraft, Luftwaffe
  Bf 109 (Me 109) 23, 26, 32, 39,
  45, 65, 66, 68, 69, 71, 86, 87,
  93, 107, 108, 109, 145, 167,
  251–252
  Bf 110 (Me 110) 18
  Do 17 43, 74
  Fw 190 26, 65, 71, 72, 73–74,
  75, 76, 78, 79, 80, 86, 87, 91,
  94, 108, 109, 145, 222–3,
  238–9, 248, 250–2
  He 111 47, 48
  Ju 86P 79
  Ju 87 32
  Ju 88 30, 32, 41–2, 126
  Me 262 87, 98–9
Aircraft, Japanese 22, 26,
  113–19, 149–50
Aicraft, RAF/FAA
  Baltimore 110
  Barracuda 145
  Beaufighter 81, 106, 165
  Blenheim 37, 38, 48, 65, 156,
  210, 211, 212
  Boston 81
  Bristol Fighter 18
  Camel 18
  Corsair 152
  Defiant 37, 38, 211
  Eurofighter Typhoon 169
  Fulmar 124, 212
  Gladiator 37, 212
  Harvard 62
  Havoc 81
  Hurricane 19, 21, 23, 27, 30,
  31, 37, 38, 40, 48, 49–50, 62,
  63, 69, 81, 104, 106, 112,
  116, 117, 152, 169, 210, 211,
  212
  Liberator 123
  Master 59, 63, 151, 152
  Mohawk 121
  Mosquito 81, 161
  Mustang (P-51) 23, 81, 82, 85,
  89, 91, 95, 146, 157, 240–3

P-47 Thunderbolt 95
Roc 125
Seafang 100, 102
Sea Fury 153
Spiteful 100–2
Tempest 166, 248
Typhoon 23, 63, 81, 87, 94
'Valiant' 101–2
Vampire 165
'Victor' 101
Walrus 214
Whirlwind 81
Wildcat 152
Aircraft carriers 85, 103, 126,
  127, 145, 146, 148, 151–5
Aircraft performance, combat
  requirements for 26, 38, 68
Aircrew training, 1942
  conference on 53–5
Air Defence of Great Britain
  (ADGB) 65–6, 83, 88
Airfields, RAF, UK
  Acklington 46, 47, 212, 213,
  217
  Aldergrove 212
  Andreas 213
  Angle 213
  Arbroath 126
  Aston Down 59, 214
  Ayr 70, 213, 214
  Benson 160, 161, 215, 216,
  217
  Bentwaters 217
  Biggin Hill 46, 47, 69, 211,
  213, 214
  Bircham Newton 211, 215
  Bolt Head 71, 214
  Boscombe Down 34, 77, 78,
  210
  Bradwell Bay 215, 216
  Brize Norton 164
  Castle Bromwich 31, 34, 79
  Castletown 212, 214
  Catfoss 61
  Catterick 46, 70, 212, 213, 214
  Chedworth 63
  Chilbolton 217
  Church Fenton 41, 212
  Church Stanton 213, 214
  Collyweston 211
  Coltishall 39, 46, 47, 211, 213,
  214, 216
  Coningsby 169
  Croydon 46, 211
  Culmhead 215
  Deanland 215
  Debden 73, 211, 213
  Detling 41, 94, 211
  Digby 45, 47, 66, 213, 214,
  216
  Driffield 213

Duxford 28, 44, 46, 47, 60, 86,
  211, 213
Drem 33, 46, 212, 214, 217
Dyce 214, 217
Eastchurch 46
Eglinton 214
Eshott 59, 214, 215
Exeter 210, 213
Fairlop 214
Fairwood Common 213, 214
Farnborough 126
Ford 215
Fowlmere 46, 211, 213
Friston 215, 216
Funtingdon 215
Grangemouth 58, 59, 212,
  213, 214, 215
Gravesend 46, 211, 213, 214
Harrowbeer 213, 214, 216,
  217
Hawarden 57, 58, 213, 214
Hawkinge 40, 43, 213, 214
Hendon 160
Henstridge 151, 152
Heston 213, 214
High Ercall 85, 214
Honington 47
Hornchurch 15, 44, 46, 211,
  213, 214
Hutton Cranswick 213, 214,
  217
Ibsley 213, 214
Keevil 217
Kenley 43, 46, 47, 72, 82, 211,
  213, 214
Kirkistown 214
Kings Cliffe 78, 213
Kirton-in-Lindsey 46, 47,
  211, 213, 214, 215
Lasham 217
Leconfield 41, 46, 47, 212
Leeming 212
Lee-on-Solent 146, 216
Llandow 59, 214
Long Kesh 214
Ludham 213, 214, 217
Lympne 40, 215
Manston 40, 99, 211, 216, 217
Martlesham Heath 27, 28,
  211, 213, 214, 219–21
Merston 213, 214, 216
Middle Wallop 46, 47, 210
Mildenhall 47
Millfield 63, 214, 215
Montrose 212, 214
Morpeth 217
Northolt 13, 79, 211, 213, 214,
  215
North Weald 78, 211, 213,
  214, 229
Odiham 215
Pembrey 46, 71, 210

Perranporth 213, 214
Peterhead 214
Portreath 213
Predannack 216
Prestwick 212, 213
Redhill 72, 213, 214
Rednal 59, 214, 215
Rochford 46, 47, 213, 214
St Eval 46, 210, 213, 216
St Merryn 152
Selsey 215
Shoreham 216
Skeabrae 214, 216, 217
Southend (see Rochford)
Stapleford Tawney 211
Sumburgh 212
Tain 214
Tangmere 46, 72, 211, 213,
  214, 215
Turnhouse 30, 46, 212, 213,
  214, 217
Usworth 212
Warmwell 46, 61, 210, 213,
  216, 217
Wellingore 211
Westhampnett 46, 211, 213,
  214
West Malling 46, 215, 216
Wick 212, 213
Wittering 46, 63, 211, 213
Woodvale 213
Worthy Down 126
Yeovilton 152
Airfields, RAF, overseas
  Aboukir 105
  Alghero 216
  Alipore 116, 117, 118, 216,
  217
  Amarda Road 218
  Baigachi 118, 216
  Bazenville (B2) 215
  Bellaria 217
  Beny sur Mer (B4) 215
  Bersis 216
  Biferno 216
  Brindisi 216
  Brown 217
  Bu Amud 216
  Calenzana 111, 216
  Calvi 111, 216
  Canne 217
  Catania 216
  Chettinad 123
  Chittagong 116, 117, 216
  Constantine 215
  Dabaing 218
  Darwin 217
  Dedelsdorf (B155) 217
  Dohazari 118
  Drigh Road 116
  Drope (B105) 217
  Dum Dum 215

Eindhoven (B78) 217
El Ballah 62
Hal Far 215, 216
Falconara 217
Fassberg (B152) 217
Fermo 111, 216
Florence 217
Foggia 216
Follonica 111, 216
Forli 217
Gambut 105
Gardemoen 217
Gibraltar 104
Grossachenheim 217
Hazbub 215
Heliopolis 105
Hong Kong 165
Hustedt (B113) 217
Husum (B172) 217
Imphal 216
Knocke le Zout (B83) 217
Krendi 15
Kuala Lumpur 164
Kumbhirgram 216
Kwetnge 218
Kyaukpyu 218
Longues (B11) 215
Luneburg 217
Luqa 108, 215
Madna 110
Madura 123
Maison Blanche 106, 215
Matariya 215
Mersa Matruh 216
Minneriya 216
Nanvy 217
Nidania 218
Pachino 108
Palel 216
Palermo 216
Perugia 111, 216
Petah Tiqva 165
Pontedera 217
Piombino 111, 216
Ramat David 165
Ramu 118, 121
Ratmalana 216, 218
Rimini 217
Rosignano 217
San Severo 216, 217
Seclin 30, 157
Sersheim 217
Sinthe 218
St Croix sur Mer (B3) 93
Sommervieu (B8) 215
Soul el Arba 106
Souk el Khemis 106, 215
Takoradi 105
Tingley 215
Tulihal 118
Varrelsbuch (B113) 217
Vavuniya 218
Venafro 111, 216
Wunstorf (B116) 217
Air Fighting Committee 21, 105
Air Fighting Development
    Establishment (AFDE) 13
Air Fighting Development
    Unit (AFDU) 13, 71, 76–7,
    80, 81–2, 85, 86–7, 99, 109
AFDU, trials reports 222–57
Air Fighting Training Unit
    (AFTU) 116
Air-Sea Rescue 35
Air Service Training 126
Air Spotting Pool 92, 146–8
Allied Expeditionary Air Force
    83, 215
Andaman Islands 148

Arab-Israeli war (1948) 165–6
Arakan, Battle of 112, 116,
    118–20
Armament trials 1935 21
Armoured glass 22, 24
Armour plating 22, 23, 232
Army Co-operation Command
    215
Avalanche, Operation 128

Balkan Air Force (BAF) 217
Barking Creek, 'Battle of' 30
Battle of Britain 18, 25, 26, 35,
    36–52, 67, 125
    1965 film 15, 59–60
    RAF Spitfire squadron
        claims/losses 46–7
    Memorial Flight (BBMF) 169
Battle of France 31–2
Blacking-out, effects of
    positive-G 56–7
Black Swan, HMS 36
British Expeditionary Force 30
British Pacific Fleet 148
Burma, ops over 112, 167
Burmese Air Force 167

Cameras, aerial 156, 157, 161,
    162, 181, 190, 196, 197
Central Fighter Establishment
    (CFE) 63, 99
Central Gunnery School (CGS)
    61–2
Central Gunnery School
    (Middle East) 62
Churchill 43, 73, 113
Circus, operation 65
Clipped wings, use of 80,
    224–5
Coastal Command 213, 215,
    216, 217
Cockpit, comfort 23–4, 221
Cockpit, visibility from 12, 18,
    23–5, 220, 231–3, 250, 255
Coffman starter cartridge
    34, 45
Contrails, problems of 159
Coventry Ordnance Works
    (COW) gun 20
Cunliffe-Owen, production of
    Seafires 145

Darwin 112, 113
Day Fighter Development
    Squadron (DFDS) 63
D-Day 89–94, 146–8
De Havilland 33
Dieppe, Operation Jubilee
    73–4, 78, 90
Director of Naval Air
    Organisation 153–4
Dragoon, Operation 146, 148
Dunkirk, evacuation from 32
Dutch Air Force 59, 123, 165

Eagle squadrons 73
East Indies Fleet 148–9
Egyptian Air Force 59, 164, 166
El Alamein offensive 106
Ensland, MV, sinking of 145
European Theatre of
    Operations (ETO) 103

Fighter armament 16–18,
    19–20, 21–2, 27–8, 34–5, 68,
    83, 85–6, 94, 95–6, 126, 145,
    163, 173–5, 177, 178, 181,
    182, 189, 190, 191, 196, 197,
    199, 200, 201, 202, 203, 204,

205, 206, 207, 208, 209, 236,
    244, 254, 258
Fighter armament, problems
    with cannon 33–4, 60, 66
Fighter Command Armament
    Section 21–2
Fighter Command Battle
    Orders 22
Fighter Command School of
    Tactics 63
Fighter Command tactics
    26–7, 44
Fighter doctrine, evolution
    of 16–18
Fighter Interception Unit
    (FIU) 37
Fighter Leaders School (FLS)
    63, 215
Flights, FAA 127
Flights, RAF 25, 160, 216
Floats, Spitfire use of 125
Force H 110, 127
Force V 110, 127
'Forget-me-Nots for Fighters'
    12–13
French Indo-China 123, 165
Fuel:
    octane rating 33
    provision of and problems
        with 19, 45, 83–5, 93, 104,
        157, 162
    protection of tanks 22, 119

Glycol 23, 34, 45, 55, 93
Groups, RAF: (Fighter
    Command Groups are
    only indexed for annexes)
    No 9 Gp 213, 215
    No 10 Gp 210, 213, 214, 215
    No 11 Gp 211, 213, 214, 216,
        217
    No 12 Gp 211, 213, 214, 216,
        217
    No 13 Gp 212, 213–14, 216,
        217
    No 16 Gp 215
    No 81 Gp 213, 214
    No 82 Gp 214
    No 83 Gp 215, 217
    No 84 Gp 98, 215, 217
    No 85 Gp 98, 215, 217
    No 88 Gp 217
    No 106 Gp 217
    No 214 Gp 216
    No 221 Gp 216, 218
    No 222 Gp 218
    No 224 Gp 216, 218
    No 228 Gp 218
    No 231 Gp 216
    No 242 Gp 106, 216
Gunsights 22, 28, 60, 232

Harmonisation of guns
    21–2, 34
Heston Flight 156
High Altitude Flight 78, 171
High-flying raiders 77–8
Hitler 43, 44
Hong Kong Auxiliary Air
    Force 164
Husky, Operation 128

Iceberg, Operation 149–50
Indian Air Force 59
India Command 215
Inmate, Operation 149–50
Irish Air Force 59
Israeli Air Force 165–6

Kamikaze attacks 149
Korean War 154, 163, 165

Laminar wing, introduction of
    100, 102
Lobelle hood 162
Loss rates, comparison of
    Spitfire and Hurricane
    49–51
Luftwaffe units 30, 36, 41–2. 43.
    47, 66, 71, 74

Malaya, anti-terrorist ops 123,
    154, 162, 163, 164–5, 167
Malta, fighters for 85, 103–4
Mediterranean Air Command
    15
Mediterranean and Allied
    (Coastal) Air Force
    (MA(C)AF) 109, 216, 217
Middle East Command 215

NAS Patuxant River 148
Naval Air Fighting
    Development Unit
    (NAFDU) 231
Naval Air Fighting School
    151, 152
Negative-G, problems of 26, 33

Operational Training Units
    57, 58, 59, 63, 152, 213,
    214, 215
Oxygen, importance of 54–5,
    56, 77, 111

People:
    Arnold, Gen 84
    Aylott, F/L 93
    Ball, A. 11
    Ball, G. 48
    Banham, G. 58
    Barker, R. 61
    Barnett, D. 119–20
    Barnett, R. 46
    Bavis, P/O 93
    Bell 41, 43
    Berg, R. 98
    Bernard, Lt 88
    Bocock, E. 70
    Brewster 41
    Brodie, C. 65
    Burton, H. 47
    Bush, F/O 93
    Caldwell, C. 113
    Carroll, P/O 117
    Casson 41–2
    Christie, G. 65
    Clerc, P/O 78–9
    Clostermann, P. 91
    Cobden, P/O 39
    Collins, A. 46
    Conway, G. 122–3
    Cooke, D. 46
    Cotton, S. 156
    Cozens, H. 28
    Crosley, M. 146–7, 149–50
    Curry, J. 60
    Darley, H. 47
    Denholm, G. 46
    Devitt, P. 46
    Douglas, Sholto 57, 67
    Dowding, Hugh 30, 31, 51
    Draisbach, H. 36
    Dundas 41–2, 43
    Dunworth, T. 46
    Ellis, J. 47
    Ernst, R. 36
    Finlay, D. 46

Foubert, F/O 93
Fraser-Harris, A. 127
Freeman, Sir W. 100
Galitzine, P/O 79
Galland, A. 11–12, 15, 38–9
Gaze, A. 78
Gillam, D. 41–2
Goering, H. 15
Goodlin 166
Graham, E. 46
Green, G. 158
Guthrie, G. 148
Hall, S. 126
Healy, D. 123
Hellyer 41
Henshaw, A. 20
Hill, J. 46
Holdsworth, F/O 111
Holland, A. 46
Hood, R. 46
Hopewell 41, 42
Hunnard, J. 46
Jameson, P. 46
Jarrold, J. 60, 62, 93–4
Jennings, F/O 78–9
Johnson, J. 33, 39, 57, 60, 82–3
Johnstone, A. 46
Kent, J. 46
Koch, F. 36
Lane, B. 46
Law, D. 148
Leathart, J. 46
Lees, R. 46
Leigh, R. 46
Lenehan, WO 88
Leonard, P/O 117
Levett, G. 167
Liskutin, M. 34–5, 58, 70, 71, 91
Lister, R. 46
Long, A. 127
Longbottom, 30, 156–7
Louis, P. 116
Lynne S/L
McComb, J. 47
MacDonald, W/C 62
Macdonnell, A. 46
Maclachlan, A. 46
Mackie, R. 24, 53, 61, 62
Malan, A. G. 11, 32, 46, 47–8, 49, 61
Marples, R. 41
Mermagen, H. 46
Middleton, W. 158
Millen. F/O 157
Mitchell, R. 28
Moberley 41, 42, 43
Molders, W. 33
Morris, D. 96
Morrison, D. 73–4
Murray 41
Niven, J. 70
O'Brien, J. 46
Odbert, N. 46
Park, Sir K. 104
Peart, A. 121
Petre, J. 48
Pinkerton, G. 46
Pinkham, R. 34, 46
Portal, ACM 84
Proudman, G. 66
Quill, J. 20, 23–5, 52, 66, 85, 86, 109, 127–8, 150–1
Reid, P/O 88
Reynolds, F/O 105
Ridley 43
Robinson, M. 41–2, 47
Rommel, E. 89

Sampson, R. 58, 70, 74, 97, 98
Sanders, P. 46
Saul, AVM 12–13
Saunders, G. 46
Sawyer, H. 46
Shea-Simmonds 163–4
Smik, O. 91, 96
Smith, A. 47
Smith, J. 28
Smith 41, 42
Smith, D. 66
Sorley 19, 101
Spencer, D. 46
Spurdle, 28, 44, 57
Stevens, E. 46
Summers, M. 20
Taylor, A. 158
Tobin, S/L 100
Tuttle, G. 158
Verney, A/C 19–20
Walker 41
Wareing 43
Weber, A. 36
Weggerty, S. 116
Wells, S/L 72
Westmorland 41, 42
Wheeler, N. 158–60
White, F. 46
Wilkinson, R. 46
Woollett, J. 121–2
Zurakowski, J. 39
Photographic Development Unit (PDU) 157
Photographic Reconnaissance Unit (PRU) 105, 112, 157, 161, 213
Principles of Air Combat 11–12
Propeller, problems 33
Prune's guide for living 75–6

Rhodesian Air Force 161
Rhubarb, offensive sweep 65
Royal Flying Corps 16
Royal Naval Volunteer Reserve 153, 154
Russian Air Force 59, 73

Scapa Flow, air defence of 125
Servicing Commando 93
Service Trials Unit 126
Singapore, fall of 112
South-West Pacific Area 113, 114
Spanish Civil War 38
Specification, aircraft requirement 16–19, 100

Special Service Flight 79
Spitfire, cost of 27
Spitfire Fund 15, 27, 40
Spitfire v Hurricane, comparison by Fighter Command 31–2, 49–50
Spitfire production 29, 31, 35, 45, 67, 76, 79, 87, 145, 161, 164, 170–2
production problems 28–9
attack on Woolston Works 45
attack on Westland Yeovil Works 45
Spotter, Operation 85
Squadrons, Fleet Air Arm:
700 Sqn 172, 203, 204, 205, 206, 208
701 Sqn 206, 207
703 Sqn 207, 208
706 Sqn 205, 206
708 Sqn 203, 204, 205
709 Sqn 205, 206, 207, 208

715 Sqn 152, 188, 203, 209
718 Sqn 152, 197, 204, 205
719 Sqn 152, 188, 203, 204
721 Sqn 205, 206
727 Sqn 207
728 Sqn 204, 205, 206, 207
731 Sqn 203, 204
733 Sqn 205, 206
736 Sqn 205, 206, 207, 209
737 Sqn 206, 207
738 Sqn 208, 209
740 Sqn 205
741 Sqn 205
744 Sqn 205
746 Sqn 208
748 Sqn 152, 178, 188, 203, 204, 205
751 Sqn 206
757 Sqn 205
759 Sqn 152, 178, 180, 188, 203, 204, 205, 206, 208, 209
760 Sqn 206
761 Sqn 151, 178, 188, 197, 200, 203, 204, 205, 206, 208
762 Sqn 178
764 Sqn 208
766 Sqn 205, 207, 208
767 Sqn 205, 207, 209
768 Sqn 188, 203, 204, 205, 207
770 Sqn 204
771 Sqn 205, 207, 208, 209
772 Sqn 205
773 Sqn 207
775 Sqn 178, 189, 203, 204
776 Sqn 204
777 Sqn 172, 205, 207, 208, 209
778 Sqn 188, 195, 197, 203, 204, 205, 207, 208, 209
779 Sqn 203
780 Sqn 207, 208
781 Sqn 203, 205, 207, 208, 209
782 Sqn 205
787 Sqn 188, 203, 204, 205, 207, 208, 209
790 Sqn 188, 203, 204, 205, 207
791 Sqn 178, 207
794 Sqn 178, 188, 204, 206
798 Sqn 188, 195, 203, 204
799 Sqn 206, 207, 208
800 Sqn 154, 207, 208, 209
801 Sqn 106, 126, 149, 150, 152, 155, 188, 203, 204, 206, 207
802 Sqn 155, 172, 206, 207
803 Sqn 155, 206, 207
804 Sqn 38, 155, 172, 207, 209, 212
805 Sqn 155, 206, 207, 208
806 Sqn 155, 206, 207
807 Sqn 106, 125, 126, 127, 128, 145, 149, 155, 172, 203, 204, 206, 208
808 Sqn 38, 90, 145, 155, 188, 197, 204, 206, 212
809 Sqn 145, 149, 155, 188, 203, 204, 206, 207, 208
816 Sqn 155, 203, 804
827 Sqn 155
833 Sqn 204
834 Sqn 148, 155, 204
842 Sqn 203, 204
879 Sqn 145, 155, 188, 203, 204, 206, 208
880 Sqn 126, 149, 150, 155, 178, 188, 204, 206

883 Sqn 153, 206, 207
884 Sqn 126, 155, 188, 204
885 Sqn 90, 126, 127, 155, 188, 203, 204, 206
886 Sqn 90, 145, 188, 197, 204, 206
887 Sqn 145, 148, 149, 155, 172, 188, 204, 206
889 Sqn 204, 206
894 Sqn 145, 149, 155, 203, 204, 206
895 Sqn 204
897 Sqn 145, 155, 178, 189, 203, 205
899 Sqn 148, 155, 189, 205, 206
1700 Sqn 205
1830 Sqn 208
1831 Sqn 207, 208
1832 Sqn 205, 206, 207, 208, 209
1833 Sqn 207, 208, 209
Squadrons, RAF:
1 Sqn 37, 192, 201, 211, 215
2 Sqn 90, 162, 192, 197, 198, 201
3 Sqn 38, 212
4 Sqn 196, 197, 213, 215
5 Sqn 199
6 Sqn 192
11 Sqn 123, 198
13 Sqn 196
16 Sqn 92, 181, 192, 196, 198, 199, 201, 215
17 Sqn 37, 123, 190, 198, 199, 211, 216
19 Sqn 28, 29, 32, 33–4, 38, 46, 47, 48, 60, 66, 171, 177, 179, 183, 186, 192, 199, 211, 213, 214
20 Sqn 190, 198, 199
23 Sqn 37, 48, 211
25 Sqn 37, 211
26 Sqn 90, 183, 196, 198, 216
28 Sqn 164, 190, 196, 198, 200
29 Sqn 37, 211
31 Sqn 199, 201
32 Sqn 37, 165, 186, 190, 192, 200, 211, 212, 216
33 Sqn 183, 186, 192, 216
34 Sqn 199
41 Sqn 37, 46, 85, 171, 177, 179, 183, 196, 197, 198, 201, 211, 212, 213, 214, 215
43 Sqn 186, 190, 192, 216
46 Sqn 37, 211
54 Sqn 38, 46, 177, 179, 180, 183, 186, 190, 212, 214
56 Sqn 37, 92, 192, 210, 211
60 Sqn 164, 200
63 Sqn 90, 183, 199, 216
64 Sqn 37, 46, 79, 171, 177, 179, 183, 186, 191, 192, 211, 212, 213, 214, 216
65 Sqn 15, 25, 33, 37, 40, 46, 177, 179, 180, 183, 192, 199, 211, 213, 214
66 Sqn 28, 32, 38, 39, 45, 46, 65, 177, 179, 183, 186, 189, 192, 199, 211, 213, 214, 215
67 Sqn 190, 216
69 Sqn 181
71 Sqn 179, 183, 213
72 Sqn 25, 38, 44–5, 46, 106, 108, 111, 177, 179, 180, 183, 186, 192, 198, 211, 212, 213, 215, 216
73 Sqn 38, 163, 172, 186, 190, 191, 193, 202, 212

74 Sqn 11, 28, 30, 32, 37, 39, 44, 46, 47, 49, 92, 177, 179, 183, 186, 193, 199, 211, 213, 214, 216
79 Sqn 38, 211, 212
80 Sqn 60, 62, 93–4, 106, 110–11, 164, 172, 173, 183, 186, 192, 202, 216
81 Sqn 106, 118, 121, 162, 164, 165, 183, 186, 190, 192, 200, 201, 214, 216
82 Sqn 201
85 Sqn 37, 211
87 Sqn 37, 183, 186, 190, 192, 210, 216
91 Sqn 90, 172, 179, 183, 192, 197, 198, 201, 213, 214, 215
92 Sqn 37, 44, 46, 66, 69, 106, 111, 171, 177, 183, 186, 190, 192, 210, 213, 215, 216
93 Sqn 192, 216
94 Sqn 183, 186, 190, 192, 216
111 Sqn 21, 37, 40, 177, 179, 183, 186, 192, 211, 213, 215, 216
118 Sqn 45, 177, 179, 180, 183, 189, 190, 192, 213, 214, 216
121 Sqn 179, 183, 213
122 Sqn 177, 179, 180, 183, 192, 201, 213, 214
123 Sqn 177, 179, 184, 186, 192, 214
124 Sqn 78, 90, 177, 180, 184, 189, 190, 192, 213, 214, 215
126 Sqn 104, 184, 186, 192, 198, 215
127 Sqn 96, 184, 186, 192, 198
129 Sqn 73, 177, 179, 184, 186, 189, 193, 213, 214
130 Sqn 179, 184, 186, 193, 198, 213, 214, 216
131 Sqn 177, 179, 184, 186–7, 190, 191, 193, 214, 215
132 Sqn 92, 177, 180, 184, 187, 189, 191, 193, 198, 214, 215
133 Sqn 179, 184, 193, 213
134 Sqn 179, 184, 213
136 Sqn 112, 116, 118, 119, 187, 191, 198, 216
140 Sqn 160, 171, 177, 181, 191, 196, 215
141 Sqn 38, 212
144 Sqn 90
145 Sqn 34, 37, 70, 105, 108, 111, 171, 177, 179, 180, 184, 190, 191, 193, 211, 212, 213, 215, 216
151 Sqn 37, 211
152 Sqn 37, 45, 46, 118, 177, 179, 184, 187, 191, 193, 198, 210, 213, 214, 215, 216
153 Sqn 191, 193
154 Sqn 106, 111, 179, 180, 184, 187, 190, 191, 193, 213, 216
155 Sqn 118, 121–3, 191, 198, 216
164 Sqn 183, 184, 193, 199
165 Sqn 183, 184, 197, 193, 214, 215
167 Sqn 184, 187, 214
185 Sqn 187, 191, 193, 215, 216
208 Sqn 111, 165, 166, 171, 187, 191, 193, 200, 216
212 Sqn 157, 177

213 Sqn 37, 187, 193, 210
219 Sqn 38, 212
222 Sqn 34, 38, 46, 87–8, 91, 92, 177, 179, 180, 184, 193, 211, 213, 214, 215
225 Sqn 106, 111, 184, 187, 194, 216
229 Sqn 37, 187, 193, 199, 211, 215, 216
232 Sqn 38, 111, 184, 187, 193, 212, 215, 216
234 Sqn 37, 39, 46, 88, 178, 179, 181, 184, 187, 189, 193, 210, 213, 214, 216
236 Sqn 210
237 Sqn 111, 184, 187, 183, 216
238 Sqn 37, 111, 178, 184, 187, 191, 193, 210, 216
241 Sqn 111, 187, 191, 193, 216
242 Sqn 37, 106, 111, 184, 187, 193, 211, 215, 216
243 Sqn 184, 187, 193, 15, 216
245 Sqn 38, 212, 215
249 Sqn 38, 178, 184, 187, 193, 211, 212, 215
253 Sqn 38, 111, 184, 187, 190, 191, 193, 196, 211, 216
255 Sqn 106
256 Sqn 191, 193
257 Sqn 178, 184, 211
263 Sqn 38, 212
264 Sqn 32, 38, 211
266 Sqn 37, 46, 178, 179, 180, 184, 211, 213
268 Sqn 90, 198, 201
269 Sqn 183
273 Sqn 123, 191, 198, 216
274 Sqn 93, 184, 187, 193, 216
275 Sqn 187, 216
276 Sqn 179, 184, 214
277 Sqn 92, 179, 180, 184, 214, 216
278 Sqn 179, 184, 216
287 Sqn 193, 199
288 Sqn 184, 199
290 Sqn 184
302 Sqn 92, 179, 184, 187, 193, 199, 212, 213, 214, 215
303 Sqn 48, 178, 179, 180, 185, 193, 198, 213, 214, 216
306 Sqn 179, 180, 185, 193, 213, 214
308 Sqn 92, 178, 179, 185, 193, 198, 213, 214, 215
310 Sqn 179, 185, 187, 189, 193, 211, 213, 214, 215
312 Sqn 70, 179, 180, 185, 187, 193, 214, 315
313 Sqn 178, 179, 185, 187, 189, 190, 194, 213, 214, 215
315 Sqn 179, 180, 185, 194, 213, 214
316 Sqn 179, 185, 194, 213, 214
317 Sqn 92, 185, 194, 198, 213, 214, 215
318 Sqn 111, 185, 187, 194, 216
322 Sqn 90, 165, 185, 187, 194, 198, 199, 215
326 Sqn 191, 194
327 Sqn 187, 191, 194
328 Sqn 187, 191, 194
329 Sqn 92, 185, 187, 194, 199, 215

331 Sqn 179, 185, 194, 214, 215
332 Sqn 183, 185, 194, 213, 214, 215, 229
335 Sqn 185, 187, 216
336 Sqn 194, 215, 216
340 Sqn 92, 180, 185, 194, 199, 213, 214, 215
341 Sqn 92, 185, 194, 199, 214, 215
345 Sqn 185, 194, 199, 216
349 Sqn 92, 183, 185, 187, 194, 199, 215
350 Sqn 180, 185, 187, 194, 198, 199, 213, 214, 216
352 Sqn 187
400 Sqn 92, 196, 197, 215
401 Sqn 73–4, 92, 180, 185, 195, 198, 199, 213, 214, 215
402 Sqn 90, 93, 185, 187, 195, 198, 199, 213, 214, 216
403 Sqn 92, 178, 180, 185, 194, 199, 213, 214, 215
411 Sqn 178, 180, 185, 194, 198, 199, 213, 214, 215
414 Sqn 215
412 Sqn 180, 185, 194, 198, 199, 213, 214, 215
416 Sqn 91, 92, 180, 185, 187, 194, 198, 199, 214
417 Sqn 180, 185, 187, 191, 194, 214, 216
421 Sqn 92, 183, 185, 194, 199, 214, 215
430 Sqn 162, 198
441 Sqn 91, 92, 185, 194, 215
442 Sqn 92, 185, 194, 215
443 Sqn 91, 92, 185, 194, 198, 199
451 Sqn 111, 188, 191, 195, 198, 216
452 Sqn 178, 180, 188, 191, 213
453 Sqn 91, 92, 185, 188, 195, 198, 199, 214, 215
457 Sqn 72, 178, 180, 185, 188, 191, 213
485 Sqn 72, 92, 180, 186, 195, 213, 214, 215
500 Sqn 202
501 Sqn 37, 178, 180, 186, 188, 195, 199, 211, 213, 214, 216
502 Sqn 202
504 Sqn 38, 180, 186, 188, 189, 195, 202, 212, 214, 216
510 Sqn 178
518 Sqn 190
519 Sqn 189, 190
520 Sqn 188
521 Sqn 181, 195, 215
527 Sqn 186
538 Sqn 181, 196
540 Sqn 161, 181
541 Sqn 161, 162, 171, 177, 181, 195, 196, 197, 201, 215, 216
542 Sqn 161, 162, 172, 181, 195, 196, 197, 200, 201, 215, 216
543 Sqn 161, 181, 196, 215
544 Sqn 161, 181, 196, 215, 216
548 Sqn 191
549 Sqn 191
567 Sqn 186, 199
577 Sqn 186, 199
587 Sqn 200

595 Sqn 186, 195, 196, 197, 200, 201
600 Sqn 37, 198, 201, 202, 211
601 Sqn 37, 186, 188, 191, 195, 200, 211, 215, 216
602 Sqn 30, 38, 46, 70, 72, 89, 91, 92, 178, 180, 183, 186, 188, 189, 198, 200, 201, 202, 212, 213, 214, 215
603 Sqn 30, 38, 46, 178, 180, 183, 186, 188, 200, 202, 211, 212, 213, 214
604 Sqn 37, 200, 210
605 Sqn 38, 212
607 Sqn 38, 112, 116, 118, 188, 191, 198, 202, 211, 212, 216
609 Sqn 25, 37, 47, 178, 180, 186, 200, 202, 210, 213
610 Sqn 37, 47, 171, 178, 180, 186, 188, 197, 198, 202, 211, 212, 213, 214, 215
611 Sqn 34, 38, 45, 47, 66, 92, 171, 179, 180, 183, 186, 190, 195, 198, 202, 211, 213, 214, 216
612 Sqn 198, 200
613 Sqn 198, 202
614 Sqn 202
615 Sqn 112, 116, 117, 118, 188, 191, 198, 200, 201, 202, 211, 216
616 Sqn 38, 41–2, 43, 47, 78, 171, 178, 180, 186, 189, 190, 211, 212, 213, 214, 215
631 Sqn 188, 200
667 Sqn 200
680 Sqn 181, 189, 195, 196, 215
681 Sqn 181, 196, 201, 215, 216
682 Sqn 111, 181, 196, 201, 215, 216
683 Sqn 181, 196, 201, 215
684 Sqn 195
691 Sqn 200
695 Sqn 183, 200
1435 Sqn 188, 195, 215, 216
Squadrons, RCAF:
  1 Sqn 211
Squadrons, Israeli:
  101 Sqn 166, 167
  105 Sqn 166
Staxton Wold, radar 41
Syrian Air Force 161

Tactical Air Force, 2nd TAF 65–6, 83, 87, 88, 89, 95–7, 98
  Tactical Paper 258–66
Tactical Air Force, 3rd TAF 118, 215
Tactical Exercise Unit (TEU) 215
Ten Rules of Air Fighting 11–12
Tirpitz, operations against 146
Torch, Operation 106, 126, 127–8
Train-busting 97–8

USAAF units 73
USN units 90, 146

Vokes filter 105
V-weapons 87, 89, 94
Wings, FAA 146, 148, 149
Wings, RAAF 113
Wings, RAF 106, 111, 217